TRUE STORIES OF
LAW & ORDER:
SPECIAL VICTIMS UNIT

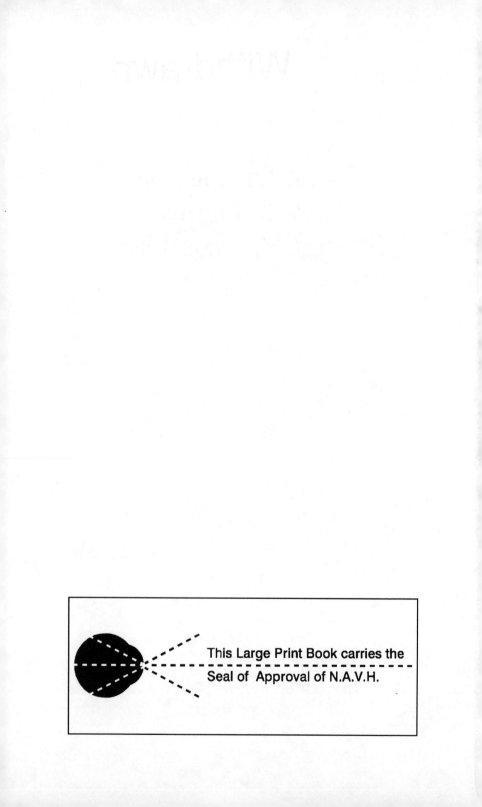
This Large Print Book carries the
Seal of Approval of N.A.V.H.

TRUE STORIES OF LAW & ORDER: SPECIAL VICTIMS UNIT

THE REAL CRIMES BEHIND THE BEST EPISODES OF THE HIT TV SHOW

KEVIN DWYER
AND JURÉ FIORILLO

THORNDIKE PRESS

A part of Gale, Cengage Learning

GALE
CENGAGE Learning

Detroit • New York • San Francisco • New Haven, Conn • Waterville, Maine • London

GALE
CENGAGE Learning

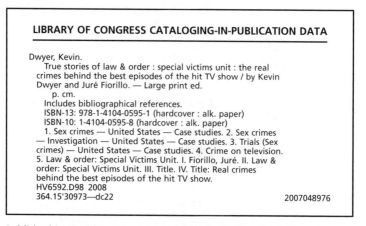

LIBRARY OF CONGRESS CATALOGING-IN-PUBLICATION DATA

Dwyer, Kevin.
  True stories of law & order : special victims unit : the real crimes behind the best episodes of the hit TV show / by Kevin Dwyer and Juré Fiorillo. — Large print ed.
    p. cm.
  Includes bibliographical references.
  ISBN-13: 978-1-4104-0595-1 (hardcover : alk. paper)
  ISBN-10: 1-4104-0595-8 (hardcover : alk. paper)
  1. Sex crimes — United States — Case studies. 2. Sex crimes — Investigation — United States — Case studies. 3. Trials (Sex crimes) — United States — Case studies. 4. Crime on television. 5. Law & order: Special Victims Unit. I. Fiorillo, Juré. II. Law & order: Special Victims Unit. III. Title. IV. Title: Real crimes behind the best episodes of the hit TV show.
  HV6592.D98 2008
  364.15'30973—dc22   2007048976

Published in 2008 by arrangement with The Berkley Publishing Group, a member of Penguin Group (USA) Inc.

CONTENTS

**L&O SVU: ("Control,"
Season 5)** *A man who
kidnaps and keeps women as
sex slaves is castrated in a
subway. Later, he's found
murdered in a hotel room.*
TRUE STORY: *"Dungeon
Master" John Jamelske built
an underground soundproof
room in his backyard, and
held several young women as
sex slaves for months and
years at a time.*

L&O SVU: ("Baby Killer,"
Season 2) *A young boy uses
a stolen gun to shoot and kill
a female classmate during
recess.*

TRUE STORY: *Six-year-old
Kayla Rolland was killed by
classmate Dedric Owens in
Michigan. The gun used in
the crime had been stolen by
a family friend.*

L&O SVU: ("Redemption,"
Season 3) *Released from
prison after eighteen years,
the "Soho Strangler" is
suspected in a string of new
sex crimes.*

TRUE STORY: *Dubbed the
"Boston Strangler," Albert
DeSalvo was a suspect in the
deaths of thirteen women.
DeSalvo died in jail before he
could be tried, and numerous
questions remain to this day
about the Boston Strangler's
true identity.*

L&O SVU: ("Chameleon," Season 4) *A prostitute turns the tables on a man who is sexually assaulting women on the street, but detectives soon discover that the woman isn't the victim she appears to be.*

TRUE STORY: *Truck-stop hooker Aileen Wuornos murdered seven men in and around Florida. Wuornos pleaded self-defense, claiming each victim tried to rape her.*

L&O SVU: ("Charisma," Season 6) *The leader of a doomsday cult sexually abuses his young congregants. The cult has also amassed an arsenal.*

TRUE STORY: *David Koresh and his Branch Davidian cult engaged in a deadly shootout with the ATF, and later battled the FBI. Koresh and many of his followers were killed, as were several government agents.*

L&O SVU: ("Game," Season 6) *Teenagers take their obsession with videogames to the point of murder.*

TRUE STORY: *Alabama teen Devin Moore killed two police officers and a dispatcher after being arrested for stealing a car. Moore claimed his addiction to the videogame Grand Theft Auto led him to commit the crimes.*

L&O SVU: ("Taboo," Season 7) *A young woman charged with killing her newborn claims she didn't know she was pregnant.*

TRUE STORY: *College student Holly Ashcraft was accused of murdering her newborn baby after hiding the pregnancy.*

L&O SVU: ("Fault," Season 7) *A released sex offender kidnaps two kids and murders their parents.*

TRUE STORY: *Class III pedophile Joseph Duncan is accused of stalking and murdering members of the Groene family to abduct eight-year-old Shasta and nine-year-old Dylan. He allegedly killed Dylan soon after, and brought Shasta back to her hometown.*

***L&O SVU:* ("Perfect,"
Season 4)** *When a
fourteen-year-old
Pennsylvania girl goes
missing, police suspect she's
been kidnapped. Eight
months later, she turns up
dead in New York.*

TRUE STORY:
*Fourteen-year-old Elizabeth
Smart was kidnapped from
her Utah home by two
Mormon fundamentalists. She
was found alive nine months
later.*

INTRODUCTION

When we were asked to write a second volume of *True Stories of Law & Order,* based on the *SVU* series, we naturally (and enthusiastically) said yes. While the format is the same as the original — twenty-five episodes, twenty-five true crimes, twenty-five chapters — the research and writing processes were not quite as clear-cut. As we began looking into which cases inspired which episodes, we quickly learned that the writers of *Law & Order: SVU* use the "ripped from the headlines" slogan more loosely than the *L&O* writers do. That is, the *SVU* writers will often take one detail of a crime and run with it, unlike their counterparts, whose plots more closely match the true crime.

For instance, chapter eight covers the murder of Kendra Webdale by a schizophrenic man named Andrew Goldstein, who pushed her in front of the New York City subway train in January 1999. Goldstein was not on his medication and claimed to have been in a psychotic state during the incident. The *L&O: SVU* episode "Uncle" revolves around the murder of a mother and daughter in their home; it ends with a mentally ill homeless man pushing the killer in front of a subway. "Uncle" isn't exclusively about the subway murder, but there is a clear parallel. And because the case was important enough to prompt legislators to pass Kendra's Law, which allows a family to force treatment upon a mentally ill relative, we decided to write about it. (The "Uncle" episode ran on October 10, 2006, the day Andrew Goldstein pleaded guilty in court, almost eight years after his crime.)

We also covered a few crimes that have been highly publicized — cases that, we assume, you're familiar with. In such instances, we've focused on certain aspects of the case that you might not know about. In our chapter about the Boston Strangler murders of the 1960s, we cover the crimes, of course, but dedicate much of the chapter to the well-argued theory that the man who is traditionally blamed for the killings, Albert DeSalvo, was most likely not the only killer. And in our section about Elizabeth Smart, we do cover her abduction by Brian

David Mitchell and Wanda Barzee, but we spend equal time on the fascinating legal argument about whether Mitchell was mentally competent to stand trial.

This brings us to another point. By the time of publication, not every case here has been resolved. We will, however, post occasional updates on our website www.True StoriesLawOrder.com. This site is our own and is not in any way affiliated with our publisher, Berkley/Penguin.

As in our last book, the crimes here defy imagination. Kidnappings, vicious sexual assaults, serial murder, human traffickers — the levels of depravity human beings are capable of never cease to amaze us. No wonder the writers consult true crimes for inspiration. Where else but from an actual criminal *could* these bizarre ideas come from? If this book can be said to have a theme, it's the same as the last: Truth is, without a doubt, more chilling than fiction.

ONE

L&O SVU: ("Control," Season 5) A man who kidnaps and keeps women as sex slaves is castrated in a subway. Later, he's found murdered in a hotel room.

TRUE STORY: "Dungeon Master" John Jamelske built an underground, sound-proof room in his backyard, and held several young women as sex slaves for months and years at a time.

Officer Damon had hosted some odd ducks in his patrol car, but there was something special about this guy. Bald on top with neatly trimmed white hair on the sides, the man in the rearview mirror appeared to be in his mid to late sixties. He had a narrow, weathered face with pronounced cheekbones and a trimmed white beard, and he looked like he was in pretty good shape. The old guy didn't seem all that nervous,

23

considering he had just been arrested. He wasn't a crackhead talking nonsense, nor did he seem mentally imbalanced; he wasn't seeing monsters under the seat or conversing with people who weren't there. In fact, his words were coming out calmly, rationally, pensively. He had been talking for a few minutes about the sixteen-year-old girl who moments ago had run across a parking lot to Damon begging for help. "We have a lot in common," the old man said, referring to his so-called girlfriend. "The only thing she liked that I don't is blue cheese."[1]

As they got closer to the police department, the man began matter-of-factly describing the activities he and the girl enjoyed together — walking the dog, dancing, singing karaoke. He was proud of the fact that guys in the bar would salute him with congratulatory high fives for hanging out with the young girl — a real coup in that crowd. Officer Damon kept driving, and listening, wondering if the man in the back seat was a sociopath. He had heard both sides of the story that had led to this scene, and the girl's version of events was quite different from the man's. But it would be up to the detectives, the DA, the judge, and possibly a jury to make it official. Now, he just had to get the old man to the precinct and book him.

John Jamelske was born in a suburb of Syracuse, New York, and he never left it — a "local" through and through. In high school, he was the kid no one wanted to stand very close to. Considered strange and a little skanky, he stood out from the crowd with his awful case of acne. One day someone called him "Germ" Jamelske. The nickname stuck. Former classmates don't recall Jamelske being picked on by bullies, but they don't remember him having any friends, either. One classmate put it well: "He went through school sideways."[2]

Jamelske's version of his high school years was different. According to him, he was one of the most popular guys in school and, he liked to tell his sons, he even dated a gal who won the Miss New York Pageant. It almost seems that Jamelske was delusional, but unfortunately he was anything but. "Germ" Jamelske knew exactly the way things were. But rather than deal with the pain of being a loser, he forced others to deal with it.

Jamelske began crafting his new past by telling small lies, like the tales of past glory he told to his children. The more he saw that people believed his fantastic stories, though, the bigger the lies got, and, in later life, he would actually begin making these vagaries come true.

His own achievements were modest to be sure. But, surprisingly, other aspects of his life made Jamelske seem moderately successful. His wife Dorothy, whom he married in 1959, was an elementary school teacher, and two of his three sons built impressive careers in the field of education — one, Paul, became a high school principal; the other, Eric, earned his doctorate in economics and taught at the University of Wisconsin. The third son, Brian, stayed in the Syracuse area, working odd jobs and helping his father out at home. Brian would later be his father's closest son.* He was the only one of the three to agree to be inter-

---

*One day, fifteen years before his arrest, John Jamelske asked Brian to drive a friend to the airport. The friend turned out to be a teenage girl, and she was blindfolded. Brian asked his father what was going on. Jamelske told his son that he was just taking part in a prank; there was nothing to worry about. Trusting his father, Brian performed the errand. Some time later, Brian helped his father build a soundproof room three feet under the backyard, which John told Brian was a bomb shelter.

26

viewed about his father's life, and the only one to visit the old man in prison.[3]

Regardless of his inability to forge a career for himself, Jamelske was financially well-off. His father, a watch and clock repairer, had amassed a small fortune in the form of antique clocks. (Jamelske himself had earned a degree in watchmaking, but he could never handle a real job.) As an only child, Jamelske inherited the clocks and the house, which he lived in with his wife and family. This solid financial base, along with his legendary cheapness[†] provided Jamelske with exactly what he needed to fulfill his wildest fantasies: property, money, and free time.

The fourteen-year-old girl didn't recognize the man and couldn't figure out what was happening. All she knew was that she had been walking down the street when someone pulled her into a car and sped off, and that she was now in a stuffy, cement-walled room with him. She didn't dare kick or punch him to get free: he had told her that

[†]John Jamelske, who cringed at the thought of spending seventy-five cents for a newspaper, would engage in weekly bullying sessions to extort the local librarians out of the Sunday coupons.[4]

if she struggled, he would kill her little brother. How he even knew about her brother she had no idea. But she thought the best thing was to wait it out and help would come. Or maybe he wanted money. Someone would pay him and then he would let her go.

Jamelske wasn't looking for money. He wanted something far more precious: control. Total control over a woman. Of Jamelske's five victims, the details of his first victim's ordeal are the vaguest. What is known is that she was abducted at the age of fourteen in October 1988 and set free at the age of seventeen, and that Jamelske controlled her actions largely with threats to her brother. The girl, now a woman, suffered severe anxiety for years after. For reasons of her and her family's own, the victim didn't report the abduction to the police.

Jamelske abducted his second victim, another fourteen-year-old, in March 1995. The girl, who had run away from home, was approached by Jamelske on the street. He said that he had a package he needed delivered anonymously. He would pay her handsomely if she would deliver it for him. The girl got in his car, happy to be making some easy money. As they drove into Jamelske's suburban neighborhood, he asked her to duck down so no one would see her; the package delivery had to be kept totally secret. The teenager did as she was asked.

When he pulled up to his house, Jamelske explained that the package was in his basement and that she'd have to come inside to get it. It was the last anyone would see of the girl for over two years. Then one day, out of nowhere, Jamelske blindfolded her, drove her to a random street in Syracuse and dropped her off.

On August 31, 1997, a fifty-three-year-old woman was walking down the street when Jamelske grabbed her and forced her into his car. He drove her to an abandoned area, tied her down, and raped her. He then drove the woman to his home and brought her to his dungeon, where he held the woman for nearly ten months. When he finally released her, at a bus station in the middle of the night, he handed her fifty dollars and drove off.[*]

[*]The woman immediately reported her abduction to the police, describing Jamelske's appearance and telling them he drove a tan 1974 Comet. The police checked out all the '74 Comets in the area and came up with nothing. They didn't, however, check Comets from other years. It turned out that

John Jamelske, who spent fifteen years kidnapping women and holding them as sex slaves in his home-made dungeon, will live out the rest of his years in a five-by-ten dungeon run by the New York State Department of Correctional Services.

Jamelske's Comet was a '75. The woman would later claim that the police never believed her in the first place; the cops say they took her claims very seriously.[5]

Three years later, a twenty-year-old mother of two was on her way to a friend's house in Syracuse. Her route took her through a rough neighborhood, where she noticed some young guys following her. When John Jamelske pulled up to the curb and asked if she needed a lift, she jumped in. She couldn't believe her luck.

The woman spent two months in Jamelske's captivity. Her family reported her missing, but detectives again were unable to find any leads. The only thing that kept the woman going was the old man's promises that he would eventually let her go. He even gave her a Bible to read when he wasn't present. One night, he tied a blindfold around her eyes and led her out of the dungeon. They drove for fifteen minutes and he stopped the car. He reached across her, opened her door, and said she was free to leave. When she removed the blindfold and got her bearings straight, she realized she was standing in front of her mother's house.

In October 2002, Jamelske abducted his final victim. Sixteen years old and another runaway, she accepted a ride in his car and was held captive for six months. During this time, Jamelske actually took her out in public, no doubt to flaunt his prize and receive precious high fives from his friends. His reign of glory, though, was about to come to an end.

On April 3, 2003, Jamelske took his prisoner out to the F-M Returnables, a bottle recycling depot in the town of Manlius, about ten miles east of Syracuse. When he turned his back on the girl to count his nickels, she scooted off to an office phone and called her older sister's cell phone. She didn't have much time and talked fast. She was unable to communicate exactly where she was and then abruptly hung up. The sister called back. The woman who worked in the office, Terry Carncross, answered the phone.[*]

The victim's sister quickly explained everything she knew and, fortunately, Carncross believed her. Jamelske happened to mention that his next stop was Pets R People Too down the street. Carncross dialed the pet store owner, Keith Alexander, who she happened to be friends with, and explained the situation. Jamelske was in the store during the conversation. Alexander played it safe and didn't confront Jamelske

[*]In an incredible coincidence, Carncross's husband Jamie delivered the concrete Jamelske used to build his dungeon twenty years earlier.[6]

32

on the spot. He called the police.[7]

Meanwhile, the older sister had by now driven from Syracuse to Manlius and was talking to Carncross and a police officer at F-M Returnables. Her cell phone rang; it was her sister, who had again managed to find a phone. She still didn't know where she was, but described everything around her, including a Dodge sign and a yellow car. Terri's husband Jamie was at F-M, too. He had come to pick up his wife. When he overheard the words "Dodge" and "yellow," he immediately remembered that he and Terry had recently seen a bright yellow Dodge Neon and joked that they should buy it. "Hey, they're at Fayettville Dodge!" he exclaimed.[8]

After Jamelske's arrest, police obtained a warrant to search his property. The bulldozers were brought in and neighbors watched in horror as Jamelske's dungeon was unearthed. This was no hastily renovated basement. It was two separate rooms, each measuring twelve by twelve, located three feet underground in his backyard and connected to his basement by a twelve-foot tunnel.

Inside, the cops found a cold-water hose and a bathtub, which functioned as the victims' "shower," a five-gallon bucket the women were forced to use for a toilet, a dirty mattress on the floor, a microwave, and some scattered belongings. In the house, they found photos of women chained against walls, as well as diaries Jamelske forced his prisoners to keep, which included records of exactly when they bathed and brushed their teeth.

Twenty years earlier, when neighbors had asked why he and his son were building an underground bunker, Jamelske said that it was a bomb shelter; that someday he'd have to go down there when America went to war with the Chinese or the Arabs.

But if Jamelske thought he could get out of doing hard time by playing the loon, he was sorely mistaken. This was a man who planned well; he spent fifteen years yanking women off the street and playing very clever psychological games to keep them from attempting to escape or even fighting him when he crawled into the dungeon to rape them, which he did on a daily basis.

He told his victims that contacting the police would be fruitless because the cops were in on it, too. He had partnered with them in a secret slavery trade, he said. Using a particularly devious tactic, Jamelske often referred to his "boss" during conversations with the women. The boss wanted him to chain them to the wall, the boss demanded he have sex with them every day, the boss insisted they mark on the calendar the date and time they had sex. This resulted in victims who not only believed they were ensnared by a cabal involving who knew how many people, but it may have also misdirected their hatred for their captor. Jamelske was just a cog in the wheel, perhaps a victim himself. This furthered the rapist's fantasy that these women were his "girlfriends." It was also an insurance policy for his secret when he'd decide to take one out for a walk with his dogs or to the bar for karaoke night.

Creating this relationship allowed Jamelske to have a better time with the women. On some nights, when he wasn't watching his favorite TV program, *The Man Show,* he would creep through the tunnel for a "date." He videotaped at least one of them, in which his victim teaches the old man how to dance, rap, and talk "street." *Please John,* she might have thought, *and I might please the boss. Then maybe I'll get out of here.* But when Jamelske retires to the other room for a moment, the victim turns her attention to the camera and pleads directly to the "boss" to let her go soon. Little does she know that the only person who would be viewing her appeal was her captor.

The only thing that might have made Jamelske physically vulnerable to attack was the entrance into the dungeon, which was necessarily headfirst. But he came up with a system to prevent that. When he entered the tunnel through his basement, he would turn around and lock the door behind him, using a combination lock. If his victim cracked his skull open with the microwave or something as he slithered into the dungeon from the tunnel, the lock's combination would die with him — and the woman would die alone in the underground, soundproof cement box.[9]

So where was Jamelske's wife, Dorothy, during all this? Upstairs in her bed dying. Dorothy had become very sick in the late eighties, and was later diagnosed with colon cancer. From the beginning of her illness, her interest in sex waned. By the time she was diagnosed with cancer, she was bedridden. Although Jamelske protests to this day that he adored his wife to the day she died in 1999, he says that he had to have sex with *someone*. If his wife couldn't do it, he would find someone who could. That's why he built the dungeon in the first place, he said.

John Jamelske pleaded guilty to five counts of kidnapping and got eighteen years to life. Although he admits he did "something wrong," he qualifies his guilt with statements about how the women lied about some of the details. He insists that he never hurt anyone. When pressed to account for the high number of rapes he was accused of, he backpedals, admitting that what he did wasn't legal, but saying that he didn't inflict pain on anyone. He even claims to this day that he was unaware that abducting women and chaining them to his dungeon wall was a felony. "I did something wrong, but I figured it's like unlawful imprisonment, maybe thirty hours of community service or something of that nature," Jamelske said.[10] In a prison interview with MSNBC, he said, "I would not mind living [in the dungeon]. It's absolutely beautiful down there."

But when push came to shove, when Jamelske stood before a judge instead of a reporter, when there were no more questions to be asked, just prison sentences to be announced, Jamelske displayed his softer side. After the judge read the sentence and berated the rapist in front of the courtroom and television cameras, Jamelske tried to respond. He began to say that he knew he did something wrong, but then broke into tears and couldn't speak. The tears, though, weren't for his victims. John Jamelske's soft side exists for one person: John Jamleske. "I wanted to puke when he started to cry in court," said a relative of the first victim.[11]

John Jamelske quickly began showing his age in prison. His face became more gaunt and he started moving much slower. He formed a walking club with some of the older inmates, and they go for strolls together to keep the blood circulating. But Jamelske's days of hip-hop dancing with girls and singing karaoke at Freddie's Bar in Syracuse are over. He'll most likely die in prison — for once, doing something to please his victims and their families.

Two

L&O SVU: ("Baby Killer," Season 2) A young boy uses a stolen gun to shoot and kill a female classmate during recess.

TRUE STORY: Six-year-old Kayla Rolland was killed by classmate Dedric Owens in Michigan. The gun used in the crime had been stolen by a family friend.

Kayla Rolland was a happy little girl who liked to tell knock-knock jokes and hold tea parties for her dolls in her yard in Mount Morris, Michigan. Kayla had short brown hair and smiled a lot. But lately, she'd been upset about a problem she was having with a classmate. Like Kayla, Dedric Owens was six years old and in the first grade. He was a troublemaker who often spit and cursed at the other first-graders. Recently, Kayla had become his target. He pushed her and taunted her. Kayla didn't like Dedric —

hardly any of the kids did — but she wasn't afraid of him. When he bothered her, she would yell at him to stop. Unfortunately, he wasn't getting the message. On February 28, 2000, Kayla told her mother Dedric was harassing her at school. Thinking it was normal kids' play, her mother advised Kayla to report the boy to the teacher. Kayla thought about it all day. That night, before falling asleep, Kayla decided to follow her mother's advice; she would tell the teacher tomorrow.

Down the street, Dedric Owen was having trouble sleeping again. The sofa bed he shared with his eight-year-old brother was lumpy and uncomfortable. If Dedric managed to fall asleep at all, he was usually jarred awake by one of the many visitors stopping by the house. It was his uncle's place; Dedric and his brother had been there for two weeks — ever since the Owens family was evicted. His mother and his sister were staying with another relative. His father was in jail. Dedric and his brother had to fend for themselves.

Their uncle didn't bother the two boys; he spent most of his time dealing with the people who dropped by — skinny adults with bad skin and half closed eyes and hands that shook when they lit their cigarettes. Sometimes they'd crash at the house, other times they'd stop by for a few minutes and leave. Dedric was free to do what he wanted. He watched whatever he felt like watching on TV. He liked violent movies best.

Dedric didn't get much sleep and was often tired during the day. He didn't like his uncle's house; he didn't like school much either. He was only six years old, and had already earned a reputation as a bully at Theo Buell Elementary School. He cursed all the time, pushed other kids, and stabbed a girl in the arm with a pencil. He frequently had to stay after school for detention. His father asked him once why he was always fighting with other kids. "I hate them," Dedric had replied.

His father had tried to get Dedric to stop fighting, but in January he was sent back to jail and Dedric hadn't seen him since. He didn't see much of his mother either; she worked a lot and Dedric wasn't even sure where she was living. Drugs had torn his family apart. He missed his parents and his sister. He missed his old house too. He was angry about the way things were.

Dedric took that anger out on a girl in his first grade class named Kayla Rolland. He started picking on and teasing her whenever he saw her. One day, he tried to kiss her. Kayla rebuffed him. Enraged, Dedric spat on her desk. In retaliation, she hit him in the arm. He went home that night and hatched a plot to get even with Kayla. He had seen his uncle's roommate Jamelle James loading and unloading a gun and twirling it in his hands. Jamelle kept the gun in a shoebox under his bed. Dedric planned to use the gun to scare Kayla.

On February 29, 2000, Dedric got dressed for school and tucked a .32-caliber semi-automatic handgun into his pants pocket. For good measure, he took along three bullets and a knife. Dedric went to school and acted as if everything was normal. Shortly before ten a.m., teacher Alicia Judd escorted the class to the computer lab on the second floor. Kayla was a few steps ahead of Dedric in the stairwell. Dedric pulled the gun out of his pocket and waved it around, halfheartedly pointing it at some other kids. He called out to Kayla: "I don't like you!" Kayla turned around and shrugged. "So what!" she replied. As she turned back around, Dedric aimed the gun at her and pulled the trigger. The bullet hit Kayla in the arm and traveled through her stomach. Kayla collapsed in a pool of blood in the stairwell. Dedric took off running. He tossed the gun into a garbage can and ducked into the boys' bathroom.

Ms. Judd scrambled for her cell phone and called 911. She begged the dispatcher to send help immediately. Kayla was convulsing and gasping for air. Judd stayed with Kayla, waiting for paramedics to arrive. There was little the emergency workers could do to save the little girl. Kayla Rolland died at 10:20 a.m.

Dedric Owens was found hiding in the boys' lavatory. He was taken into police custody. At the police station, Dedric denied shooting Kayla; he blamed it on another child. When pressed, he admitted that he had brought the gun to school to scare Kayla. He said that he was playing with the gun and shot Kayla by accident. "When we got past the fact that he knew he did it, he said he was trying to scare people in his class. He thought this was like television, meaning people don't really die. He was expressing to police he didn't understand it was real," said Police Chief Eric King.

A dozen children had witnessed the shooting. The story they told police contradicted Dedric's. Classmate Haili Durbin said that another boy had egged Dedric into loading the gun with the bullet he had in his pocket. Dedric had aimed the gun at her first,

43

before settling on Kayla. "He was pointing it at me and then at Kayla and it went into her," Haili said. She told police that Dedric often "hit people and cursed and stuck up his middle finger," and that "he didn't like Kayla because she was mean and yelled at him."[1]

When he killed Kayla, Dedric became the youngest school shooter in American history, and Kayla, the youngest victim. Ironically, Theo Buell Elementary had been chosen as a pilot school for the Primary Mental Health Project, an intervention program designed to detect and treat troubled and potentially violent children. Dedric had been identified as a problem student; he was scheduled to see a school psychologist. A week before the appointment, he shot Kayla Rolland. The system had failed both children.

Because of Dedric's age, there was little chance he would be prosecuted for killing Kayla. Six-year-olds are not criminally liable for crimes they commit. In 1893, the U.S. Supreme Court ruled that children "under the age of 7 years could not be guilty of felony, or punished for any capital offense, for within that age the infant was conclusively presumed to be incapable of committing the crime."

"A six-year-old can't form criminal intent," Steve Drizin, a lawyer at Northwestern University's Children and Family Justice Center in Chicago told reporters. "A six-year-old still believes in the tooth fairy, the Easter bunny, and Santa Claus. They don't make the connections between their actions and the consequences. They have no sense of permanence or death."[2]

As authorities tried to figure out what to do with Dedric, the boy sat at a table in the precinct drawing pictures with a box of crayons an officer had given him. He was calm and did not seem to understand the severity of his actions. "His actions were naughty, in his mindset. He realized a bad thing happened, but at six years old it's hard to form mentally the intent to kill," Genesee County prosecutor Arthur Busch said. However, he added, "That's not to say we're going to do nothing."[3]

The police had a tough time locating Dedric's mother. The address the school had for her and Dedric was outdated. She had not informed the school that her children had moved in with their uncle. Police discovered that the boys had been staying in a run-down crack house frequented by addicts looking to trade guns and other items for crack cocaine. The property was littered with empty beer bottles and trash; a dilapidated car was parked in the front yard, a dirty mattress rested against the side of the house. A police raid turned up a shotgun and a stash of narcotics. Dedric "was basically living in hell," Sheriff Robert Picerell said.[4] The neighbors had repeatedly called the police and social services about the boys next door. No one came out to investigate until it was too late for Kayla Rolland. "It took a killing to get these people out here," one neighbor said.[5]

Busch, a no-nonsense prosecutor with a reputation for being tough on defendants, was moved by Dedric's case. The boy had been dealt a lousy hand in life. At six years old, he was living in squalor and left to fend for himself. Dedric was "a victim of a drug culture and house that's really in chaos," Busch said. "He is as much of a victim, in my opinion, as the little girl. We need to put our arms around him and love him."[6] Charles Patrick Ewing, author of *Kids Who Kill,* agreed. "This kid has been victimized by a family that basically neglected him and put him in a position of danger. If the legal system takes any action, it should be to protect him, not punish him," he said.[7]

The community struggled to understand

how such a terrible tragedy could happen. Newspapers ran stories asking "Who Killed Kayla?" Dedric killed Kayla, of course, but he wasn't legally responsible. Without a villain to prosecute, the community and the Rolland family were denied closure. The question on everyone's lips was where did Dedric get the gun? The shooting inspired President Bill Clinton to renew his call for mandatory safety locks on guns. He pointed out that the rate of gun deaths among U.S. children is nine times higher than the world's twenty-five other largest nations combined. "The child was six years old. How'd that child get that gun? Why could the child fire the gun?" Clinton asked. "If we have the technology today to put in these child safety locks, why don't we do it?"[8]

The murder weapon was traced back to nineteen-year-old Jamelle James. He was taken into custody along with Dedric's uncle Sir Marcus Winfrey, twenty-two. As it turned out, James and Winfrey had outstanding warrants on other charges. They were indicted on federal charges for possession of the gun Dedric used to kill Kayla. Winfrey pleaded guilty and was sentenced to a year in prison. James was also charged with involuntary manslaughter; the prosecutor said James's failure to secure the gun made him culpable for Kayla's murder. James pleaded no contest to the charges and served three years in prison; he was paroled in 2003.

Dedric never returned to his uncle's house. In October 2001, Tamarla Owens agreed to waive her parental rights to her three children. At a custody hearing, prosecutors had introduced evidence that she had beaten one of the children and regularly smoked marijuana in front of all of them. Dedric and his brother were placed in foster care. Tamarla Owens later regained custody of the boys' younger sister. "The day [Dedric] was born, he went from hospital to crack house. He never had a chance," a police investigator said.[9]

The Real SVU

As in the TV show, detectives of the NYPD's Special Victims Squads investigate sexual assault and abuse crimes involving children, and handle all rape cases. Unlike the TV program, these detectives are never the lead investigators on murder cases, which are always handled by homicide detectives. However, if the murder involved sexual assault, Special Victims Squad detectives will often work the case with the lead investigators.

A Special Victims Squad is located in four of New York City's five boroughs: Manhattan, the Bronx, Brooklyn, and Queens; Staten Island does not have such a squad, but the NYPD plans to form one there soon. Though part of the NYPD, each squad retains its own headquarters.

The district attorney's office also has bureaus dedicated solely to prosecuting sex crimes. According to the Manhattan DA's office, its Sex Crimes Unit convicts about one hundred defendants every year and has an overall conviction rate of 90 percent.

THREE

L&O SVU: ("Redemption," Season 3) Released from prison after eighteen years, the "Soho Strangler" is suspected in a string of new sex crimes.

TRUE STORY: Dubbed the "Boston Strangler," Albert DeSalvo was a suspect in the deaths of thirteen women. DeSalvo died in jail before he could be tried, and numerous questions remain to this day about the Boston Strangler's true identity.

Anna Slesers turned on the phonograph and put one of her favorite records on the turntable — *Tristan und Isolde,* Richard Wagner's opera of the great tragic romance. Her son was coming over later to bring her to church, and she wanted to take a bath before he arrived. The church was holding a memorial in honor of the Latvians who died in World War II. Slesers, now fifty-five years old, had lived in Latvia during those violent years when hundreds of thousands of her countrymen were murdered, first by the Communists, then the Nazis. She had managed to survive the war that destroyed her country, and she emigrated to America shortly after. Her apartment was nothing fancy. She lived in a low-income neighborhood of Boston, but Slesers, a seamstress, didn't complain. She had steady work and enough money to get by, and most importantly, she was safe. What more could a person ask for? She put her robe on and tied the belt tightly around her slim waist.

As she was preparing for her bath, she heard someone knock. It was too early to be her son. Hesitantly, she opened the door . . .

For eighteen months, from June 1962 until January 1964, the so-called Boston Strangler was a black cloud over the City on a Hill. Thirteen women were murdered in their homes, and the police were powerless to do anything about it. Serial killings weren't totally unknown to Americans at the time, but they weren't as common as the phenomenon is today. (The phrase "serial killer" wouldn't even be invented until the next decade.) And the glorification of

51

serial murderers — the lovable movie serial killer, the "ironic" Ted Bundy T-shirt, rock songs written about legendary psychos — was nonexistent. The Boston Strangler changed all that.

Until this point Jack the Ripper, who preyed on prostitutes in England nearly a century earlier, was the most notorious serial killer in the American sensibility. The Boston Strangler replaced him. Unlike the Ripper, the Strangler didn't target prostitutes, but like his English counter-part, he did work in a relatively limited area, he always targeted women, and his victims usually lived in lower-income neighborhoods.[1] The two men had another thing in common: They were never identified beyond a reasonable doubt. Jack the Ripper's murders were never solved, and some of the Boston Strangler murder cases remain open to this day.

Anna Slesers wouldn't live to hear the end of her favorite opera. When her son arrived in the early evening, his mother didn't answer the door. Odd, he thought. Maybe she just stepped out to the store for something. He left for a few minutes and came back. When his knocking again went unanswered, he began to panic. He broke the

52

door open and saw Anna lying on the floor, her legs spread and her head in a pool of blood. Her robe was opened wide, exposing her body; the belt was tied tightly around her neck.

There was no sign of forced entry, so police concluded that Slesers had let her killer in. Her son insisted that she was shy and cautious and would never let a stranger into her home. But a work crew had been working on the apartment facade — scaffolding covered the front of the building — so perhaps a laborer, or a man posing as a laborer, had told Slesers he needed access to her apartment.

Exactly two weeks later, on June 28, an eighty-five-year-old woman named Mary Mullen answered a knock at her door. The man most likely told her that he was doing work on the building and needed access to her apartment. She let him in. When the stranger came up from behind and put his arm around her neck, Mary Mullen instantly had a heart attack and died on the spot.[*]

[*]Many details of how the murders took place have been reported using Albert DeSalvo's detailed confessions. Since the publication of most books on the subject, however, much evidence has

53

On June 30, the Boston Strangler killed two women: Helen Blake and Nina Nichols, sixty-five and sixty-eight years old, respectively. Blake was found strangled, with one of her stockings tied into a bow around her neck, and raped with an unknown object in her apartment north of Boston. Nichols was found lying on her back with her legs spread, facing the doorway, probably to heighten the shock for anyone who entered the apartment. The killer had tied a stocking around her throat, too. Forensic experts concluded that he had used a wine bottle to rape her.

A pattern was emerging. In addition to similar means of death and the sexual nature of the crimes, all five victims were older women living in apartments. Investigators believed someone was going on a rampage targeting mother figures, but they weren't sure. The women of Boston, young and old, weren't going to wait and find out. They began buying up all the dead bolts in

---

emerged clearing DeSalvo of some, if not all, of the murders, and the Boston attorney general's office has reopened some of the cases. We've chosen to assume DeSalvo was lying about some or all of the murders and, therefore, have not used any of his descriptions of the murders.

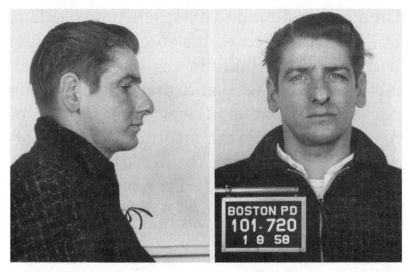

The Boston Strangler? Maybe not. Albert DeSalvo claimed to have been responsible for thirteen murders, but compelling new evidence suggests that at least some of his confessions were bogus.

town, and the locksmith business boomed. Animal shelters were sending out adoptive dogs faster than they were coming in. And if a woman was a few minutes late to work, the police might very well get a call from a frantic coworker.

The panic was well-founded. Two more women were soon murdered. Ida Irga, seventy-five, was killed on August 19. Again, the killer clearly wanted to shock the first people through the apartment door. He had torn her dress open, spread her legs, and placed each one on a chair. Around her neck, he had tied a pillow case. Eleven days later, police found sixty-seven-year-old Jane Sullivan strangled with a stocking. The killer had placed her body in the bathtub, kneeling and face down, and then filled the tub partway with water. Local police, FBI profilers, and the Boston attorney general's office were scrambling to find the killer, but were totally stymied. Tragically, all they could do at this point was wait for the next murder.

Three and a half months passed without a sign of the Boston Strangler. Then on December 5, twenty-year-old Sophie Clark was killed, the seventh victim. Someone had gained entry to her home, then raped and killed her. Clark's body was positioned similarly to other victims, and she had three stockings tied around her neck — which fit with the Strangler's general pattern. More important to many investigators, however, was Clark's young age and her race. She was black. Such killers rarely cross racial boundaries and, most often, when a pattern is set — in this case, the general age and race of the six previous victims — they don't often deviate from it. Nonetheless, police erred on the side of caution, focusing on the means of the murder, and the positioning of the body. Clark was officially considered the seventh victim of the

Boston Strangler.

The new year would bring no peace to Boston. On December 31, Patricia Bissette was strangled with a stocking. The twenty-three-year-old white woman was found dead in her bed with the sheets pulled up to her chin. Investigators were more baffled than before. About two months later, in the beginning of March 1963, Mary Brown, a sixty-nine-year-old woman, was found in her apartment with her dress torn open. She had been beaten to death with a blunt object and placed on her bed, where the killer covered her with a sheet. He then stabbed her in the breast with a fork. Again, this was officially considered the work of the Boston Strangler — nine brutal murders in less than one year.

A month later, the body of Beverly Samans, a woman in her early twenties, was discovered in her home. Her clothes had been removed and the killer had placed a blouse across her shoulders. Like earlier murder victims, Samans was positioned with her legs spread apart, and a stocking was tied in a bow around her neck, but her hands had been tied behind her back and a piece of cloth pushed into her mouth. She had been stabbed more than twenty times.

The eleventh murder of those credited to the Boston Strangler occurred on September 8. The victim was Evelyn Corbin, fifty-eight years old, found with her hands tied in front of her and strangled with a stocking, which was tied around her neck; another one was tied around her ankle. Corbin had been positioned with her legs spread.

On November 24, 1963, two days after the assassination of John F. Kennedy, twenty-three-year-old Joann Graff was strangled. She was found lying on her bed with two stockings and a leotard tied around her neck.

Four days into 1964, the thirteenth victim of the Boston Strangler lost her life. Mary Sullivan was nineteen years old when she was murdered. Investigators found her on the bed in a sitting position. Her knees were up, her legs were spread, and a broom handle had been placed into her vagina; a stocking and scarf were tied in bows around her neck. The killer had ejaculated into her mouth. Perhaps the most gruesome scene left behind by the Boston Strangler, the murder of Mary Sullivan was the last. The murders ended as abruptly as they began.

And, still, police didn't know where to turn.

One man's name — Albert DeSalvo — would eventually be connected to all the murders, and for nearly forty years most of the world considered him the one and only Boston Strangler. Although he confessed to all thirteen murders, he was never convicted — he was stabbed to death in jail before he could be tried. The Massachusetts attorney general's office considered it an open-and-shut case. They had nearly one-hundred hours worth of confession on tape. But at the beginning of the new century, and with revolutionary gains in DNA research, many people would begin to question not only if DeSalvo committed all the crimes, but whether he had committed *any* of them.

Albert DeSalvo was no doubt a sexual predator. Raised on the outskirts of Boston, DeSalvo's home life was about as bad as it gets. His father Frank was an angry, thieving alcoholic who taught young Albert to steal when he was five years old. Frank liked to get drunk and beat either his children or his wife, who had married Frank when she was fifteen years old.[2] After he was apprehended for the Strangler killings, Albert told police how he once witnessed his father hit his mother in the face, knocking some of her teeth out. Then he took her hand and snapped her fingers one by one. And he once told a psychiatrist that his father often brought home prostitutes and had sex with them in front of the family.

DeSalvo's upbringing was tailor-made to create a sexual predator. And, as many serial killer experts point out, exposure to this type of family violence is exactly what helps create serial killers. According to an exhaustive FBI study, the majority of serial killers come from homes in which at least one parent suffers from alcoholism and has a criminal record, and over 80 percent of serial killers began stealing at an early age.[3] DeSalvo had all the elements in spades.

In 1943, at the age of twelve, Albert was sent to reform school for burglary. When he was released in his early teens he continued stealing, claiming in a later interview that the rush he got from breaking into people's homes was sexual in nature. When he wasn't burglarizing, DeSalvo spent much of his time looking through peoples' windows in an attempt to see them having sex, or at least changing their clothes.

In 1948, the Bean Town Peeping Tom joined the army and was deployed to Germany. A woman named Irma from Frankfurt had the misfortune of meeting and falling in love with DeSalvo. The two got married and returned to the States in 1954. Within less than a year, DeSalvo twice knocked on random front doors and attempted to enter the peoples' homes. On the first occasion, he told the woman of the house that he had seen someone trying to break into her home as he drove by. Frightened, the woman allowed him in to check, but as he began asking personal questions, she started to realize that it was DeSalvo himself she should fear. She went into another room and locked the door, and DeSalvo eventually left.

A couple of weeks later, he knocked on a door and a nine-year-old girl answered. When he learned her mother wasn't home, he explained that he was the landlord and had come to get the rent. The girl let him in. The mother arrived home shortly after, by which time DeSalvo had groped her daughter. The mother called the police. DeSalvo was tracked down and fined one thousand dollars.

All this creepiness was only a foreshadow of things to come. In 1960, having received an honorable discharge from the army, DeSalvo began working as a laborer. It was during this period that Boston newspapers gave him the nickname the "Measuring Man." Albert would go around knocking on apartment doors. When a good-looking woman answered, he would pretend to be a modeling scout canvassing the neighborhood for beautiful women. Amazingly enough, he often succeeded in talking his way into the home and getting permission to take the woman's measurements — which of course gave him the opportunity to touch the women's breasts and other body parts. Then he would leave, and the women would never hear from the mysterious modeling scout again.

Caught breaking into a house in 1961, DeSalvo confessed to being the Measuring Man, for which he received a year and a half prison sentence. He was released six months early for good behavior. Two months later, Anna Slesers was murdered.

During the string of killings, the Boston Police Department set up a Boston Strangler task force. The investigators were able to come up with some suspects, but they couldn't get anything to stick. Then, a miracle occurred. A year after the murder of Mary Sullivan, the final victim of the Boston Strangler, a man who had been breaking into women's homes and sexually assaulting them was caught. The "Green Man" (he always wore green pants during his assaults) turned out to be Albert De-Salvo. What made these crimes so bizarrely different from the Strangler murders was that DeSalvo would often apologize as he assaulted his victim.

While in custody for the Green Man rapes and assaults, DeSalvo told police that he had broken into as many as four hundred homes. Later, after being placed in Bridge-water State Hospital, an insane asylum, he ratcheted that number up to a whopping one thousand break-ins. This, in a period of two years? DeSalvo was clearly full of it, but there was no doubt in anyone's mind that he was a dangerous predator. The psychiatrist who interviewed DeSalvo, Dr. Ames Robey, diagnosed him as a sociopath and eventually considered the suspect unfit for trial.[4]

DeSalvo didn't care for Bridgewater, but it was certainly better than prison. This is where DeSalvo met George Nassar, a conscienceless multiple murderer with coal-black lifeless eyes, a high IQ, and a deep hatred for women. Compared to the frigid, spooky, and unapproachable Nassar, De-Salvo came across as a doe-eyed doofus. Yet the two were inseparable and reportedly discussed the Boston Strangler murders ad nauseum. (Nassar had lived in the vicinity of a number of the murders, and police had found a police and a doctor's uniform in his closet.)[5]

Eventually, Nassar introduced DeSalvo to his lawyer, a promising young attorney named F. Lee Bailey, who later explained that when Nassar first told him about De-Salvo, he (Nassar) inquired whether a criminal could legally make money from a book describing the crimes. At the time there were no laws against this, so Bailey said yes, but qualified that a confession on paper wouldn't be a good idea.[6] Bailey eventually agreed to represent DeSalvo for the Green Man crimes. He would use an insanity defense in order to keep DeSalvo out of prison — his client's greatest fear in life. While he had no problem dominating women in the dead of night, DeSalvo was petrified of the characters he knew he'd meet in prison.

In his book *A Rose for Mary,* Casey Sherman, the nephew of Mary Sullivan, details the circumstances behind DeSalvo's confession. First of all, Sherman points out, the Bridgewater psychiatrist said that DeSalvo didn't fit the profile of the Boston Strangler; Nassar, though, was a dead ringer. And one of the head detectives on the Boston Strangler Task Force didn't believe DeSalvo's confession for a minute: not just because it didn't ring true, but because he had another suspect in mind with a real motive in at least two of the murders. Also, no physical evidence connected DeSalvo to any of the thirteen murders.

The most shocking aspect of the investigation involved the interrogations of DeSalvo conducted by John Bottomly, a real estate lawyer and the Massachusetts attorney general's appointed head of the Boston Strangler Task Force. In transcripts of more than sixty hours of interviews, Bottomly, clearly untrained in the art of interrogation, often leads DeSalvo to the answer he's looking for. And DeSalvo, when questioned on facts of the murders that weren't printed in the papers, gets numerous details wrong.

These tapes were not released to the public, however, and DeSalvo insisted he had committed the murders. He truly believed he would get rich off a book deal; somehow, he got it into his head that he could sell pieces of information on the murders for ten grand each, and that wasn't including movie rights.

Thanks to DeSalvo's public posturing as the Boston Strangler, the newspapers and, as a result, the public in general accepted him at his word. In January 1967, as he and

Bailey expected, he was convicted for the Green Man rapes. Only he was sentenced to life in Walpole State Prison — not in a mental hospital.

Although he wasn't living in the environment he had hoped for, DeSalvo *was* able to sell his story to author Gerold Frank. DeSalvo basked in his newfound importance. After Frank's book *The Boston Strangler* climbed to the top of the bestseller list, DeSalvo recorded a song in prison — "Strangler in the Night" — and sold commemorative choker necklaces in the prison's gift shop, made by "Albert DeSalvo, the Boston Strangler."[7] As he had hoped for all along, DeSalvo was making money based on his status as the most notorious killer in the country.

But when Hollywood producers decided there was a lucrative market for the story, they didn't come to DeSalvo with their checkbooks out. They did, though, pay DeSalvo's wife for the right to use her children's names; a number of others involved in the investigation and "prosecution" of the Boston Strangler were paid for their stories, as well, including John Bottomly.[8] *The Boston Strangler,* starring Tony Curtis and Henry Fonda, opened in October 1968 to packed houses. And while most

"Queen for a Day"

On television, we often see a defense attorney or suspect request that what they're about to say be "off the record." The prosecutor usually grants the request. In the real world, though, everything has to be on the record.

This doesn't mean, however, that the prosecutor will always use the suspect's words against him. In order to successfully investigate a case, there has to be some give and take. A written contract called "queen for a day" allows a suspect to reveal knowledge of a crime with the promise that it won't be used against him in those particular proceedings. (The suspect's words can, however, be used to gather evidence against him in other investigations.)

Although the goal of "queen for a day" on the suspect's part is immunity, it doesn't necessarily work out that way. The agreement is really just the first step toward that end; it allows the prosecutor to decide if the quality of information gained is worth passing on an indictment.

of it was a crock, audiences lapped it up as gospel truth. Newspapers and court rulings are one thing, a movie is another. Although never tried for the Boston Strangler murders, Albert DeSalvo was then in the public's opinion the infamous killer — beyond a reasonable doubt. So while his wife and investigators were raking in the cash, munching on popcorn, and watching themselves portrayed on the big screen, DeSalvo was sitting on his prison bunk counting his pennies from the proceeds of cheap necklaces he had hawked to a few self-indulgent customers.

He was not happy. The whole thing had turned out to be a financial disaster. During the next five years, DeSalvo tried to find a way out. He attempted to sue the film's producers for portraying him unfairly and ruining his reputation. The case was thrown out. DeSalvo was becoming frantic. He started behaving strangely during visits with his brother, the only relative who maintained ties with him. Constantly shadowed by his sinister friend George Nassar — even during these visits — DeSalvo nevertheless began to change his tune. One day he rhetorically asked his brother if he wanted to know who the real Boston Strangler was, and then playfully poked Nassar, for which he received a hard look.[9] DeSalvo immediately shut his mouth.[*]

Then, after not hearing from DeSalvo for years, Ames Robey received a call from him. DeSalvo asked him to come to the prison as soon as he could, adding that he wanted to "tell the real story" of the Boston Strangler.[10]

DeSalvo wouldn't live to tell his secret. Not long after he hung up the phone, he was found in the infirmary lying in a pool of blood, stabbed to death just hours before he was to reveal his secret. Two men were tried for the murder, but not convicted. No one ever answered for DeSalvo's murder.

Upon cleaning out his cell, guards found a poem DeSalvo had penned. It begins:

Here is the story of the Strangler, yet
  untold
The man who claims he killed thirteen
  women, young and old.
The elusive Strangler, there he goes.
Where his wanderlust sends him, no one
  knows.

[*]Albert DeSalvo reportedly told Tom Troy, an attorney he hired after firing F. Lee Bailey, that he was not the Boston Strangler. (*A Rose for Mary,* 100)

The poem goes on to describe how the Strangler avoided capture for so long — a testament to his genius — and then discusses a secret he has never revealed:

> Today he sits in a prison cell,
> Deep inside only a secret can he tell.
> People everywhere are still in doubt,
> Is the Strangler in prison, or roaming about?

DeSalvo was certainly not the next Robert Lowell, but his scrawl, although not exactly a retraction of his confession, is cryptic enough to raise eyebrows.

The fact that DeSalvo was never convicted for any of the Boston Strangler murders has piqued the curiosity of the more inquisitive people familiar with the case. When Casey Sherman got through with his twelve-year crusade to find the real killer of his aunt, Mary Sullivan, all bets on DeSalvo's status as the Boston Strangler were off.

Sherman painstakingly compared the transcripts and tapes of DeSalvo's confession with the real facts of the murders. He came up with one inaccuracy after another, ranging from incorrect descriptions of murder scenes to claims that he raped certain victims when no evidence of rape had occurred.[11] In the case of his aunt's murder, Sherman noticed, DeSalvo claimed to have strangled her with his hands, but she had really been strangled with a stocking and scarf. In each murder DeSalvo confessed to, he got more than one thing wrong. These inaccuracies, combined with Bottomly's "interrogations" (if they can be called that; Bottomly, either due to inexperience or the desire to get DeSalvo behind bars as quickly as possible, consistently suggested the real answers to DeSalvo through the wording of his questions), convinced Casey of what he had believed for a long time. Albert DeSalvo didn't murder his aunt.

Others who investigated the case maintain that DeSalvo was without a doubt the Boston Strangler, including a long-time reporter for the *Boston Record* named Eddie Corsetti, who cites minute details about the crime scenes that even the police didn't notice until they talked to DeSalvo and then went back to verify his claims. For instance, DeSalvo pointed out that the bathtub faucets in Jane Sullivan's apartment were backwards: the hot faucet emitted cold water and vice versa. DeSalvo noticed also that Patricia Bisette's door violated city codes because it opened outward instead of in, a detail the police apparently hadn't noted until DeSalvo mentioned it.[12]

The controversy came to a head in 2000. Convinced he had enough proof of DeSalvo's innocence in the case of Mary Sullivan's murder, Sherman contacted the Boston Police Department to get his hands on the crime scene evidence. They said they couldn't find it. And even if they did have it, Sherman and his family didn't necessarily have a right to it. Sherman hired a lawyer and contacted one of the best forensic scientists in the business. The use of DNA was relatively new at the time, but cases across the country were being reopened because of it. Sherman sued the Commonwealth of Massachusetts to gain possession of the evidence and conduct his own investigation of the thirty-five-year-old crime.

While the argument was waylaid in the court system, Sherman tracked down De-Salvo's brother Richard who, after much coaxing, agreed to donate his DNA to the private investigation. (DNA from siblings always contains certain similarities) Sherman wasn't going to sit around and wait for the court's decision. Convinced that the Commonwealth would tie it up for as long as possible, which could easily be years, Sherman received permission from his mother (Mary's sister) to exhume Sullivan's body. He learned that the corpse had been embalmed, which meant that there was a good chance that any DNA left by the killer would still be present. Soon after, Massachusetts Attorney General Tom Reilly announced that his office had tracked down sperm samples that had been taken from Mary's body. The Commonwealth reopened the Mary Sullivan murder, which of course complicated Sherman's lawsuit even further.

Nonetheless, Casey's investigation continued. More than a year after exhuming Mary Sullivan's body, the DNA experts working on behalf of the Shermans announced their results. First, the skull showed no blunt trauma, even though DeSalvo claimed to have hit her in the head until she was unconscious. Second, scientists found no evidence of manual strangulation; DeSalvo said he had strangled her. Third, tests of the semen they had located on her body showed it did not belong to Albert DeSalvo.

In December 2001, the court announced its verdict. Because the case of Mary Sullivan's murder was ongoing, the family could not have access to the evidence.

Nevertheless, the Attorney General refused to part with the evidence, prompting Sherman to file suit against the Commonwealth to get it. As we write, this matter has yet to be solved.

FOUR

L&O SVU: ("Mean," Season 5) Three popular but particularly nasty teenage girls brutally murder a friend and stuff her body in the trunk of a car.

TRUE STORY: Four Indiana teenagers abducted and killed twelve-year-old Shanda Sharer, an unwitting participant in a deadly love triangle.

In the fall of 1991, the halls of Hazelwood Junior High were abuzz with gossip about a new seventh-grader. Her name was Shanda Sharer and she had recently moved to Indiana from Kentucky. A pretty girl with bright eyes and golden hair, Shanda was just twelve years old but seemed older. She smiled often, a winning smile that belied her anxiety about being the new kid in school.

It's never easy being the new kid. The

experience was especially difficult for Shanda, who was also making the transition from parochial to public school. In parochial school, the students wore uniforms, raised their hands to speak in class, and respected their elders. It was stifling at times but it was also an orderly, safe environment, one in which young Shanda flourished.

Public school was a shock to her system. Kids wore what they wanted, talked in class, sassed their teachers. For Shanda, it was both terrifying and titillating. She did her best to fit in. At twelve, Shanda was one of the youngest students at Hazelwood, much to her chagrin. She longed to be a teenager and tried to dress and act the part, wearing tight blue jeans that complimented her slim build and adopting a cool facade. Each morning, Shanda carefully applied her makeup and painstakingly curled her blonde hair until it was just right. Her efforts did not go unnoticed.

Fifteen-year-old Amanda Heavrin was one of Shanda's more ardent admirers. She was a quiet girl who dressed and carried herself like a boy. Amanda was a determined suitor, wooing the younger girl with love notes, phone calls, and flowers. Shanda was flattered by the attention Amanda bestowed on her. At first, she was grateful for the company. Despite her good looks, Shanda had not made many friends in her new school. But soon, she and Amanda became friends. Shanda had always liked boys but found herself drawn to Amanda; the older girl was so persistent and so nice to her. Their friendship blossomed into romance.

The two girls began spending time together after school. When they weren't together, they wrote notes back and forth or talked on the phone. Shanda's mother, Jackie Vaught, found the friendship unsettling. She didn't approve of Amanda and felt the girl was too old to be hanging around her twelve-year-old daughter. But Shanda was so lonely and Amanda seemed to be the only friend she had in Indiana. Jackie had her misgivings but allowed Shanda to socialize with Amanda.

Jackie Vaught wasn't the only one who was bothered by Shanda and Amanda's burgeoning friendship. Melinda Loveless was seething over it. Amanda was Melinda's girlfriend and the two had been seriously dating for some time — until Shanda arrived on the scene.

A lovely doe-eyed girl with cascading dark curls, Melinda was a consummate flirt with a raunchy sense of humor. She dressed in the latest fashions and turned heads wher-

Leader of the group that murdered Shanda Sharer, Melinda Loveless smiles for the policeman.

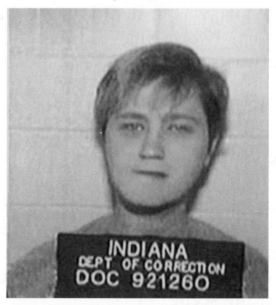

Prior to the murder, Laurie Tackett told friends how she dreamed of drinking human blood and setting someone on fire.

Dazed and confused-looking Toni Lawrence is often credited with being least involved in the slaying of Shanda Sharer.

ever she went. Melinda wasn't used to competition. She considered Amanda her "wife" and was stunned to see her fawning over Shanda. She swallowed her pride and dashed off a letter to her rival. "Amanda and I are going together & she loves me & I love her & she only wants to be friends with you. You need to accept that!" she wrote. "You need to find you a boyfriend cause Amanda is mine."[1]

Amanda, however, continued to encourage Shanda's affections. They went on outings together and even enjoyed sleepovers at the younger girl's house where they

Like Loveless, Hope Rippey seems more than happy to have her mugshot taken. Rippey poured gasoline on Shanda.

danced together and shared secret kisses. Shanda was so different from Melinda, her opposite in many ways. For starters, Shanda was blonde and innocent; Melinda, a brunette seductress. Shanda was easygoing, Melinda possessive. Shanda was a naïf just beginning to discover her sexuality. Melinda, on the other hand, had experimented with both boys and girls before deciding she was gay.

The drama went on for several months with Amanda flip-flopping between Shanda and Melinda. It was difficult to keep her meetings with her two girlfriends secret. All three girls attended the same school and things got ugly fast. Melinda menaced Shanda in the lunchroom and in the common hallways. Though smaller and younger, Shanda did not back down. Amanda watched as things spiraled out of control. "I don't think I would ever tell Melinda we are going out together," Amanda warned Shanda. "She would probably kill you."[2]

Shanda had always been a good student who participated in sports and school activities. Since transferring to Hazelwood, her grades had plummeted. She'd become quiet and secretive. Jackie was worried. While cleaning her daughter's room, she stumbled upon a stash of letters Amanda had written to Shanda. The content and the sexual tone alarmed her. Jackie forbade Shanda from seeing Amanda and arranged to have her transferred to a local parochial school. She hoped the change of venue would solve Shanda's social problems. It did. Shanda perked up, made new friends, and even joined the school's basketball team. Jackie was relieved.

What Jackie didn't know, however, was that Shanda and Amanda continued to exchange letters, talk on the phone, and sneak off to be together whenever they could. Melinda suspected Amanda was still seeing Shanda. One night she caught the two of them together. Furious, she demanded that Amanda choose whom she wanted to be with. Amanda chose Melinda. "If you even try to talk to Amanda again, I'm going to fucking kill you," a triumphant Melinda warned Shanda.[3] Amanda promised not to see the younger girl again. It was a promise she did not keep.

By January 1992, Melinda Loveless was adamant: she wanted Shanda Sharer dead. Her new friend Laurie Tackett listened with rapt attention as Melinda explained why Shanda had to go. Seventeen-year-old Laurie was a tough-looking girl with short blonde hair and a penchant for the occult. She was from Madison and had met Melinda through mutual friends. Laurie told people she could channel the dead. She had a preoccupation with fire and said she wanted to see someone burn to death. Most people thought Laurie was weird. Melinda liked her and knew Laurie was eager to prove her loyalty to her.

On Friday, January 10, Laurie arrived at Melinda's house with two friends in tow. Fifteen-year-olds Toni Lawrence and Hope Rippey had never met Melinda but they'd heard a lot about her from Laurie. Toni was a tiny girl with mousy brown hair; a pair of large glasses obscured much of her face. Hope was thin and had long brown hair that hung down past her shoulders. The four girls holed up in Melinda's room for a while before deciding to go to a punk rock show nearby. But first, they had to make a detour.

Shanda Sharer was spending the weekend with her father and his new family. After dinner, there was a knock on the door. Shanda opened the door to find two teenaged girls she had never seen before. They told her they were Amanda's friends, Hope and Toni, and that Amanda wanted to see her. Shanda hadn't seen Amanda in a while and was eager to reconnect with her. She asked the girls to come back around midnight when her family would be asleep.

A few hours later Hope was back. This time, Laurie, another stranger to Shanda, accompanied her. Shanda tiptoed outside to meet them, careful not to slam the door behind her. The girls ushered Shanda to their car. Laurie sat in the backseat; Shanda was asked to sit in front between Toni and Hope, who was driving. "Where's Amanda?" Shanda asked. Amanda, the girls said, was waiting for her at the Witches' Castle, an abandoned, rundown cottage where neighborhood teens hung out. They would take Shanda to her. Shanda hadn't planned on staying out but before she could reply, Hope was steering the car onto the road.

Toni was silent, staring out the passenger window through her huge glasses. Hope was chatty and smiled a lot, exposing a gap between her two front teeth. Hope asked Shanda about her relationship with Amanda. Shanda told her that she and Amanda were close and that they had been dating for a few months.

Just then a fourth figure appeared in the backseat. It was Melinda Loveless. She had been hiding under a blanket the whole time. Laurie snickered as Melinda lunged forward with a kitchen knife. She held the blade against Shanda's throat and ordered the twelve-year-old to tell her when she had last seen Amanda. Terrified, Shanda began to shake and cry. "Amanda knows I'm going to kill you," Melinda taunted. "She wants you dead just as much as I do!"[4]

At the Witches' Castle, the girls dragged Shanda out of the car. Melinda tied her wrists and ankles with rope. As Toni watched, the other girls took turns terrorizing Shanda with the knife. They kicked and punched her and threatened to cut off her hair. Hope took Shanda's Mickey

Mouse watch and put it on. Laurie told Shanda they were going to set her on fire. Sobbing uncontrollably, Shanda begged them to let her go.

Spooked by some passing cars, the girls pushed Shanda back into the car and left the Witches' Castle. They decided to make the one-hour journey out to Laurie's house in Madison. Along the way, they stopped at a gas station to fuel up the car and fill a plastic soda bottle with gasoline. Toni made a few calls to friends but never mentioned Shanda.

On the way to Madison, Shanda was subjected to more violence. They made her strip down to her underwear. While Hope held her down, Melinda attempted to cut Shanda's throat with the kitchen knife. The knife proved too dull, so Melinda and Laurie plunged it into the girl's stomach and chest instead. Then Laurie attempted to strangle her with a rope. Shanda fell silent. Thinking she was dead, they tossed her bloody, battered body back into the trunk of the car and continued on their way.

At Laurie's house, the girls opened the trunk to inspect their victim. Soaked in blood, Shanda sat up and whispered "Mommy." Laurie stabbed her some more in the chest and legs and hit her in the head several times with a tire iron. Hope sprayed Windex onto Shanda; she watched with glee as the cleanser bubbled up inside the girl's wounds.

While Toni waited with Hope at the house, Laurie and Melinda went for a ride with their human cargo. Along the way, Laurie made frequent stops to bludgeon Shanda again and again with the tire iron. Melinda sat in the car listening to the radio.

Morning was approaching when they returned to pick up Toni and Hope. The foursome piled back into the car and headed out to an abandoned soybean field. Shanda was barely breathing as the girls pulled her out of the trunk and laid her on the frozen ground. Hope doused her with the gasoline from the soda bottle. Laurie could hardly contain her excitement as she lit a match and set Shanda on fire. Afraid of getting caught, the girls made a hasty retreat.

Melinda wanted to make sure Shanda was dead. At her request, Laurie made a U-turn and headed back to the field. Melinda hopped out of the car and poured the remaining gasoline over Shanda, watching as the flames engulfed her rival's bloody body. Shanda curled into a fetal position; her tongue darted in and out of her mouth. Melinda found the sight funny. Back in the car, she told the other girls that Shanda looked like a snake. They left the field for good and went to McDonald's for breakfast.

Shanda Sharer died at dawn on January 12, 1992, after being held captive and brutalized for hours. Her body was discovered by two men out quail hunting. Shanda's face was burned beyond recognition and the medical examiner had to use dental records to determine her identity. The autopsy revealed that she had been stabbed and bludgeoned numerous times and sodomized with a foreign object before finally succumbing to smoke inhalation.

It didn't take long for the sheriff's department to solve the case — leads began pouring in before Shanda's body was even found. A teenage boy reported that he overheard some girls talking about the crime in a local bowling alley. And then a hysterical Toni Lawrence came forward to report that she had "witnessed" a murder. Toni mistakenly believed that she wouldn't be held accountable for her role in Shanda's death. She was wrong. All four girls were arrested and charged with murder.

The murder stunned the citizens of Madison, a quaint community dotted with small farms, antique shops, and country inns.

Many had trouble believing that four teen-age girls were capable of committing such a heinous crime. "We're living in a state of shock and disbelief," Madison mayor Morris Wooden told reporters.[5] The fact that twelve-year-old Shanda was the victim in a deadly homosexual love triangle was difficult for some residents to accept. In 1992, the word "lesbian" was not "native to everyday speech in Madison," a local reporter wrote. "So some prefer to interpret the competition between Sharer and Loveless for a third girl's affection as the kind of platonic crushes teenage girls cycle through on their way to maturity."[6]

Prosecutor Guy Townsend had a mountain of evidence against all four girls; he was eager to broker plea deals with them and avoid lengthy court trials. Toni was the first to accept Townsend's deal, agreeing to plead guilty to the lesser charge of criminal confinement. She was also required to testify against her coconspirators. Initially, the other three girls refused to cut a deal with the prosecutor. Melinda claimed that Laurie had masterminded the murder; and Laurie, in turn, put the blame on Melinda. Hope insisted she was innocent. Townsend was frustrated by their insistence to go to trial. He played his trump card: he filed notice to seek the death penalty against Melinda and Laurie, and a life sentence for Hope (like Toni, Hope was ineligible for the death penalty because she was just fifteen at the time of the crime). The ruse worked. All three girls eventually pleaded guilty.

During the sentencing hearings, defense attorneys introduced evidence that the girls had been subjected to sexual, physical, and psychological abuse as children. The hope was that the judges would take these mitigating factors into consideration before meting out sentences. Melinda, the court learned, hailed from a deeply dysfunctional family; her father was a sexual deviant who beat his wife and molested each of his three daughters.[*] Laurie took the stand and testified that she had been repeatedly molested as a child but under cross-examination refused to name her attackers.

In Hope's case, the defense argued that she was too emotionally immature to understand the grievous nature of her actions. A defense psychologist said Hope had acted out of peer pressure. As for Toni, defense witnesses testified in court that she had

[*]Shortly after Melinda's sentencing trial, Larry Loveless was convicted of multiple counts of child sexual abuse.

been raped a year earlier by a boy who went unpunished. The defense strategy disgusted Jackie Vaught. "I see attorneys trying to convince everyone that these girls were all victims. The victim here is Shanda Renee Sharer and her family and friends."[7]

Although the defendants had already pleaded guilty, prosecutor Townsend wanted to be sure the judges gave them the harshest sentences allowed. He did his best to underscore the depravity of their crimes at the sentencing hearings. A number of the girls' friends were called to testify. Kary Pope, who knew both Melinda and Laurie, testified that Melinda told her "if she had the chance she would kill Shanda." According to Pope and subsequent witnesses, Laurie was fascinated with fire and with blood, going so far as to cut her arms and drink her own blood. Pope said Laurie told her she fantasized about sticking a knife in someone's stomach and thought it would be "fun just to kill someone."[8]

At her sentencing hearing, Toni testified that her actions the night of the murder were prompted by fear. She said that she believed the girls would kill her if she intervened on Shanda's behalf. Townsend pointed out that Toni had several opportunities to call for help — at the gas station when she phoned some friends and then in Madison when Laurie and Melinda left her and Hope at Laurie's house — but did nothing to stop the attack.

Hope, who was sentenced last, declined to take the stand. Townsend read her police statement to the court in which Hope admitted to luring Shanda into the car and later pouring gasoline on her. Before rendering Hope's sentence, the judge told the court that Hope's "lack of mercy, of tender courage, is a horrifying lesson to us all."[9]

In the end, Toni Lawrence was sentenced to twenty years in prison. For her part in the murder, Hope Rippey was given a fifty-year sentence. Melinda and Laurie were each sentenced to sixty years in prison. "It's like you took the Leopold and Loeb case, recast it for girls and set it in Main Street, USA," said *Madison Courier* reporter Wayne Eagle.[10]

Under Indiana's "good time" rule, prisoners are awarded one day of credit off their sentences for each day of good behavior. By towing the line, a well-behaved prisoner can slash his or her sentence in half. And so in 2000, with half of her sentence left, Toni Lawrence walked out of prison a free woman. Hope Rippey was released in 2006

91

after serving just thirteen years of her original fifty-year sentence. Apparently, the girl who had sprayed Windex into the wounds of a dying twelve-year-old was a model prisoner, one whom the prison board felt deserved a second chance. Melinda Loveless and Laurie Tackett will be eligible for parole in 2022.

The Medical Examiner

Medical examiners don't get out much. If they ever do visit the scene of a crime, it's long afterward, at the request of a prosecutor or detective for a specific reason involving the investigation.

If anyone from the ME's office is going to see police lights flashing at the crime scene, it will be the medical-legal investigator. A medical-legal investigator isn't a coroner but rather a person with extensive education and training in forensic anthropology who works more closely with police from the outset of an investigation than a medical examiner does.

FIVE

L&O SVU: ("Serendipity," Season 5) A doctor puts a tube of his patient's blood in his arm to fool a paternity test.

TRUE CRIME: Canadian doctor John Schneeberger implanted a tube of blood in his arm to foil a DNA test and clear himself of rape charges.

Some people might say Candace Foley had a short temper, others would say she was feisty. There was no question, though, that Candace could get extraordinarily pissed off at people, and on this particular night, no one knew it better than her boyfriend. It was Halloween 1992, and twenty-three-year-old Candace was fuming because she couldn't get out of work.[1] All her friends were out having a great time, and here she was sitting behind a stupid counter selling cigarettes, gum, coffee, and sodas on one of

93

the best party nights of the year. There wasn't a hell of a lot to do in her tiny Saskatchewan town, so a Halloween party was a real event. But there were cigarettes to be smoked, gum to be chewed, and Cokes to be slurped — the really important things in life — so she'd have to wait until the next party. Hopefully, her boss wouldn't schedule her for that day, too.

At one point early in the night, her boyfriend came in to visit her at the gas station. They began talking and then had some words. One thing led to another, and Candace lost it. They started yelling, and Candace stormed out of the gas station and drove off. Before she knew it, she arrived at the local medical center where her friend was working. She was still visibly upset when she entered the hospital and found her friend. As she was describing the fight at the gas station, a nurse noticed how upset Candace was and called the Foley family doctor, John Schneeberger, who was working at the hospital that night.

Schneeberger, a Zambian-born physician, had moved to Canada in 1987 and was in the middle of his citizenship application. He knew the Foleys well — in fact, he had delivered Candace's baby not long ago.

Candace calmed down a bit as Schneeberger gently edged her toward an examination room and offered to help her. The next thing Candace knew, the doctor was preparing a syringe. She wasn't expecting a shot; she figured he'd give her some pills. But he was the doctor and she assumed he knew what was best for her. Schneeberger didn't tell Candace what he was giving her, and she didn't ask. Even if he had told her it was midazolam, it wouldn't have meant much to her, anyway. But midazolam is a very powerful drug used to sedate pre-op patients and treat epileptic seizures. And the drug contains properties that cause amnesia but allow the patient to take instructions, making it ideal as an anesthetic during certain procedures.

By the time Schneeberger was disposing of the needle and putting the syringe away, Candace was already feeling the drug's effects. "My eyes were wide open," she later said in a television interview. "They were, like, stuck wide open. I couldn't even shut them. It was like I was paralyzed."[2] The midazolam had shut down her ability to control her body, but her mind was working normally — a normal effect from a shot at that dosage — so she was fully aware of what was happening when Schneeberger raped her. Soon afterward, she passed out and spent the night in the hospital.

When Candace woke up the next morning, she wondered for a second if she had been dreaming. But when she realized she was in the hospital, she knew that it was no dream. Unfortunately for the good doctor, Candace didn't experience the amnesiac effects that usually come with midazolam.

When Schneeberger came in to check on Candace, he asked her if she had had some "wild dreams." In the rare event that she did remember something about the previous night, he thought, he'd try to plant it in her head that it was all just a dream. It was a sleazy move, and it didn't work.

Candace quietly left the hospital. When she got home, she wisely put the clothes she was wearing into a plastic bag and drove to the city of Regina to have herself examined as a rape victim.

Schneeberger knew this whole thing might catch up to him. He could only hope that Candace would be a compliant victim. He could hope all he wanted, but Candace wasn't just horrified, she was pissed off. And when Candace got pissed off, she let people know about it.

But John Schneeberger wasn't a passive person either; he didn't just let things happen to him. He had two daughters, a step-daughter, and a beautiful wife. He liked his job; it felt good to be one of only a few doctors in his small town. People looked up to him, he was paid well, and he had a new pool. He was a man of action and was going to do what it took to make sure this young woman didn't ruin his career and marriage. Schneeberger didn't have it in him to "dispose" of Candace, though. Besides, in such a small town, he would never get away with it. He was no murderer . . . but he was a doctor and if he put his mind to it, he was sure he could foil any rape charges Candace Foley filed against him.

It wasn't long before Schneeberger got a visit from the local police informing him he had been accused of rape. Nonsense, Schneeberger said. He would be more than happy to surrender some of his blood for a DNA test and put this preposterous charge behind him. He allowed medical personnel to take a blood sample from his left arm and send it out for testing.

When the results came back a few months later, Candace was anxious to see the doctor exposed for what he was: a cruel and manipulative rapist. But to her shock, the test results were negative — no match was found between the semen on her clothes and the DNA in Schneeberger's blood. How could this be? She was raped. She was awake and saw it happen. This didn't make any sense.

Some people might begin to question their own sanity at this point, or even entertain the thought that it had been a "wild dream." Not Candace. Someone must have tampered with the blood, or the evidence. Schneeberger had a lot of contacts in the hospitals. It wasn't too far-fetched to believe he could have an inside person mix up some blood samples.[3] Or perhaps he knew one of the local cops, who could have tinkered with the rape kit. Someone was up to something, and Candace was going to find out. She hired a lawyer.

There was no legal basis for Candace and her lawyer's insistence that Schneeberger take another test, but the doctor wanted this problem to go away, so he agreed to roll his sleeve up once again and take a needle.

Result: Negative. Candace's family was stunned; Candace was filled with righteous indignation. The Schneeberger case was closed. There was no way he was going to submit to another test. So now she hired a private investigator who sought, by any means necessary, a sample of Schneeberg-

DNA I

As a suspect escorts Detective Benson from his office in an episode of *Law & Order: SVU,* Benson tells him there's a hair on the lapel of his expensive suit, and then plucks it off. She isn't being motherly. She's getting his DNA.

This method of gathering evidence would most likely not get past a judge. Because the hair was on the suspect's jacket, a judge would say that the hair belonged to him and that the detective illegally seized the evidence. (It might not even be the suspect's hair in the first place.) Even if she had found the hair on the office floor, a judge might rule it was an illegal seizure.

But in real life, can Benson use that illegally seized evidence strictly for investigative purposes? Not legally. And it would be pretty difficult to get DNA analysis performed on a contraband piece of evidence, anyway. Plus, if the prosecutor found out about it, he or she would be obliged to report the detective's breach of conduct.

er's DNA. The PI broke into Schneeberger's car and stole a vial of chapstick.[4] Candace's lawyer submitted a sample for DNA testing, and this time it came back positive.

Once again, four years after raping Candace Foley, Schneeberger rolled up his sleeve and provided a blood sample. But this time, when the blood was extracted, it was almost black, as if it had been taken from a cadaver. The doctor extracting the blood was puzzled. "Yeah, that was a little strange, that one, eh?" said a Canadian Mountie in the room.[5] The DNA test on the weird, dark blood was inconclusive.

Lisa Schneeberger was a single mother of one daughter when she married her second husband. She had done well. John was a highly respected small-town doctor who was not only a loving husband, but a good provider. Plus, he was always on call for the family. Lisa's daughter and the two girls she had with John never had to worry about colds and flus. John was always there with some kind of pill or syringe filled with something or other to make them feel better.

Lisa was furious that this Candace Foley girl would bring up these ridiculous charges against her husband, and then drag them out for so many years. Didn't she know when she had been defeated? But now that John was vindicated — whether he had corpse blood coursing through his veins or not — the Schneeberger family could get back to their ordinary life.

Then one day, Lisa's teenage daughter told her mother about strange dreams she had been having that revolved around a needle and syringe. Lisa didn't think too much of it until her daughter showed her some used condoms she had found in her bed. Lisa's head spun as she put two and two together. She couldn't believe she had been vociferously defending and worrying about her husband when now, it seemed, he had been molesting her daughter in the next room! Instantly, it all made sense. A quick search of her husband's medical supplies revealed the drugs, needles, and condoms law enforcement would need to nail the doctor for drugging and molesting his stepdaughter and, most likely, for raping Candace Foley.

A new blood sample was taken from a different part of his body. It was a beautiful shade of red, a stunning crimson. Dr. John Schneeberger's jig was up.

At his trial, Schneeberger admitted to

101

stealing blood from a male patient and storing it in vials in his home. When he found out that he was going to be forced to submit blood for DNA testing based on Candace Foley's allegations, he filled a surgical tube with some of the blood, slit his bicep open, and slipped the blood-filled tube down into his forearm. He made sure to do this early enough to give his arm a chance to heal before the testing.

In a sad show of desperation, though, Schneeberger said he performed this self-surgery because he was being framed. He didn't know exactly why Candace Foley was out to get him, but she must have broken into his house, found a sample of his semen, and rubbed it on her clothes. He knew that his own DNA would match the DNA in the rape kit, so he had had to take precautions. Of course, this didn't explain his stepdaughter's dreams.

John Schneeberger was found guilty of two counts of sexual assault, one count of using a drug to commit assault, and one count of obstruction of justice. He was found not guilty of administering drugs to his stepdaughter. Seven years after raping Candace Foley, Schneeberger began his sentence of six years, to be followed by deportation back to Africa.

Notwithstanding the relatively light sentence, everyone in the courtroom was pleased. When the judge uttered the word "guilty," spectators filled the courtroom with the sound of a soft, hissing "Yes."

"That was wonderful. I just had to wait around and see that," Candace said as Schneeberger was led out in handcuffs.[6]

SIX

L&O SVU: ("Chameleon," Season 4) A prostitute turns the tables on a man who is sexually assaulting women on the street, but detectives soon discover that the woman isn't the victim she appears to be.

TRUE STORY: Truck-stop hooker Aileen Wuornos murdered seven men in and around Florida. Wuornos pleaded self-defense, claiming each victim tried to rape her.

She was standing on the side of the road, thumbing a ride. He didn't usually pick up hitchhikers but it had been a long trip and he could use the company. Plus, she looked like she could use a friend. He pulled the car to the side and the woman jumped in. She'd been out there all day, she told him. She was grateful that he stopped.

Up close, the woman looked older, and

harder than she did from the road. She said her name was Cammie and that she was just trying to get home to her kids. He felt badly for her. She looked like she'd fallen on hard times. Cammie confirmed this, telling him about her recent run of bad luck, recounting in a loud, excited voice how her car had broken down making it impossible to get to her job. Now she was out of work and trying to regain custody of her two children. He tried to reassure her that things would get better. She looked at him quizzically, then leaned forward and played with the radio dial, switching the stations until she found a song she liked. Cammie tapped her fingers on the dashboard in time, sang along with the radio. Midsong, she turned and told him that she really needed a break, needed to make some fast cash. When he didn't respond, she put her hand on his thigh and said something about helping each other out.

He was uncomfortable and tried to make light of her proposition. He knew she was dead serious but he pretended he thought she was kidding around. Cammie was silent. It felt like an eternity before she asked if he could stop the car so she could relieve herself. Something in her eyes spooked him. It was silly; he was a grown man and all. He pulled the car onto the shoulder of the road. She jumped out and headed toward some trees. "Come on!" she called. He put the car in gear and got out of there as fast as he could. He could hear her cursing at him as he drove away.

Cammie got back on the road. Eventually, she caught another ride and made another proposition. This time, the driver accepted. He steered the car off the highway and into a wooded area. It was dark and quiet except for the rhythmic song of some nearby crickets. Without hesitation, Cammie stepped out of the car and out of her clothes. She stood naked under the starless sky. The driver got out of the car and retrieved a blanket from his trunk. He spread the blanket on the ground and sat down. Cammie wanted him to strip; he refused. This irked her. He grabbed for her and that made her angrier. She pulled away and reached for her jeans. She cursed and took something from her pocket. It was a gun. She pointed it at him and demanded his wallet. He jumped up and she moved closer to him; she aimed the gun at his head. He tossed his wallet onto the blanket. She didn't seem to notice. He pleaded with her: Take the money, take the car. Please, just let me go. Cammie pulled the trigger. Years

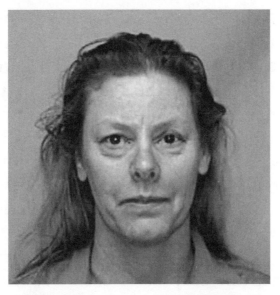

Aileen Wuronos, a prostitute who murdered five people, was incorrectly dubbed the "first female serial killer." She was executed in 2002.

ago — a lifetime really — she'd been tossed away like garbage. Now she was in control. She pulled the trigger again and again. The air smelled of gunpowder. She dressed quickly. It was getting easier each time.

In reality, "Cammie" was Aileen Wuornos, a thirty-four-year-old drifter who made a living as a truck stop prostitute. Her earnings were barely enough to support herself and her lover, Tyria Moore. Wuornos had once been pretty but that was long ago. Worn and haggard, her face was a road map of hardship, hard living, and hard drinking. Wuornos had a history. She also had a gun.

She told Moore the gun was for protection. There were a lot of creeps and psychos out on the road, men who enjoyed hurting women. Wuornos had been raped and had never really recovered. Moore believed her at first but then Aileen, whom friends knew as "Lee," started coming home with big money and an assortment of cars. Lee explained the surplus of cash was the result of a good day at work. The cars? They were loaners from friends. Moore didn't ask too many questions. She not only loved Lee, she relied on her to support her.

Aileen Wuornos and Tyria Moore met in a gay bar in Daytona, Florida, in 1986. Wuornos had come to Florida from her native Michigan for the warm weather and to ply her trade as a prostitute. Her life up to that point had been marked by disappointment and dysfunction. Her mother had abandoned her when she was a child. She never knew her father, a convicted child molester who hanged himself in jail. Aileen and her brother were raised to believe their grandparents were their parents. Aileen was twelve when she learned the truth.

By all accounts, Wournos's childhood was

a stormy one. Her grandparents were strict and her grandfather, Lauri, was a heavy drinker and reportedly beat Aileen with a belt when she disobeyed him. He constantly told her she was "evil" and "never should have been born." Aileen "wasn't worthy of the air she breathed," he said.[1]

Wuornos had other disadvantages besides her home life — she had a very low IQ and a violent, uncontrollable temper. The frequent verbal and physical beatings at the hands of her grandfather damaged her already low self-esteem. She was desperate for acceptance but would lash out if rejected. Wuornos was eleven when she had sex for the first time. Many years later, she would say that she had been raped. She learned quickly that the neighborhood boys would pay her for sexual favors. Wuornos traded sex for cigarette money, earning her the cruel moniker "Cigarette Pig."[2] The boys sought her out for sex, paying her in quarters and dimes. Afterward, they teased her and refused to be seen in public with her. Aileen put on a tough facade and acted like she didn't care. Secretly, she was crushed by their rejection.

At fourteen, Wuornos became pregnant. Lauri sent her to live in a state home for unwed mothers. She gave birth to a baby boy who was given up for adoption. Lauri didn't want Wuornos back in the house. She lived in cars and in a fort in the woods behind her house. She drank like a fish and fought like a tiger, traits that landed her in numerous county jails. When she was sixteen she hitchhiked across the state, selling her body on the highway. Along the way she added burglary, disorderly conduct, and assault to her growing rap sheet and was in and out of jail. Winters were cold for the homeless Wuornos and after a few years, she decided to relocate to Florida. Her criminal activities continued and she spent a year in prison for the armed robbery of a convenience store. Three years after hooking up with twenty-four-year-old Tyria Moore in 1986, bodies began turning up along the highways of the Sunshine State.

Richard Mallory had been missing for two weeks. The fifty-one-year-old liked to party. It was not uncommon for him to close up his electronics repair shop and take off for a week on a sex and alcohol bender. On December 13, 1989, two men scouting for scrap metal along Interstate 95 in Florida's Volusia County stumbled upon a dead body wrapped in a carpet. Police identified the body as Richard Mallory. He had been shot three times with a .22. An early suspect, a stripper named Chastity, was cleared after police verified her alibi.

Six months later, the body of forty-three-year-old construction worker David Spears was found off U.S. 19 in Citrus County, Florida. Except for a baseball cap on his head, Spears was naked. Used condoms were found next to him on the ground. He had been shot six times with a .22. Spears's truck was found abandoned several weeks later in another county.

Thirty miles away, and five days later, Tennessee resident Charles Carskaddon was found shot to death off the interstate. Carskaddon had been traveling to Tampa to pick up his fiancé. His car was found the following day, the same day a man named Peter Siems was reported missing. The police feared that a serial killer was trolling the Florida highways.

On Independence Day, Rhonda Bailey watched a car swerve off the road in front of her house and crash into some trees into the woods. Two women piled out of the car and began arguing. Bailey approached them and asked if they needed help. The car's windshield was smashed and one of the women, the tall blonde, was bleeding from her arm. She told Bailey her father lived up the road and asked her not to report the accident. The blonde woman got back into the car, and her short, stocky brunette companion followed suit. They drove the car a few feet before it stalled. The women left the car on the road and set out on foot. The car was traced back to murder victim Peter Siems, and police put out an all points bulletin for the two women.

Before the year was over, three more middle-aged men were found dead off Florida's highways: Former Alabama police chief Charles Humphreys, fifty-six; trucker Troy Burress, fifty; and security guard Walter Gino Antonio, sixty. All three men had been shot to death with a .22.

Aileen Wuornos and her lover Tyria Moore moved across Florida, exchanging one flea-bag motel for another. Money was tight and they were occasionally homeless. They slept in the woods and stowed their meager belongings in a storage facility. Wuornos had grown increasingly erratic. Moore could no longer live in denial; she knew Wuornos was involved in the highway killings. She began to fear for her own life. Moore moved back home to her parents' house in Pennsylvania. Wuornos was alone and depressed. She pleaded with Moore to return. Moore refused.

Meanwhile, the police had untangled

Wuornos's web of aliases — Cammie Greene, Lori Grody, Susan Blahovec — and they were closing in on her. Wuornos had hocked several items belonging to victims Richard Mallory and David Spears. By law, pawnbrokers are required to obtain a fingerprint from sellers. The print from the pawn receipt and another found in Peter Siems's car were put into the system. They came up as a match for Aileen Wuornos.

By January 1991, Aileen was broke. She didn't have enough money for a motel room and was lost without Tyria. She spent what little money she had left on beer at a biker bar called the Last Resort. The bartender took pity on her and let her crash on a couch inside the bar. Wuornos wasn't aware of it but she was under police surveillance. For days, two undercover police officers had been tracking her every movement. Their plan was to befriend her and get her to incriminate herself. They also wanted to take her in without a fuss. Posing as drug dealers, Officers Mike Joyner and Dick Martin chatted her up at the Last Resort. The officers bought her drinks and she told them about her situation — her lover had left her and she was homeless. They made plans to meet her at the bar the next day. On January 9, the decision was made to arrest Wuornos. Joyner and Martin returned to the bar. Wuornos was still there — she had slept at the bar. She was in bad shape. They asked her if she wanted to come back to their motel room to get cleaned up. Wuornos accepted the offer and the three left. Outside, she was arrested by officers from the Volusia County Sheriff's Department. She was told that she was being taken in for an outstanding warrant. They did not tell her she was their prime suspect in the highway murders.

The next day, Tyria Moore was taken into custody in Scranton, Pennsylvania. She admitted that she knew Wuornos had committed the highway murders but insisted that she had not been involved. Wuornos had wanted to talk about the killings but Moore had silenced her, telling her, "I don't want to hear about it." Moore was not arrested but remained under suspicion. To clear herself, Moore agreed to try to coax Wuornos into confessing to the crimes. She accompanied the officers back to Florida. She was housed in a motel room and coached on what to say. Moore did not have to face Wuornos; instead, she spoke to her on the phone. Their conversations were recorded.

Wuornos believed she was being held in

jail on an old weapons charge. Moore told her that the police suspected them in the highway murders. She said that she had been interrogated in Pennsylvania, and that police were convinced she was guilty. Wuornos attempted to reassure her but Moore would not be placated. This pattern went on for three days. Moore, coached by the detectives in the room with her, played on Wuornos's affection for her. She cried and said she was frightened. Finally, Wuornos told her, "Just go ahead and let them know what they want to know . . . and I will cover for you, because you're innocent. I'm not going to let you go to jail. Listen, if I have to confess, I will."[3]

True to her word, Wuornos confessed to the murders two days later. She claimed that all of the victims had tried to rape her and that the killings were done in self-defense. She said that she had been raped nine times in her life. "I had lots of guys, maybe ten to twelve a day. I could have killed all of them but I didn't want to," she said. "I'm really just a nice person. I'm describing a normal day to you here, but a killing day would be just about the same. On a normal day we would just do it by the side of the road . . . On a killing day, those guys always wanted to go way, way back in the woods. Now I know why they did it: they were gonna hurt me."[4]

Wuornos's crimes propelled her into the limelight. She was being touted as the first female serial killer — a claim that was untrue but sold newspapers. Book and movie deals poured in and several documentaries were made about her case.

In January 1992, she was tried and convicted for the first-degree murder of Richard Mallory. Tyria Moore was the prosecution's star witness. As she was being led from the courtroom, Wuornos shouted, "I'm innocent! I was raped! I hope you get raped! Scumbags of America!" At sentencing, expert psychiatrists for the defense testified that Wuornos was mentally unstable and had been diagnosed as having a borderline personality disorder. The jury recommended that Wuornos be sentenced to death. The judge agreed.

Later that year, a *Dateline NBC* reporter uncovered evidence that Mallory had been convicted of violent rape and had served a decade in jail in another state. Wuornos's attorneys used this information to appeal for a retrial. The appeal was denied.

Wuornos was indicted for the murders of Dick Humphreys, David Spears, and Troy Burress in March 1992. Already on death

The Multiple Murderer

While all three types of murderers — serial killers, mass murderers, and spree killers — kill multiple people, there are major differences between each type. Although every rule has its exceptions, each generally has its own characteristics, the knowledge of which is instrumental to finding, arresting, and prosecuting him or her.

Serial killers are usually motivated largely by violent urges revolving around sex. They tend to carefully plan out each murder and take time to "cool off" between each one (see chapter 13). Predators in the most literal sense of the word, serial killers are usually diagnosed as psychopaths (as opposed to psychotic) and tend to come across as normal, even likeable, people who lead ordinary lives. Experts disagree about the number of victims a person must murder before being deemed a serial killer, but three is generally the accepted number.

A mass murderer kills multiple people in one place. Motive doesn't figure as much into defining someone as a mass murderer. Anyone from high-ranking Nazis during World War II to Julio Gonzalez, who set a fire killing eighty-seven people at the Happy Land social club in the Bronx, can be considered a mass murderer.

Spree killers are more spontaneous than serial killers, and they kill in at least two different locations, unlike mass murderers. Andrew Cunanan, who murdered five people, including legendary clothing designer Gianni Versace, over the course of three months, is an example of a spree killer.

row, she pleaded no contest. "I wanted to confess to you that Richard Mallory did rape me as I've told you. But these others did not. They only began to start to," she told the court. The judge gave her three more death sentences. Wuornos responded by calling him a "motherfucker." She received two additional death sentences for the murders of Charles Caskaddon and Walter Gino Antonio. Peter Siems's body was never found; Wuornos was not charged with his murder.

By law, death sentences are automatically appealed. For a few years, Wuornos fought to have her death sentences overturned. Then in 2001 she had a change of mind and demanded that the state hasten her execution. "I killed those men, robbed them as cold as ice. And I'd do it again, too. There's no chance in keeping me alive or anything because I'd kill again. I have hate crawling through my system," Wuornos said. Her attorney argued that "Wuornos is using the court as merely a vehicle for state-assisted suicide."[5]

Wuornos was subjected to a psychiatric test to determine if she was mentally competent. After the fifteen-minute test, the state declared her competent, and she moved one step closer to the death chamber. Many people believed she was mentally ill. Filmmaker Nick Broomfield interviewed Wuornos on death row. Wuornos spoke with an odd affect and repeatedly contradicted herself. She ranted on illogically, her eyes wide and vacant. Afterward, Broomfield concluded that Wuornos was "mad" and had "totally lost her mind."[6]

Of her impending doom, Wuornos said, "I'd just like to say I'm sailing with the Rock and I'll be back like Independence Day with Jesus, June 6, like the movie, big mother-ship and all. I'll be back." Aileen Wuornos was executed by lethal injection on October 9, 2002.

Seven

L&O SVU: ("Charisma," Season 6) The leader of a doomsday cult sexually abuses his young congregants. The cult has also amassed an arsenal.

TRUE STORY: David Koresh and his Branch Davidian cult engaged in a deadly shootout with the ATF, and later battled the FBI. Koresh and many of his followers were killed, as were several government agents.

George Roden was grateful to his mother for giving birth to him, but there comes a point in every man's life when he needs to make a stand. The meek don't always inherit the Earth. The church had been in limbo for long enough, and he was going to do something about it. His father, who founded the sect, had been a strong leader, but when he died in 1978 George's mother Lois took the reins. Her crazy idea that God was both male and female, and that Jesus would appear at the Second Coming in the form of a woman, was too shocking for most members to accept. George took the opportunity to sidle into the leadership position. It was only right that he, a prophet of God, lead the flock. He would soon be receiving messages revealing the secrets of Armageddon.

Roden's new position of authority, though, was being challenged by another member of the flock — a drifter who had appeared out of nowhere in 1981. Vernon Howell was an uneducated, dyslexic rock guitarist from Houston. He was no scholar, but he knew the Bible back and forth, and more importantly, he possessed a natural charisma that drew people to him. Plus, Howell had the support of Roden's seventy-year-old mother, whom he was reportedly sleeping with.

George Roden may have been the new messiah, but he was a messiah with Texas roots. When push came to shove with Howell in 1987, he challenged his foe to a duel. But Roden's version didn't include walking ten paces and turning around with guns blazing. No, instead he dug up the body of a parishioner who had died twenty years earlier and pronounced that the one who raised her from the dead was the true leader of the church. Howell refused the challenge and left the area.

About a year later, Howell and seven members who had remained loyal to him returned, wearing camouflage and carrying rifles. The minute Roden heard about it, he reached for his Uzi and a firefight broke out. The sheriff showed up about a half hour later and broke it up. The only casualty was Roden, who had been shot in the chest, but not seriously wounded. Howell and his cohorts were arrested on attempted murder charges and released on bail. In an unrelated case, Roden was put in jail for contempt of court in 1988. Howell seized the opportunity and crowned himself church leader. Later, when a hung jury verdict was announced at the conclusion of Howell and his cohorts' trial, the elated young preacher invited everyone in the court, including the judge and jury, up to the church for some ice cream.

In 1990, Vernon Howell legally changed his name to David Koresh. He claimed to be a direct descendant of King David, from whom, it is believed, the messiah will be descended. "Koresh" is the name

Branch Davidian leader and self-proclaimed messiah, David Koresh, used his charisma to seduce the women and girls of his flock.
Courtesy of CNN

Cyrus in Hebrew; Cyrus was an Old Testament Persian king who fought and conquered the Babylonians, liberated the Jews, and sent them back to Israel to build the second Temple, presently located beneath two gigantic Muslim shrines and on the hottest thirty-five acres on Earth. His last name figured strongly into his prophecy, discussed later in this chapter.

By now Koresh was fully in charge of the Branch Davidians, a rather radical sect of

The grim aftermath. Officials begin the monumental task of gathering evidence from what's left of Mount Carmel.

Courtesy of CNN

Christianity, and their commune called Mt. Carmel, in Waco, Texas. Koresh was raised as a devout Seventh Day Adventist (SDA). Early in life, he developed an obsession with Scripture, but his interpretations didn't always match those of his church. In his twenties, he began disagreeing with church leaders' interpretations. Rather than accept the "correct" interpretations of the church, he would argue incessantly — to the point where he was disfellowshipped. With a Bible in his pocket and a head full of ideas, the young man hit the road. In 1981 he found the Davidians, which

A memorial to the Branch Davidian dead erected by the Northeast Texas Regional Militia of Texarkana, Texas. It reads: "On February 28, 1993, a church and its members known as Branch Davidians came under attack by ATF and FBI agents. For 51 days, the Davidians and their leader, David Koresh, stood proudly."

Courtesy of CNN

had broken from the SDA in 1955. He entered Mt. Carmel for the first time and met with the Rodens. Howell was immediately drawn to the Davidian's brand of apocalypticism and, very likely, their status as SDA "outlaws." The church's founder, Victor Houteff (who was long dead by the time Howell found the church) had himself been disfellowshipped from

SDA for his radical teachings.* No doubt, Howell felt a certain kinship with the church's erstwhile leader.

Koresh threw himself completely into his life's mission: putting every last Davidian on the path to salvation — with himself proudly marching in front. Under the Rodens, the group had been organized into a clanlike system. Various families within the church enjoyed different levels of power, depending for the most part on how much money they put in the church coffers, while the Rodens, claiming direct descent to the Old Testament's King David, strictly controlled biblical interpretation and prophecy.[1] With his overthrow of George Roden (the

---

*Florence Houteff, wife of Davidian founder Victor Houteff, took over the church upon her husband's death in 1955. Based on her interpretation of the Book of Revelation, she predicted the end of the world would come on April 22, 1959. Branch Davidians sold their homes and businesses, packed up what little was left and converged on Mt. Carmel to wait for the sky to open. When the clock struck midnight, and Jesus was nowhere to be seen, Florence Houteff's reputation went down the toilet. Benjamin Roden, George's father, took advantage of the great disappointment and seized control of the religion.

third Roden to lead the Davidians), David Koresh transformed the organization into what most people call a cult. Under the Rodens, there was much political infighting; under Koresh, there would be none of that.

Like any good leader, Koresh began to improve his followers' quality of life. Prophecy is important, but so are food and electricity. Members donated belongings and pooled their money (in some cases, hundreds of thousands of dollars) to shore up the compound's infrastructure. Mt. Carmel was making the switch from community to commune. But the donations were never quite enough. In order to keep the cash flow moving, Koresh and his followers launched several small businesses, mostly involving repairing cars and trading in firearms and survival equipment. These ventures were an important element in transforming the Davidians into the radical and ultimately self-destructive group that it became. The group's existence was determined less by the wealthier families and more by the community itself — with Koresh as the uncontested authoritarian.[2] More biblically astute than Lois Roden and more charismatic than George Roden, Koresh enjoyed a level of power that no previous Davidian leader had even dreamed of. And with his dominance firmly established, Koresh moved on to the crux of what drove him: visions of glory and End Times prophecy.

The planet, according to Koresh, was slouching toward oblivion, its time had come at last. Like so many religious fundamentalists before him, the Davidian leader claimed to receive visions from God that the end was imminent. Koresh was continuing a tradition that he grew up with. The SDA church was founded largely on the teachings of Ellen G. White, a nineteenth-century self-declared prophet who often had visions of herself and her fellow congregants drenched in blinding holy light, marching through the gates of Heaven. Lois Roden, as well, saw visions. When she took over the church after her husband died, she claimed to have seen the Holy Spirit as a "shimmering silvery angel" in feminine form.

Koresh's visions and Bible interpretations, though, were a little more self-serving than those of his predecessors. Previously, the leaders — the Houteffs and the Rodens — provided leadership, but spirituality was focused on the "church" in the purest sense of the word: the body of congregants. Koresh turned it around, placing himself at the center of his members' worshipping practice. Nothing makes this more evident than his "New Light Doctrine" — the claim that he was the new messiah.

David Koresh would stand for hours in front of his congregation, dressed in jeans and a denim shirt, passionately reading Bible passages and offering his interpretations. After a number of marathon Bible sessions, he successfully convinced his followers that he was the Lamb of God, who in the Book of Revelation opens the seven seals of God's scrolls, unleashing plagues, fires, earthquakes, meteors, and showers of blood on humanity. Most people are killed during the days of reckoning; only a chosen few are allowed to help in the reconstruction of a perfect world. These, according to Koresh, were the Davidians.

Somehow, Koresh leaped to the conclusion that all of this meant that he, and he alone, was allowed to have sex with the female congregants — old or young, married or single. And many of them agreed. His reasoning went like this: As messiah, he had the duty to father twenty-four children in order to create a new, divine race. If he didn't do it, who would? Surely not the other males of the church; they were not pure like him, and so their children wouldn't be pure. Because these children were destined to begin the next race (twenty-four

Adams and Eves, as it were), Koresh was willing to take no chances. The Davidian men — "Mighty Men,"* as their leader called them — weren't left out in the cold, though. Koresh announced that they would be united with their dream women later on, in Heaven.

Koresh, now twenty-nine years old, wasted no time. He soon married Rachel Jones, the daughter of two followers. Rachel was fourteen years old and spawned the first two of Koresh's planned tribe of twenty-four. Whether he decided that it would be unfair to require twenty-two more births from his young wife or he just wanted more women, Koresh began sleeping around within the compound. God had told him that, like King David of yore, he must build a harem. Most parents not only gave their consent, but were honored that their daughters figured so directly into End Times. Koresh lined up his prospective wives, including his

*In the King James version of the Song of Solomon, sixty "mighty men" stand around King Solomon's bed, guarding their leader. A connection with Solomon only made sense for Koresh. The Bible says that Solomon was entitled to sixty wives, eighty concubines, and as many virgins as he wanted.

wife's twelve-year-old sister, Michelle, his stated "favorite." These "chosen ones" walked around the compound wearing a Star of David around their necks.

Some parents objected. A Branch Davidian's ex-husband, who lived in Michigan, sued for custody when he found out that his ten-year-old daughter was wearing the Star. He won the case and took the girl to his home in Michigan. Little did he know at the time that he had not only rescued her from Koresh's advances but from almost certain death, as well.

Davidian services weren't the kind where everyone held hands and sang "Kumbaya." When Koresh spoke, he expected people to listen. During one of his lengthy sermons, a two-year-old girl fell asleep on a bench. An infuriated Koresh grabbed her by the arm and spanked her in front of the congregation.[3]

In one of his many convoluted and self-serving Bible interpretations, Koresh quoted from Psalm 45[*], in particular a passage stating that the king will be anointed with "the

[*] It's no wonder Koresh was a fan of Psalm 45, which speaks of the king as "the most handsome of men" and instructs the women of his kingdom to "forget also thine own people and thy father's

oil of gladness." In biblical times, one's forehead was the most common spot on the body to be anointed. In the time of Koresh, though, the head of his penis was declared the spot that would be anointed, and the "oil" in question was vaginal secretions.[4] One woman whom Koresh tried to convert said he claimed to be the Son of God — and that his Father was lonely and wanted grandchildren![5] In 1989, a couple of Australian Davidians, apparently deeply disturbed by the New Light Doctrine, went home. In an attempt to woo them back to Waco, Koresh sent them an audiotape defending his beliefs saying, "You have only one seed that can deliver you from death . . . There's only one hard-on in this whole universe who really loves you and wants to say good things about you. Remember Mary and God? Yeah? God couldn't make any advances because the world would misjudge."[6] Koresh even told a Davidian couple that God had given him their daughter as a wife; they were more than happy to have a new Son-in-law.[7]

Day after day, Koresh preached about the end of the world to his flock. By the early

---

house/So shall the king greatly desire your beauty." (*King James Bible*)

1990s, the group's membership numbered about seventy-five, people having come from as far away as Australia and New Zealand. Some members must have been terrified. The idea that God Himself was going to pour death and destruction upon Earth must have been terrifying even to those with the heartiest religious beliefs. But Koresh succeeded in convincing them that those meteors would land elsewhere and the plagues would stop at the gates of the compound, which in 1992 he renamed Ranch Apocalypse. Nevertheless, the Branch Davidians thought it might be prudent to learn some survival tactics. It might be a long haul, and no one said God was going to keep the rabble away from their food pantries. When the barbarians decided to storm the gates, the Davidian God would be there waiting — looking more like an AK–47 than an old man with a beard.

As if things at Mt. Carmel/Ranch Apocalypse weren't weird enough — what with Koresh fathering children left and right and reportedly sleeping with preteen girls — the guitar-playing savant began to take his role as church leader even further. He demanded that followers eat what he said they should. One couple was excommunicated for eating french fries against Koresh's will, another for treating themselves to chocolate chip ice cream. One day, he would declare that bananas were the only fruit anyone was allowed to eat. Then, later, they couldn't eat oranges or grapes; raisins, however, were okay. For a while, Koresh was the only one permitted to eat meat. And at one point, "God" said that only David Koresh could have a Coke on ice.[8]

It got to the point where some previously avowed followers of Koresh were starting to get creeped out. They wanted to leave. But they were afraid. They were apprehensive about taking a chance that Koresh's prophecy was not correct. What if Koresh was right, and they had willingly walked away from him? How many people had done the same thing to Jesus and the prophets? Where did they end up? Gehenna, no doubt. Koresh liked to talk about what life would be like in Hell. He offered graphic depictions of skin being ripped off with nail clippers. And then he would scream at the top of his lungs. And keep screaming.[9] Physically, the continued screaming was hard to listen to; psychologically, it was hard to forget. Being one of the faithful and then abandoning the messiah was just too perfect an irony to discount. The questioning

Branch Davidians played it safe and stayed put.

Koresh made it clear to his followers that this wasn't a game. They were all going to die early deaths. The payoff would be beyond their wildest dreams, but death was coming and they better be prepared. According to the testimony of former Davidian children, Koresh even taught them the best way to commit suicide with a gun: don't put the barrel to the temple, put it in the mouth.[10]

Meanwhile, Koresh had placed armed sentries to guard the premises in shifts; everyone performed guard duty, unless they had a good excuse not to. The place was filling up with weapons for use when the end of the world came. The complex — which by the early nineties was really a fort, turrets and all — was an increasingly hostile place to live.

One day in May 1992, a UPS worker in Waco noticed something a little odd with one of his packages. A bunch of hand grenades was spilling from a box that had been accidentally broken open. The delivery address was for Koresh's compound. The deliveryman prudently contacted the Waco sheriff's department, which put in a call to the Bureau of Alcohol, Tobacco, and Firearms. A federal investigation was quickly launched. The ATF learned through UPS shipping forms that the compound in Waco had received shipments of guns, gun parts, and bomb-making material — over $40,000 worth.[*] The Branch Davidians, it seemed, had more on their minds than the fantastic prophecies of their long-haired leader.

In 1993, the bureau asked for and received one warrant for Koresh's arrest and another for a search of Ranch Apocalypse. Given

[*]In addition, the ATF determined, mainly through the use of informants, that the Davidians had a methamphetamine lab inside the compound. They used this supposed evidence as leverage (the "War on Drugs" was still the rage at this time) to get the Texas National Guard to provide them with aerial surveillance of the compound. According to Senator John C. Danforth's report on the matter to the Attorney General, published in July 2000, "an informal analysis of the thermal imaging data done by a Guard airman who was not a qualified infrared image interpreter revealed a 'hot spot' which he thought to be consistent with the existence of a methamphetamine laboratory at the complex." The ATF took this info and ran with it. Follow-up aerial recon missions were flown by the Texas and Alabama National Guards.

the amount of weaponry law enforcement agents were convinced the Davidians had, along with their nutty religious beliefs, the ATF wasn't taking any chances. On February 28, 1993, it deployed an army of agents toting automatic weapons and dressed in paramilitary garb to issue the warrants.

Unfortunately, the ATF totally lost the element of surprise, key in their plan to search the compound. The mile-long convoy of ATF vehicles and Texas National Guard helicopters buzzing around caught the attention of everyone in Waco. The previous day, a Waco paramedic informed a reporter that the ATF had asked the hospital to gear up for something major. Word spread quickly, eventually to the ears of a local mailman — David Jones, one of Koresh's many brothers-in-law. Reporters and cameramen simply followed the ATF to the compound.

What made matters worse was that the ATF knew that Koresh knew they were coming. Even though commanders were fully aware that they had lost the element of surprise, they launched the mission anyway. When a ball this size gets rolling, it takes some very talented, determined people to stop it. No one stepped up. At 9:30 a.m. on February 28, the agents went in.

Who shot first? Who knows. Put people with guns into a buggy situation like this, and someone's fingers are bound to get itchy, whether they belong to trained federal agents or apocalyptic renegades. In this case, the fog of war was thick and both detractors and defenders of the government claimed perfectly clear vision on the matter. Koresh reportedly opened the front door of the main building when the commandos approached, screaming for them to go away. When agents shouted for him to freeze, he shut the door. And the bullets started flying — from ATF agents and Davidians holed up inside the structures.

At 9:48 a.m., the Davidians called the local police, pleading for them to have the assault called off. The deputy sheriff said they would do what they could, but in reality they couldn't do much. In the taped conversation, the caller, a Davidian named Wayne Martin, is articulate, calm, and convincing as he explains how frightened everyone is inside the compound. The only thing they know, he says, is that a swarm of ATF agents wearing black ski masks are descending on the buildings and firing their weapons through windows, doors, and walls, heedless to the fact that women and children were inside.

The operation was not just compromised by the loss of surprise, ATF agents were also sorely outgunned. The Davidians had been hoarding weapons for years and possessed numerous illegal automatic firearms. Four agents were killed and twenty were wounded. In turn, they killed three Davidians and wounded five, including David Koresh. Three more Davidians were killed by their own, inside Ranch Apocalypse.

The ATF's mission was an absolute disaster from the get-go, and control was transferred to the FBI the very next day. As the ATF slinked away, its head hung in shame, the FBI arrived, fresh and ready to roll.

The mission changed from an assault to a siege — and sieges rarely work out well for the ones inside. The FBI surrounded the place (doing the best they could to keep prying journalists from getting a view of what was going on), strategically positioning snipers and cutting the phone lines. FBI negotiators arrived and established a private telephone link to Koresh. The FBI leadership, meanwhile, obtained Bradley fighting vehicles, trucks, jeeps, and other supplies from the Texas National Guard. From the U.S. Army, they received high-tech sensing equipment, helicopters, and two Abrams tanks with their offensive capabilities disabled.

For weeks, negotiators were treated to Koresh's Bible interpretations. These communiqués weren't so much conversations as they were monologues, and agents soon labeled Koresh's dissertations "Bible Babble." But during the first few weeks, over thirty women and kids came out and surrendered (a fact often forgotten by the FBI's harshest critics). Agents immediately arrested the adults and charged them with murder, but the negotiators convinced them to drop the charges.

Early on in the negotiations, the FBI had what seemed a major breakthrough. Absolutely convinced that Koresh truly believed in his role in the End Times, they gave him an offer they were sure he wouldn't refuse. He could explain his theology on tape and the FBI would arrange to have it aired nationally on the Christian Broadcast Network radio. After it aired, he would have to surrender. Koresh made the deal, and for about an hour, American radio listeners got an earful of Koresh's prophecy (the part about having sex with Davidian women and children being omitted, of course).

When Koresh's screed ended, news cameramen focused their lenses on the doors of

Mt. Carmel, waiting for the great exodus. Hostage negotiators primed themselves for some serious high-fives. And the TV viewing public waited anxiously to see what these crazy "chosen people" actually looked like.

Nothing.

The FBI put in a call to Mt. Carmel and asked what time they all were planning to come out. Koresh's spokesmen informed the FBI that God had told Koresh to wait; it wasn't time yet. Koresh would have to wait for further instruction from God, and no one could say how long it would be. In the realm of Branch Davidianism, this explanation made complete sense; in the realm of law enforcement, it meant that Koresh had pretty much destroyed any credibility he might have had.

Soon after, the FBI leadership, which had been champing at the bit, concluded that the negotiations were going nowhere fast, and they decided to kick things up a notch. They cut off the complex's electricity and then sent in military vehicles to crush "obstacles" that might impede operations, such as Davidians' cars parked near the buildings, propane tanks, and sheds — and the grave of a Davidian who had been killed in the initial assault. The tanks rolled over it, back and forth, showing that as far as they were concerned, negotiation time was over. And agents on the ground were getting themselves primed for combat. When a Davidian would look out a window, he or she would often see a group of agents giving the finger or dropping their pants and mooning the cult member.

At night, the FBI's psychological warfare included directing blinding floodlights at the houses and cranking deafening music and other noises. When they were in a kindhearted mood, agents played the chants of Tibetan monks. When they got tired of that, they blared Christmas music. And when agents felt particularly sadistic, they cranked a disturbing audio mix of rabbits being slaughtered and the sounds of industrial machinery. All of it, of course, was designed to break down the wills of Koresh and his followers, but their beliefs in their leader as the messiah and in themselves as the chosen people were iron-clad. Koresh was so angered by the FBI's tactics that he told negotiators to screw themselves — no one would be coming out of the complex ever again.

Enter Janet Reno, a relatively unknown DA from Florida chosen by President Clinton for United States Attorney General. She was confirmed in mid-March, just as things were beginning to heat up between the FBI negotiation team and hostage rescue team. While the negotiators were calling for patience from everyone, members of the tactical rescue team were loading their weapons, revving the Bradleys, and posing for their buddies' cameras, holding up their automatic weapons Rambo-style. Negotiators would spend hours on the phone feigning interest in Koresh's warped theology just to build the slightest bit of trust and, hopefully, secure the release of one or two more children. Then the tactics guys would do something like crank up another hot mix of screeching animals, ensuring that no one in Ranch Apocalypse got a good night's sleep. For the Davidians, these methods of intimidation surely affirmed the prophecy of their leader; the Apocalypse had begun.

Reno had few close contacts in Washington, and the government confirmation committee had denied her the two deputy AGs she had requested. She was alone, and the standoff in Waco was now her baby.

Reno's boss, President Clinton, said he wanted a peaceful end to the situation no matter how long it took. With pressure squeezing in on her from both ends — "Be patient," "Act now!" — Reno initially sided with the negotiators. They would get all the time they needed for peaceful resolution. Reno had daily meetings with FBI leadership in the middle of April. Convinced that Koresh was intractable in his stance, the FBI representatives were pushing for an OK from the attorney general to use tear gas on the Davidians and then send in the FBI elite rescue team.

David Koresh then contacted the negotiators with a proposal. Forget the fact that he had gone back on his original promise to surrender. He was now working on his interpretation of the Seven Seals, from the Bible's Book of Revelation. When he completed it, he and his followers would come out of the compound. The FBI had no problem with that, so long as they didn't all kill themselves in there. The delay would also give the FBI time to iron out the details of the assault plan.

Koresh had initially promised to send out drafts of his magnum opus. As the days dragged on, though, the FBI saw no religious tracts, no earth-shattering prophecies, no brilliant scriptural interpretations. Koresh was unaware that for all intents and purposes the bureau had already abandoned the tactic of talking. It was time for action.

Then, at Reno's request, the FBI provided her with a full brief on the situation, which alluded to the subject of child abuse — a hot-button topic for Reno, who had been well known in Florida as a passionate child advocate.* The document alleged that Koresh was beating children and even making some of them his "wives."[11] Reno gave the go-ahead to use tear gas and storm the compound.

Early in the morning of April 19, Branch Davidians looked out their window and saw CEVs (Combat Engineer Vehicles) rolling across the lawn at Mt. Carmel. The presence of military vehicles wasn't an unusual sight. For weeks, the FBI showed its presence by destroying cars and sheds with their tanks. But this time, it was different. The

*It's important to note that the allegations at the time were less founded than they are today. Some former Davidians had claimed they or their children were abused. But State of Texas child welfare workers who had visited Ranch Apocalypse found no evidence of child abuse. In addition, the head of child psychiatry at the Texas Children's Hospital, who interviewed Davidian children who had been released during the siege, concluded that the children had not been sexually abused.

tanks were heading straight for the building, and they weren't slowing down. Suddenly, the phone rang. It was the FBI, announcing that they were about to fill the complex with tear gas and that Koresh should surrender now. The FBI insisted that this wasn't an attack on their lives, it was one final attempt at a peaceful solution. The Davidians weren't going anywhere.

The CEVs had long booms with tear gas canisters attached, allowing them to safely insert the CS gas through windows. CS gas is created by mixing a powder called Chlorobenzalmalononitrile (CS) with methylene chloride, a volatile liquid used for such things as stripping paint, welding plastics, and decaffeinating coffee, and which has been linked in lab experiments to cancer of the lungs, liver, and pancreas. Combine the two and you get a gas that can send people into such convulsions, they break their own bones. When it burns, it becomes the same substance used to kill death row inmates in gas chambers. Agents armed with grenade launchers were also deployed around the complex. The launchers were equipped with two types of gas shells: "ferret rounds," which burst on impact, and military rounds, which dispursed gas via extreme heat.

First aid stations were established for

wounded Davidians. Firefighters were on hand, as well, but because of the Davidians' heavy arsenal, they weren't to approach any building until they were officially given the word.

From outside the compound, the operation showed just who was in charge. The CEVs' American flags stood out starkly from the grim and drab surroundings of Mt. Carmel, which had been enshrouded in a depressing fog of doom for weeks. That fog, though, was being blown out now by the morning's sudden, frenetic activity. Action was being taken. Things were getting done. The Davidians' doom was upon them. It was Armageddon.

The Davidians' answer to the tear gas filling their rooms, corridors, and hallways was a barrage of small-arms fire. Some of the men with weapons wore gasmasks and fired out the window on the FBI's tanks and at incoming helicopters. Women and children were ordered to retreat to a concrete bunker built for a moment such as this.

The U.S. military aided the FBI in filming the event. A Nightstalker aircraft equipped with a forward-looking infrared camera (FLIR) circled above the compound, capturing images through the detection of thermal energy. In the video, bright flashes burst from the buildings, which are answered by bright flashes from around the tanks. Critics of the FBI interpret this as a firefight between the Davidians and law enforcement.[12] The FBI maintains, however, that none of its agents fired their gun during the operation, that the only shots they fired were the "ferret" rounds — gas projectiles that couldn't even penetrate a piece of plywood. The official government stance is that the flashes are "solar reflections from certain types of debris, including glass, that was strewn around the complex."*[13]

The original plan called for a gradual gas insertion over a period of forty-eight hours. Four minutes into the operation, though, the FBI decided to ramp it up to a fast and massive insertion. About six hours later, black smoke and flames began billowing out

*In 2000, families of Branch Davidians killed in the operation filed a civil case against the U.S. government. Based on the interpretation of these flashes as a firefight, the plaintiffs argued that their loved ones were pinned down by the agents' gunfire and, thus, couldn't escape the fire that spread throughout the complex during the confrontation. The government's claim that the flashes showed nothing but broken glass was supported in the civil suit.

the windows in three different areas of the complex. Though it seemed at first that the fire must have been ignited by the FBI tear-gassing operation, it turned out that the Davidians themselves had apparently started the conflagration. The FBI had succeeded in installing audio surveillance devices inside the compound prior to the operation, which picked up numerous discussions among Branch Davidian men as they prepared to set the buildings on fire. One of these conversations occurred at 7:21 a.m.:

Unidentified Male: Is there a way to spread fuel here?

Unidentified Male: OK . . . what we do . . . You don't know.

Unidentified Male: I know that won't spread . . . get some more.

Unidentified Male: So we only light it first when they come in with the tank right . . . right as they're coming in?

Unidentified Male: Right.

Unidentified Male: That's secure . . . We should get more hay in here.

Unidentified Male: I know.[14]

And then at about noon, shortly before Ranch Apocalypse burst into flames, a Branch Davidian was recorded saying:

"Keep that fire going . . . keep it."[15] It was the last thing anyone on the outside heard from the Davidians.* When the tanks ripped holes in the sides of the complex, which were designed to provide escape routes for the Davidians, the oxygen actually fed the fire, making it spread even more rapidly. One survivor said he saw fireballs blowing down the hallways, as if something huge had exploded.[16] According to the former fire chief of Houston, creating air holes in the sides of the complex during the fire in essence created a "pot belly stove."[17]

Immediately after the blaze began, FBI agents heard gunshots inside the buildings. Nine Davidians subsequently ran outside. One reentered the buildings and an agent followed her in and dragged her back outside. He asked where the children were inside, but she refused to tell him.

If the tear gas operation had been effective, perhaps April 19 wouldn't have turned out as it did. But the guys inside with the guns, fuel, and matches had gas masks.

*Survivors would later admit that Davidians started the fires, and during the investigation of the crime scene, numerous punctured Coleman fuel cans were recovered. FBI agents also reported seeing some pouring fuel.

Unaffected by the CS gas, they were able to go about their business creating their own End Time. The same can't be said for the others — those without masks.

Those without gas masks, mainly the women and children, suffered incredibly. When the CEVs rolled in, they retreated to a steel-enforced kitchen storage room. When the fires began, there was absolutely no escape. Their only protection from the CS gas, which irritates skin on contact, was, pathetically, wet blankets and towels covering their heads and skin. The victims' final moments were spent coughing, retching, and vomiting. Before they died, mothers watched their children fall into comatose states. The body of one child was found in a nearly 180-degree "U" position; he possibly broke his own back in a violent convulsive reaction to the CS gas.

At the same time, the FBI was holding the firefighters back out of fear that the Davidians would shoot them. But after only eighteen minutes, they untied the leash. Clearly, no one inside could still be alive.

What was once Mt. Carmel was now a smoldering funeral pyre. Eighty-three Davidians were dead. A number of people apparently died before the smoke and fire reached them. According to the *Danforth Report,* the U.S. government's official documentation of the event, "The autopsy reports indicate that on April 19, at least 20 Davidians were shot including at least five children under 14. Of the 20, 12 were shot in the head, two others were shot in the head and chest, three more were shot in the chest only, two were shot in the back and one, Schneider, was shot in the mouth . . . Additionally, one child was stabbed to death."[18] David Koresh's skull had a bullet hole through it.

A scene like this demanded a lot of answers from the FBI and the attorney general's office. Numerous members of the House and Senate had plenty of questions about how the standoff turned into an inferno. Everyone from Reno on down appeared at congressional hearings, answering questions from Democrats aiming to make friends with Reno's boss, President Clinton, and Republicans trying to do him in.

In addition to getting a glimpse of how crass and self-serving politicians can be, viewers of these sessions learned that the FBI did not fire any incendiary rounds — gas shells that use pyrotechnics rather than pressure to release their gas. (At this point, the origin of the fire was still a mystery.) It was the FBI's story, and they were sticking to it. Reno backed them up.

In 1999, however, it would be revealed that three spent military projectiles had been photographed at the crime scene, which meant that there were three empty shells somewhere, as well. None of it was logged in by the FBI as evidence; agents also failed to record the use of the three military gas rounds in their logbook. To be fair, Reno probably didn't know any of this when she testified, given the fact that the FBI's official report to her unequivocally claimed that no pyrotechnic devices had been fired. And in 1999, an FBI agent admitted that he had fired three incendiary gas rounds, and the FBI came clean.

In addition to its original denial about firing incendiary devices, the agency had also insisted that they didn't fire any bullets. This claim led independent investigators to scrutinize the FLIR tape. Some believed (and still do) that flashes near the CEVs denote gunshots being fired by FBI agents into the complex. They maintain that because the FLIR detects heat, not light, it would not show bright spots from a simple reflection. The controversy eventually led Congress to request its own investigation of the FLIR tapes — all three of them. Until that point the FBI and the Department of Justice maintained that only one existed, but miraculously, two more FLIR tapes — three-and-a-half-hours worth — turned up when an FBI attorney asked the bureau's aviation unit to make another search. The tapes, one of which shows the agent firing the pyrotechnic devices, were in an unlocked filing cabinet.

In the end, it was determined that the Davidians set fire to the complex, and there is no evidence that any Davidians were shot with FBI bullets. But damage had been done to a law enforcement agency that already had a reputation for taking the law into its own hands.

Many supporters of the Branch Davidians still cite the right to freedom of religion when they criticize the government for the Waco disaster. But the government's actions had nothing to do with curtailing the Davidians' freedom of religion. Had the FBI been more forthright in the aftermath, there would be much less to talk about.

Senator Danforth's report is also criticized for protecting the government. He is accused of not taking the investigation far enough and asking all the wrong questions. Perhaps. One point Danforth makes in the Introduction to his *Interim Report,* released on July 21, 2000, is that "[t]he actions of these few government employees who failed to disclose the use of pyrotechnics are reprehensible because they undermined the public confidence with which they were entrusted." In the very next sentence, Danforth says, "In today's world, however, it is perhaps understandable that government officials are reluctant to make full disclosures of information for fear that the result of candor will be personal or professional ruin."[19] Throughout his Introduction, Danforth bemoans America's lack of trust in its government. But when he, a U.S. senator, defends the same "reprehensible" acts leading to that mistrust as "understandable," what's a citizen to do?

At the turn of the millennium, a white chapel was built on the former site of the Branch Davidian compound. A legal dispute among various survivors and others connected with the Branch Davidians left the property ownership in limbo for six years. Theological rifts emerged among the Davidians, but many live on the property in peace. No shootouts over church leadership this time. One Davidian, Renos Avraam, sentenced to prison for ten years after the standoff, claims to be Koresh's successor and "The Chosen Vessel of the Remaining Bride." Most of them are waiting patiently for the resurrection and return of David Koresh. "When David comes back, that's when we'll evangelize," says Davidian Catherine Matteson. "When David comes back, you'll know it."[20]

EIGHT

L&O SVU: ("Uncle," Season 8) A mentally ill man pushes a murder suspect into an oncoming subway train.

TRUE STORY: Andrew Goldstein, a known schizophrenic, says he was in a psychotic state when he pushed Kendra Webdale in front of an oncoming train.

Andrew Goldstein was feeling down. It was January 3, 1999, and he'd spent the holidays alone in his drab basement apartment in Queens, New York. He hadn't seen his family for quite some time. The twenty-nine-year-old was lonely — the voices in his head were his only companions. The weather didn't help much either; it had been raining on and off for most of the day. Goldstein braved the rain and headed into Manhattan; it was a trip he frequently made. He was unemployed and had a lot of time on his hands — when he wasn't in the psych ward, that is. In the city, Goldstein walked around in the rain for a while. He stopped and had lunch at McDonald's and then spent a good part of the afternoon hanging out in a record store. Around 5 p.m., he decided to return home to Queens. He made his way to the subway station on 23rd Street.

Kendra Webdale hated the rain. She had planned on spending the day inside her cozy Manhattan apartment but when a friend called to invite her over, she couldn't say no. Kendra was kindhearted, a good listener who was always there to lend a hand or a shoulder to cry on. Kendra put on her coat and grabbed an umbrella. She was in a good mood, in spite of the rain. A week earlier, Kendra had traveled to her hometown in Fredonia, New York, to celebrate the holidays with her family. They all had a wonderful time and Kendra was happy to reconnect with her parents and her siblings. Kendra left her apartment and dashed through the raindrops, trying to keep dry on the way to the subway station. The station was damp and smelled musty but thankfully, it was dry. Kendra shook off the rain and pulled a magazine from her bag.

She leaned back against a post and thumbed through the pages as she waited for her train to arrive. A dozen riders milled about on the platform; Andrew Goldstein was one of them.

Goldstein was hard not to notice. He was mumbling to himself and pacing; he'd take five tiny steps forward and then, as if programmed, turn swiftly and double back five steps. Every few minutes he'd stop and stare at someone. When they met his gaze, he'd quickly avert his eyes. He was making the other riders uncomfortable, so much so that one man called out to him, "Yo, buddy, can you stop that pacing? You're making us nervous."[1] The man startled Goldstein. He stopped pacing and walked toward Kendra Webdale. He asked her if she knew the time. Kendra looked up and smiled at Goldstein, told him the time. She had a great smile — her friends and family always told her it was her best feature.

The station began to rumble; a train was approaching. Goldstein craned his neck toward the tracks. The N train was making its way into the station. He waited until the train was just about in front of them. He lunged forward and grabbed Kendra by her shoulders and shoved her into the path of the oncoming train. In less than a second,

Kendra was gone, pulled down under the train. A woman screamed and people began running away from Goldstein. The trainman slammed on the brakes; the wheels screeched as the train came to a stop. The trainman rushed down to the tracks to see who or what he had hit. He saw Kendra lying there, motionless. "Hold on! Help is coming," he told her. It was too late: Kendra Webdale was dead. She was thirty-two years old.

Andrew Goldstein made no attempt to flee the scene. He remained there at the station, pacing. When police arrived he declared, "I'm psychotic. Take me to a hospital."

Goldstein was taken into custody. He told the police detectives that he was not taking his medication and was in a psychotic state. He claimed he was possessed by a "spirit" or "ghost" who compelled him to shove Kendra in front of the train. "When I have the sensation that something is entering me, I get the urge to push, shove, or kick," he said. "What happened was this train is coming and then it goes away again, and then it comes back again. And then the train is almost there and I said, 'Oh no, it happened.' You know I go into the fit again, like I've done this in the past, and I pushed

161

the woman, not meaning to push her onto the track and I went into shock, horror."[2]

The murder of Kendra Webdale was big news in New York City. With more than 8 million residents, the city has its fair share of crimes. But the random violence of the attack unnerved even the most hardened New Yorkers. At a time when crime was down in the metropolis, people were suddenly faced with a new threat: being attacked by a mad stranger. In a city where everyone takes mass transit, subways "are the common denominator between people of different races, languages and income levels," explained reporter Harriet Ryan. "In a millisecond, Goldstein had given them a second unifier: fear . . . what could you do about a subway pusher? Everyone was vulnerable."[3]

Kendra was like so many other young people who had migrated to New York City in search of excitement, culture, and a dream job. She had come to the Big Apple from a small town to pursue a career in the recording industry. While she waited for her big break, Kendra worked as a receptionist, cheerfully meeting and greeting people with her lovely smile.

As detectives worked to piece the crime together, details about Andrew Goldstein's long and troubled history of mental illness began to emerge. Goldstein had been an exceptionally bright youngster whose intellect had gained him acceptance into the elite Bronx High School of Science. In his freshman year of college, his world fell apart. Goldstein began hearing voices and became convinced his mother was poisoning him. He attacked her and threatened to kill her. Goldstein was hospitalized; it would be the first of many trips to the hospital. Doctors determined that Goldstein was schizophrenic and suffering from paranoid delusions. A disabling brain disorder, schizophrenia affects one percent of the population around the world. Symptoms include delusions, hallucinations, disorganized thoughts and behaviors, and social isolation. It is not uncommon for schizophrenics to "hear" imaginary voices talking to them.

For the next decade, Goldstein moved in and out of state hospitals and clinics. Sometimes he checked himself in voluntarily; other times he was brought in by the police after attacking someone. He told doctors that aliens were depleting the Earth of oxygen, that his neck had disappeared, and that he was compelled to strike out at women. He asked for a pair of glasses to help him see the people whose voices he heard in his head. Doctors prescribed Haldol and Risperdal, powerful drugs used to treat schizophrenics. The antipsychotic medications quieted the voices in his head but they also made him feel sluggish and heavy, like he was seeing the world through a filter of gauze. Goldstein's hospital stays usually lasted a few days or weeks at the most, after which he was either transferred to a halfway house or released and told to visit a local clinic. He was clearly ill and desperate for help but state budget cuts had severely limited the number of patients psychiatric facilities were able to treat. There simply weren't enough beds available.

Goldstein, like many schizophrenics, often stopped taking his medication. Without his medication, he was prone to delusions, paranoia, and violence. He told a social worker that he was afraid he was a danger to others. His fears were valid: in ten years, Goldstein attacked nearly two dozen people — nurses, doctors, medical staff, and strangers. Six months before shoving Kendra in front of a train, he punched a woman in the face on a subway car. The assault landed him in the psych ward at Brookdale Hospital. During his stay, he attacked four hospital workers. Once again he was released after a few weeks.

On December 9, 1998, Goldstein was back in the hospital. The voices were getting louder and he believed someone was trying to kill him. On his medical chart, doctors noted that he was "disorganized, thought disordered, and delusional." Entries for the next two days indicate that he remained "psychotic" and "paranoid." The doctors attempted to transfer Goldstein to Creedmoor Psychiatric Center for long-term care. However, there were no vacancies and Goldstein's was put on a waiting list. Days later, the man doctors described as psychotic was set loose on an unsuspecting public. On his way out, he promised to stay on his medication. It was a promise Goldstein did not keep. Eighteen days later, he shoved Kendra Webdale in front of an N train.

There was no doubt that Goldstein had killed Webdale; numerous people had witnessed the attack and Goldstein had given police a confession. Goldstein acted alone but was not solely responsible for Webdale's death. The mental health system that had repeatedly released him — even though it was clear that he was a danger to others — bore some of that responsibility. By 1999,

Goldstein's psychiatric record had grown to a whopping 3,500 pages. Page after page, he is described as dangerous, psychotic, paranoid, and in need of treatment.

No one was surprised when Goldstein pleaded not guilty of murdering Webdale by reason of insanity. What was surprising was the prosecutor's determination to bring Goldstein to trial. While the public may not be aware of it, prosecutors almost always accept insanity defenses. According to Harriet Ryan, "[e]xperts estimate as many as 90 percent of all insanity defenses never go to trial largely because the prosecutor conceded that the defendant is insane and the case becomes a matter of treatment instead of punishment." The Goldstein case had garnered enormous publicity; and the defendant "admits to senseless killing that caused an outcry in New York, and prosecutors certainly know that an insanity defense — no matter what its merit — does not sit well with the public," says Ryan.[4]

Goldstein was charged with murder in the second degree. The jury was faced with the difficult job of determining whether Goldstein was sane or insane at the time of the crime. If the jury found he had been insane, it could vote to acquit. Goldstein would then be confined to a mental institution until doctors deemed he was no longer a threat to society. A guilty verdict, on the other hand, would be accompanied by a sentence of twenty-five years to life in a state prison.

Goldstein's defense attorneys contended that he had been in a psychotic state and unable to understand the consequences of his actions when he pushed Webdale in front of the train. They had thousands of pages of medical records to support their case. Goldstein, heavily medicated, watched impassively as his attorneys introduced evidence of his illness.

The prosecution acknowledged that Goldstein was schizophrenic but argued that he was legally sane when he attacked Webdale. Prosecution psychiatrists testified that Goldstein had been aware of what he was doing and knew it was wrong. Assistant District Attorney William Greenbaum argued the attack on Webdale had been prompted not by psychosis but by anger at another blonde woman who had shunned Goldstein in the subway. Further, Goldstein had used his illness as a shield, Greenbaum said.

The jury deadlocked 10 to 2 in favor of conviction. The judge declared a mistrial.

Reporter Michael Winerip covered the

Goldstein case for the *New York Times.* He believed the ten jurors leaning toward conviction were frightened by the prospect of Goldstein being released again. "If judged insane, he would go to a secure state psychiatric hospital. There he would be re-evaluated every two years to determine whether he was fit for discharge," Winerip explained. "And that, I believe, scared the hell out of many New Yorkers — the possibility that Andrew Goldstein could be back on the streets in a few years' time. It was, to my mind, the prosecutor's secret weapon."[5]

Goldstein was tried again in 2000. As part of his defense strategy, attorney Kevin Canfield took Goldstein off his medication for the trial. Canfield wanted this jury to see what the first jury had not, what he called "the real Andrew." Medicated, Goldstein was groggy and subdued; he was nothing like the crazed man who killed Kendra Webdale. "This is a very serious charge, and when he's on his medication, he's sedated and doesn't act like a person on trial for murder," Canfield said. "I wanted him to be able to testify and I wanted the psychiatric experts to be able to examine him while he was in a psychotic state."[6] Canfield's strategy worked too well — an unmedicated Goldstein punched a social worker before trial. The judge ordered he be put back on his medication. Goldstein did not take the stand.

As in the first trial, the key issue was Goldstein's sanity, or lack thereof, when he attacked Webdale. Defense attorney Canfield argued that the killing itself was insane because it lacked motivation, reason, or justification. "This was not the act of a cold-blooded, depraved killer. He didn't know it was wrong if he didn't know what he was doing," Canfield said.[7]

The prosecutor countered that Goldstein had "a history of insulating himself from his actions. He had done it time and time again, taking advantage of people of good will, saying, 'I'm psychotic, take me to the hospital.' " The defendant used "his insanity as a tool to insulate himself from the consequences of his actions right away."

Prosecution witness Dawn Lorenzo testified that she watched Goldstein shuffling around the station prior to the attack but that he began to walk normally as he approached Kendra. She said that Goldstein didn't push Kendra; instead, he picked her up and threw her into the path of the oncoming train. Lorenzo also said that

Goldstein made sure to regain his balance so that he would not fall with Kendra.

Dr. Spencer Eth, a defense psychiatrist, testified that he believed Goldstein attacked Webdale "when he was suffering an acute exacerbation . . . of severe psychotic symptoms," most likely caused by his failure to take his prescribed antipsychotic medication. According to Eth, the symptoms would have been so severe that Goldstein "couldn't plan, he couldn't intend, he couldn't know as we understand what know means what he was doing or that it was wrong."

Prosecution psychiatrist Angela Hegarty disagreed with Eth, insisting Goldstein had a "relatively mild" disorder "in the schizophrenic spectrum" and that his symptoms "were substantially in remission" when he attacked Webdale. Hegarty also testified about conversations she had had with people who knew Goldstein including a landlord, a roommate, and friends from college. The defense objected to her testimony — it was clearly hearsay. The objection was overruled.

In the end, it was the testimony of witness Dawn Lorenzo that had the biggest impact on the jury. Goldstein was found guilty of second-degree murder. He was sentenced to twenty-five years to life in prison. After the trial, one juror commented that they had believed Goldstein was mentally ill but "the evidence was pretty compelling" that he knew right from wrong. "He seemed to know what he was doing. He picked her up and threw her. That was not a psychotic jerk, an involuntary movement."[8]

The guilty verdict was overturned by an appeals court in 2005. The court ruled that the trial judge had erred in allowing Hegarty to testify about other people's opinions about the defendant when those people were unavailable for cross-examination. Her testimony was deemed inadmissible hearsay and a new trial was ordered.

Rather than go through a third trial, Goldstein agreed to plead guilty to the lesser charge of manslaughter. In his allocution, he told the court that Webdale "was leaning against a pole with her back to me near the edge of the platform near the tracks. I looked to see if the train was coming down the tracks. I saw that the subway train was coming into the station. When the train was almost in front of us, I placed my hands on the back of her shoulders and pushed her. My actions caused her to fall onto the tracks." In exchange for his guilty plea, Goldstein was sentenced to twenty-five years in prison, to be followed by five years

The Crime Scene

Nothing is more important to an investigation than securing the crime scene quickly and efficiently. Before the detectives arrive, the responding officer must act quickly to preserve the scene so it's exactly as it was during the time the crime was committed. That means, first, keeping anyone from leaving the area (so they can be questioned) or entering the area from the outside (so they don't disturb vital clues, or worse, so the suspect doesn't return to hinder the investigation). Even something as seemingly innocent as a nosy neighbor walking on a carpet can wipe away vital clues. If the crime scene isn't frozen in time — if someone flushes a toilet, moves a chair, or closes an open closet door — the investigation can be hampered. Much to the annoyance of homicide detectives, things like this happen all the time.

There's a certain TV show that revolves around crime scene investigations. If real crime scene units behaved like the one in the show, the police department's solve rate would be zero.

of postrelease supervision and psychiatric care.

As a result of the Andrew Goldstein case, New York State passed Kendra's Law, which allows a family to force treatment upon a mentally ill relative.

NINE

L&O: SVU: ("Slaves," Season 1) A controlling yuppie and his subservient wife hold a live-in maid captive as a sex slave.

TRUE CRIME: Pennsylvania high school student Tanya Kach was held captive as a sex slave by a security guard from her school, only a few miles from her father's house. She emerged ten years later.

Tanya Kach was getting a slow start in life. A resident of Elizabeth, Pennsylvania, a southeast suburb of Pittsburgh, she was already twenty-four years old when she got her learner's permit to drive. She didn't come from a well-off family and didn't have much money of her own, but with the help of a local charity, she was able to buy her first car. But Tanya hadn't had a good string of luck in a long time, and this time wasn't any different. The car broke down as she was driving soon after she got it. She didn't know what to do. There she was parked on the side of the road, and panic was setting in fast. What does a person do when her car breaks down? Flag someone down for help? Call the police? Call a tow truck? What does a person *do?* She couldn't think of the right answer, so she found a telephone and called her lawyer. . . .

Dealing with a broken-down car on the highway can be an unsettling experience for anyone, but for Tanya Kach it was an absolute catastrophe. Actually, it was beyond that. Considering her state of mind at this point in her life — the very concept of reality itself was enough to cause severe anxiety and confusion — she probably couldn't even label the situation. The last time she had been out in public, around other people, dealing with everyday life in a capacity that could be considered even remotely normal was ten years previous, in 1996, when she was fourteen years old — when she began dating Thomas Hose.

According to students interviewed after Tanya Kach appeared out of nowhere in 2006, Hose was the heartthrob of Cornell Middle School. The girls thought he was

175

adorable. Hose lapped up the attention, too. No other guy in the school could hold a candle to him. The odd part was that Hose didn't hold the status of star football player. He wasn't the class brainiac, and he wasn't rich. He had no prospects for a bright future in any way, shape, or form. That's because Hose wasn't a student; he was a thirty-seven-year-old security guard with a penchant for younger girls. And he had his dream job; with access to teenage girls every day, he was young enough to be cool but old enough to be considered wise and worldly. Hose played the part really well. He was the knight in shining armor.

The school had never received any complaints about how Hose performed his job. Both the administrators and the private security company he worked for considered Hose a model employee. Those who witnessed him interact with the students on a day to day basis, however, saw Hose in a different light. To them, he was a pathetic guy in his thirties who flirted with middle school girls. According to one cafeteria employee, Jeanie Krimm, the kitchen staff got a kick out of Hose. "I thought he was hilarious. He would wear his pants two sizes too small. You could see every nook and cranny."* She added that he drenched himself in so much cologne that people smelled Hose before they saw him.[1]

Hose's personal life wasn't much better than his professional life. He lived in a dumpy two-story house in the town of Mc-Keesport, Pennsylvania. He had lived there all his life, sharing the house with his parents. Hose had been married once and divorced. He had one child — a son two years younger than Tanya Kach — and his ex-wife lived a few houses away.

In 1995, Hose went beyond the boundaries of flirting. When he and Tanya Kach

---

*Krimm's daughter Kimberlie left her house at 9:00 p.m. one June night in 1998 to buy some hair coloring products. She didn't return home. About a week later, her body was found decomposing in a cemetery about a block from her house. Her jeans had been pulled down below her waist. When Tanya Kach emerged in 2006, police began investigating Thomas Hose in connection with the Krimm death, but he was later cleared as a suspect. The police are treating it as a homicide, but because Kimberlie's body was so decomposed, coroners were unable to determine the cause of death. It appears to have been a murder, though. As of the publication of this book, the case remains open.

Tanya Kach with her father during a television interview after she emerged from her decade-long captivity.
Courtesy of CNN

bumped into each other one day in the privacy of a stairwell, they got to talking. They moved closer to each other and the talking turned to kissing, according to Kach. She was in love. Thereafter, the couple saw one another as often as possible, on and off the school campus. If they tried to keep the relationship a secret, they didn't try very hard. Tanya's classmates all knew what was going on. What did she care, though? She had been unhappy as hell, and Thomas Hose, she thought, was the answer to her problems. Tanya lived with her father and stepmother and had a history of running away. In school, local police recall, she often got into fights. When this guy, this seemingly stable, good-looking guy showed interest in her, she felt her life had changed. In fact it had, but not for the better.

At the first chance, Tanya dropped everything for Thomas Hose. On February 10, 1996, a Saturday, Tanya packed her bags and left her house. Her family had seen it before. After a fight or a spell of brooding, Tanya would disappear. But she always returned a few days later. This time, though, they didn't see her for weeks, then months . . . then years. Her father and stepmother had no idea where she had gone, and neither did the police. When Tanya had been gone a few weeks, they launched an investigation. A picture of Tanya along with key information went up on missing children websites everywhere, but eventually the police gave up. Tanya's family had to accept the probability that at best she had started a new life, at worst, she was dead. Ten years later, although her family never forgot about Tanya Kach, all hope was gone. They expected never to see her again.

On March 21, 2006, a twenty-four-year-old woman named Nikki Allen walked into a deli down the block from Thomas Hose's house. The deli's owner, Joe Sparico, knew Nikki from her previous visits. A pretty girl with big, warm eyes, she had been shy at first, perhaps a little sad, but as time went on, she became more and more comfortable striking up conversations with him. On this day, though, she had a story that would blow him away.

Nikki told Sparico that she had spent the last ten years as a virtual prisoner in the bedroom of Thomas Hose. Her name wasn't really Nikki either. It was Tanya. Tanya Kach. Insane as it all sounded, Sparico believed it. He picked up the phone and called the police.

When the story broke, Tanya, who for a solid decade had next to no human contact and grew from child to woman in a single room, would now look out the window of her father's home and see a film crew approaching the front steps, or a neighbor slowing down her car to get a closer look at what was previously the nondescript house of a man whose daughter had run away ten years ago. The phone would ring and it might be an ABC TV producer asking for an interview, or a litigation lawyer offering his services. The entire world wanted to know what had happened to Tanya Kach. All her father cared about now was that she was alive and well. He couldn't believe it. More incredible still was the fact that she had been living only a few miles away the whole time.

Over the next few weeks the details unraveled. Tanya's story defied imagination. She had run off with Hose that day in February, only they didn't run very far. They went to his house and pretty much stayed there. Occasionally, during the first few months of their relationship, Tanya would sleep at the home of Hose's friend Judy Sokol, a hairdresser who cut and dyed Kach's hair so no one in town would recognize her, which was unlikely since Tanya would be carefully shuttled from one house to the other in the dead of night. But it was a chance none of them wanted to take.

After a few months, Tanya had a permanent home: Hose's bedroom. Although his parents lived in the same house, which was less than one thousand square feet, they didn't know about Tanya for the first nine years, according to Kach. She says that she was told to avoid walking on the floor as much as possible during the daytime; she had to remember which floorboards creaked so she could step over them if she absolutely had to traverse across the room. She subsisted largely on peanut butter and jelly sandwiches. She was allowed to use the bathroom in the basement (the only bathroom in the house) a couple of times a week, when the old folks were asleep or had gone out. Otherwise showers were prohibited and a bucket in the bedroom took care of everything else.

Tanya's high school prom and graduation came and went. While her friends were getting their drivers licenses and tasting real freedom for the first time in their lives, Tanya was dutifully hiding quietly in Thomas Hose's closet when she heard someone coming up the stairs. As her peers were going out on dates, exploring feelings and emotions they never knew they had, Tanya Kach was sleeping next to a middle school security guard who wore too much cologne. And while her friends who attended college were learning new ideas and outlooks that transported them intellectually light years beyond the suburbs of Pittsburgh, Tanya was stuck reading teen novels and watching educational shows on TV to keep her brain from atrophying.

Nine years after seducing a fourteen-year-old desperate to escape her dysfunctional family, and then housing her in his bedroom for the better part of a decade, Thomas Hose introduced his "girlfriend" to his parents, who reportedly had never met Tanya, nor heard any noises upstairs loud enough to prompt an investigation. Questions remain about how this could have been the case.

As Hose became more comfortable introducing Tanya to others, he allowed her certain freedoms. She was permitted to go shopping for new clothes, make trips to the deli where she met Joe Sparico, and attend church, where she did volunteer work. Her church friends, who knew Tanya as Nikki Allen, appreciated Tanya's gentle, kind manner. The more observant of them detected a sadness behind those big eyes, and began questioning her about Thomas Hose. Though Tanya didn't reveal all, she revealed enough information about her boyfriend to raise eyebrows. The relationship between Tanya and Thomas was obviously askew. It was clear from what Tanya told them that Hose possessed a severely controlling personality. Even when he wasn't around, the specter of Hose seemed always to be watching over Tanya. The young woman was frightened to death of her boyfriend, and she seemed to be the only one unaware of the extent of it.

Tanya was urged to go out and do things on her own. Her friends implored her to finish her high school education, get a drivers license, and, most of all, leave Thomas Hose. For nine months, Tanya absorbed the advice of her friends, and one day made that last trip to the deli. She was reborn.

So why didn't Tanya leave earlier? She is often described as being "locked" in a bedroom for years. But no one can literally lock someone inside a bedroom for ten years. Escaping from a suburban home is a simple process for any ambulatory person. And why did Tanya Kach not run for help the moment she was first "allowed" out of the house?

Stockholm Syndrome is often referenced in the Tanya Kach story. The term refers to a 1973 hostage situation in Stockholm, Sweden, during which some hostages experienced feelings of sympathy for their captors. One woman ended up marrying one of the hostage takers. They also shared with their captors a fear of the police who were trying to rescue them. The man who coined the term, Dr. Frank Ochberg, an American psychiatrist who specializes in post-traumatic stress disorder, lists three elements of Stockholm Syndrome: the victim has positive feelings about his or her captor; the victim experiences positive treatment from the captor; and the victim shares a fear of those who would meddle in the relationship, such as hostage negotiators and rescuers.[*]

Tanya Kach seems to have experienced these types of feelings. She was just a kid when she ran off with Thomas Hose and was very impressionable. She was physically separated from her parents, friends, and any possible future acquaintances and boyfriends. More important, though, Tanya was psychologically cut off from everything that wasn't connected to Thomas Hose. It would have been relatively easy to get out of the house any time Thomas Hose was at work, or at least shout for help. But in her state of mind, Tanya would not allow herself to do that. Kach says that Hose often told her that no one cared about her, that her family had stopped searching for her, and that he was the only one in the world who loved her.

[*]While the term was originally used to describe the experience of hostages and kidnap victims, Stockholm Syndrome is today often linked to women in abusive relationships, and historically to slaves and Holocaust victims who collaborated with their captors.

No doubt, though, Thomas Hose occasionally showed his softer side to Tanya, and in such a relationship, the victim will blow out of proportion even the smallest kindness. A small gift will be interpreted as a token of love; an expression of vulnerability will be translated as total trust. How can I leave this man who is so good to me? the victim often thinks. Whether or not Tanya Kach technically suffered from Stockholm Syndrome, she was a psychological prisoner of Thomas Hose. "He had a puppet," Tanya said in an interview, referring to herself.[2]

In April 2006, the month after Kach's reappearance, a hearing was held in an Allegheny County courtroom. Kach told the whole story under oath. Based on the testimony, the judge ordered Hose to stand trial for a number of charges, including statutory sexual assault and involuntary deviate sexual intercourse. Later more charges were added, including aggravated indecent assault, endangering the welfare of a child, and corruption of a minor. Considered an accomplice of Hose, Sokol, too, faced charges: statutory sexual assault, indecent assault, and corruption of a minor. Hose pleaded not guilty, and the judge

The Rape Kit

The very first thing police need in order to investigate a rape, and something mentioned in most *Law & Order: SVU* episodes, is a "rape kit." It is actually a kit, complete with the materials and instructions a trained hospital worker needs to compile physical evidence from a woman who reports having been raped. The evidence gathering is a terribly clinical and intrusive process that includes testing for disease and, sometimes, pregnancy, collecting hair, fingernail scrapings, semen, and other physical evidence, and conducting a complete examination of the body, which is completely documented.

Everything goes into the rape kit, which is then sealed to prevent tampering. In many cases, the rape kit is the only evidence linking the victim to the perpetrator, and with the advent of DNA testing, rape kit evidence is more useful than ever. As long as the rape kit is stored correctly, the police can always use it to prosecute a suspect, even years after the crime was committed.

In a perfect world, each rape kit would be automatically tested for DNA, and the results would be entered into the national database. Problem is, there are an estimated 350,000 rape kits in warehouses around the country that have yet to be tested. Each test costs between $500 and $1,000, and most police departments simply don't have the funds for this — which is especially sad considering that the few departments that *have* found the money to do this, including the NYPD, saw dramatic results in solving major cases, thus preventing further crimes, as well as exonerating innocent convicts.

put him under house arrest until his trial. The ramshackle house was now his prison.

Just hours before his trial was to begin on February 13, 2007, Thomas Hose stabbed himself repeatedly in the stomach and sat down in a chair. He was taken to a state mental hospital and treated for both his wounds and his mental health. His trial has been postponed on multiple occasions. As of this writing, Hose has yet to face a jury.

TEN

L&O: SVU: ("Venom," Season 7) Detective Tutola's son and nephew are implicated in the murder of a woman and child.

TRUE STORY: Raymond Levi Cobb killed a woman and her baby while robbing a house in Texas in 1993.

December 27, 1993, started like any other day for Lindsey Owings. He rose early, showered, and dressed for work, taking care not to wake his wife, Margaret, and their sixteen-month-old daughter, Kori. Before leaving the house, Owings checked on Kori; the toddler was asleep in her crib. She looked particularly adorable, dressed in a tutu-like sleep suit with the word "ballerina" stenciled across the chest, a pair of moccasins on her feet. Owings then kissed his sleeping wife good-bye and left for the Texas Department of Criminal Justice where he worked as a carpenter.

Owings put in a full day of work and returned home around dinner time. Margaret's car was still in the driveway but the house was dark. Owings opened the door and called out to his wife and child. There was no answer. He flipped on the light switch. The house was a mess. Kori's toys were strewn across the living room floor and the stereo and VCR were gone. Owings was alarmed. He searched the house and the yard but did not find Margaret and Kori. He called the Walker County Sheriff's Department to report his family missing. The police filed a missing persons report and conducted an unfruitful search of the area.

The next day, an anonymous caller phoned the sheriff's department with information linking a seventeen-year-old named Raymond Levi Cobb to the Owings' burglary. Cobb was a high school student who had recently moved across the street from the Owingses. The family had met him once, when he knocked on their door a week earlier claiming to be looking for his missing dog. Detectives took Cobb in for questioning. He denied burglarizing the Owings house and said he had no knowledge or information about the disappearance of

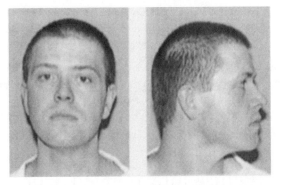

In December 1993, Raymond Cobb murdered his neighbor Margret Owings and buried her in the woods, along with her sixteen-month-old daughter, Kori, who was still alive.

Margaret and Kori. The detectives suspected he was lying but with no evidence to implicate him, they were forced to let him go.

Despite the efforts of numerous search parties, the whereabouts of Margaret and Kori Owings would remain a mystery for nearly two years.

In July 1994, Raymond Cobb was arrested on an unrelated charge. The detectives questioned him again about the Owings case; this time Cobb admitted that he had burglarized their home. However, he continued to insist he had no idea what had happened to Margaret and Kori. Cobb was released on bail. Public defender Hal Ridley was appointed Cobb's counsel.

Ridley gave the police unqualified permission to interview his client about the missing Owings woman and her child, telling them, "it was okay, if it was okay with Cobb." Police interrogated Cobb. Once again, he insisted he was guilty only of robbing the Owings' home. Cobb was indicted on burglary charges and released on bail. He moved to Odessa to live with his father while awaiting his trial.

In the meantime, Lindsey Owings was living in a perpetual state of anxiety and fear. He held on to the belief that his family was out there somewhere and would eventually come home. Owings searched the area woods and made frequent stops along the road to call out his wife's name. Twenty-three-year-old Margaret was a decorated navy veteran who had met Owings during Desert Storm. She had been assigned to a supply ship; Owings was assigned to a submarine. Owings found it mind-boggling to think that Margaret had returned unscathed from Desert Storm only to go missing from their home in quiet, rural Texas.

■ ■ ■ ■

Cobb was in Odessa just a few days before he confessed to his father that he had killed Margaret and Kori Owings when he robbed their home. His father called the police. Cobb was taken into custody and read his Miranda Rights. He had been arrested and questioned numerous times in his young life, and was keenly aware of his rights. He waived them voluntarily and agreed to speak with the detectives without a lawyer present. Cobb did not tell the detectives that he was awaiting trial in another jurisdiction for burglarizing the Owings home, or more importantly, that he already had a lawyer in that case.

Initially Cobb denied he had killed Margaret and Kori Owings. But after a while, he confessed. He told Sergeant Harold Thomas that Margaret had caught him robbing her house and jumped on his back. The two had fought and Cobb stabbed her twice in the stomach with a double-edged knife he was carrying. He then dragged Margaret's body into the woods, a few hundred yards away. "I went back to her house and I saw the baby laying on its bed," he told Thomas. "I took the baby out there and it was sleeping the whole time. I laid the baby down on the ground four or five feet away from its mother. I went back to my house and got a flat edge shovel. That's all I could find. Then I went back over to where they were and I started digging a hole between them. After I got the hole dug, the baby was awake. It started going towards its mom and it fell in the hole. I put the lady in the hole and I covered them up. I remember stabbing a different knife I had in the ground where they were. I was crying right then."

Sergeant Thomas didn't really believe Cobb had cried for his victims. The teenager struck him as being very detached and a bit strange. "The only time he showed emotion was when he was feeling sorry for himself," Thomas would say later. "He had no emotions for the victims. She was 'the lady' and he called the baby 'it.' "

Shortly after he confessed, Cobb agreed to show police where he had buried his victims. He led the officers to a wooded area about a half mile from the Owings home in Huntsville. Cadaver-locating dogs were brought in after Cobb was unable to find the exact burial site. Hours later, the shallow grave was discovered. It appeared that wild animals had dug up the victims' remains. All that was left were a few scattered pieces of clothing, a tiny pink moccasin, and bones that were later identified as belonging to Margaret Owings.

In 1997, Raymond Levi Cobb was tried for the capital murders of Margaret and Kori Owings. If convicted, Cobb faced a possible death sentence. During the trial, jurors learned that Cobb fatally stabbed Margaret Owings at least twice in the stomach before burying her in the woods. Medical examiners testified that Kori most likely suffocated when she was buried alive. Her body was never found; the medical examiner speculated that animals had devoured her remains.

The defendant's father, Charles Cobb, was the prosecution's star witness. Without him, the case may very well have never been solved. An ex-con who had served two prison sentences, the elder Cobb took the stand to recount the day Raymond confessed he had killed Margaret and Kori Owings. Charles Cobb said that he always suspected his son was somehow involved in their disappearance. "I told him I was tired of lies," Charles Cobb testified. "I told him that the only way I could help was if he told me the truth. He started crying. He said he killed her, stabbed her."[1] Charles Cobb said he was shaken by Raymond's confession. He felt bad about ratting out his son but he believed the Owings family deserved to know what had happened to their loved ones.

Sergeant Victor Sikes, another prosecution witness, testified that Cobb had confessed to stabbing Margaret and burying Kori alive. He also said he took Margaret's rings off her fingers. According to Sikes, Cobb said he had been smoking marijuana and drinking heavily on the day of the murders and "said he had a pretty good buzz."[2]

The most heartbreaking moment in the trial came when Lindsey Owings took the stand. Choking back tears, he recalled the last time he saw his wife and daughter. When the prosecutor handed him a ring to identify, Owings broke down. "That's Maggie's wedding ring," he said. Owings also identified the pink moccasin found at the burial site as belonging to a pair he had bought for his daughter.

After eight days, the prosecution rested. The defense called no witnesses. It took the jury just forty-five minutes to reach a verdict: guilty.

During the penalty phase, Cobb's mother, several of his high school teachers, and members of the church took the stand to attest that he was a good kid who "pretty much grew up in [the] church," and "loved animals and other kids." Cobb's mother cried as she begged the court to spare her son's life. "You have found him guilty and he needs to be punished. But there is no reason why a third person should die," she said.[3] Walter Quijana, the psychologist for the defense, stated that Cobb was "not likely to be a future danger to society," because he had no prior history of violence before the Owings murders.

The prosecution called psychologist Richard Mears to rebut Quijana's testimony. "No one kills twenty-four hours a day. Even dyed-in-the-wool killers take a break," Mears said. "But then one day, eight years later, they kill again."[4] He told the court that Cobb had saved newspaper clippings of his crimes and had a "fascination with death." "Once I heard about the murder of the mother, it didn't make any difference that he was a good boy in school and took all his tests. The only thing that makes any difference is the nature of the crime. The mother dying. The baby dying. I dismiss all his history as a smoke screen that some psychologists came up with," he said.[5]

The jury agreed. For the murders of Margaret and Kori Owings, Raymond Levi

Cobb was sentenced to die by lethal injection.

Although the trial had ended, the Cobb case was far from over. Represented by a new attorney, Cobb appealed his death sentence on the grounds that the trial judge should have excluded his police confession because it was obtained in violation of his Sixth Amendment right to counsel. Cobb contended that his right to counsel had attached on the burglary charge when Ridley was appointed his public defender; therefore, the Odessa police were required to obtain Ridley's permission before interrogating him.

The Texas Court of Criminal Appeals ruled in Cobb's favor, declaring that the right to counsel attached to any offense closely related to the original offense the defendant was charged with. The court found the capital murder charge to be "factually interwoven with the burglary." Therefore, it concluded, Cobb's Sixth Amendment rights had, in fact, been violated when detectives questioned him without obtaining permission from his attorney. Cobb's confession was deemed inadmissible and a new trial was ordered.

The State of Texas immediately filed an

The Interrogation

There are as many ways of interrogating a suspect as there are different personalities in the world. Everyone reacts differently to questioning, and every cop has different instincts on how best to exploit the suspect's weaknesses. One of the universally useful weapons in the police interrogator's arsenal, though, is the big fat lie.

Cops can't necessarily *do* anything they want in the interrogation room (no beatings allowed), but they can pretty much *say* anything they want. In order to get a confession out of a suspect, a cop might tell him that they have an eyewitness to the crime in the next room, that an accomplice has already spilled his guts, or that if they don't confess now, it will be much worse down the road — all of which may or may not be true. There is no law against a police officer lying to a suspect in order to extract a confession, which is why experienced criminals will usually "lawyer up" without saying a word.

appeal of its own in the U.S. Supreme Court. By a 5–4 vote, the court reversed the Criminal Appeals Court's ruling, stating that "the Sixth Amendment right to counsel is offense specific," and "cannot be invoked once for all future prosecutions, for it does not attach until a prosecution is commenced."

In the court's written decision, Chief Justice Rehnquist noted that "as defined by Texas law, burglary and capital murder are not the same offense . . . Accordingly, the Sixth Amendment right to counsel did not bar police from interrogating respondent regarding the murders, and respondent's confession was therefore admissible." He pointed out that Cobb had the right under Miranda to refuse police questioning but chose not to.

"Admissions of guilt resulting from valid Miranda waivers are more than merely desirable; they are essential to society's compelling interest in finding, convicting, and punishing those who violate the law," Rehnquist concluded.

Cobb was sent back to death row — but not for long. In 2002, in an unrelated case, the U.S. Supreme Court ruled it unconstitutional to execute prisoners for crimes committed before the age of eighteen because society views minors "as less categorically culpable than the average criminal." In response to the ruling, Texas Governor Rick Perry commuted the death sentences of twenty-eight convicts — Raymond Levi Cobb among them — who had murdered before the age of eighteen. Cobb is currently serving a life sentence. He will be eligible for parole in 2037.

ELEVEN

L&O SVU: ("Name," Season 7) The SVU detectives are faced with solving a cold case after the skeletal remains of a boy who disappeared in 1978 are found.

TRUE STORY: The identity of a dead child found on a rural Philadelphia road in 1957 is unknown, and his murder remains unsolved today.

Officer Sam Weinstein was driving in the Fox Chase section of Philadelphia when he took the call. As he proceeded down Susquehanna Road, Weinstein saw that his colleague had beaten him to the scene. Officer Elmer Palmer was standing a few feet off the side of the road in the woods looking at a large, partly crushed packing box with the word "Fragile" stamped on it. Weinstein got out of his patrol car and walked up to Palmer. For a moment the two policemen just stood there in silence. These Philly cops had seen a lot of bad things on the job, but this was the worst yet. The body of a little boy was inside the box, his head sticking out from the open end, resting on the weeds. Bruises covered his face and head, but Weinstein and Palmer could see no other obvious damage to the boy's body. The officers took note of how skinny he was, clearly malnourished. The boy, who could be no more than five or six years old, was partly covered with a thin, plaid blanket. He wasn't just tossed there; he was posed, lying on his back with his arms over his chest, as if someone had prepared him for a funeral.

The emergency call was an odd one. It was made by a twenty-six-year-old student from LaSalle, a nearby Catholic university in Philadelphia, who had been driving down Susquehanna Road and had seen a rabbit run across the road and into the woods. When he stopped his car and began chasing it, he stumbled across the box. He was shocked to see a body inside it. He couldn't tell if it was a doll or a little boy, and he didn't get any closer to find out. He ran off, he said, and called the police.

The truth is that the student had seen the body days before. He didn't call the police initially because his adventure in the woods didn't really involve the pursuit of a rabbit. He had been cutting through the woods, as he often did, to stalk the girls at a nearby school. He phoned the police only after he told his story to a priest at his college, who urged him to report it.

Officers Weinstein and Palmer didn't know any of this now, though. All they knew was that a poor little boy was dead, and that from the looks of it he had been murdered. Soon, the detectives arrived. They, too, were stunned by the sight, but they were absolutely determined to get the son-of-a-bitch who would do this to a child. The date was February 25, 1957. Police have yet to catch the killer.

Today, Susquehanna Road is wider and much busier than it was in 1957. The woods are long gone, replaced with green lawns and brick homes, and the spot where the Boy in the Box was found is now somewhere in the eastbound lane next to the entrance of a driveway. But the boy remains frozen in time. He is still the young boy (four to six years old, medical experts concluded) with a large forehead and blank look on his face. In many ways, the investigators, too, are frozen in time, and will remain so until they

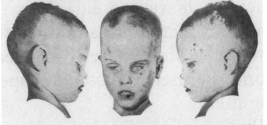

POLICE DEPARTMENT, PHILADELPHIA, PA.

INFORMATION WANTED

Photographs depict unidentified boy, whose nude body was found in a cardboard carton, in a thicket, near Susquehanna and Verree Roads, Fox Chase, Philadelphia, 3:45 p.m., Monday, February 25, 1957. Death caused by head injuries. Multiple bruises over entire body. Death estimated to have occurred from three days to two weeks prior to discovery. No clothing found. Body covered by blanket. Man's cloth cap found adjacent to body.

Description of Boy: 4 to 5 years, height 40½", weight 30 lbs., blue eyes, fair complexion; medium to light brown hair, crudely cut; full set baby teeth; no deformities; "L"-shaped scar under chin; no vaccination scar; tonsils not removed; no bone fractures; finger and toe nails neatly clipped; clothing size probably 4; shoe size, 8-D.

Blanket made of cheap cotton flannel, patterned with diamonds and blocks in green, rust and white, colors faded. Overall size 64" x 76" with section 51" x 26" missing. Clean, apparently washed recently. Mended with poor-grade cotton thread on home-type sewing machine.

Man's cap, size 7⅛, leather strap in back, royal blue corduroy material. In excellent condition, with large roll of paper tissue in sweatband. Manufacturer's stamp in lining of crown, Robbins Bald Eagle Cap, 2603 South 7th St., Philadelphia, Pa.

Carton, size 15" x 19" x 35". Originally contained white bassinet, price $7.50, sold at J. C. Penney store, 69th and Chestnut Sts., Upper Darby, Pa., between December 3, 1956 and February 16, 1957.

It is requested that citizens and law enforcement, welfare, and child caring agencies supply information concerning boys of this age and description, known to be in the custody of persons who might abuse them; also, the disappearance or absence of any child answering this description. Newspaper, radio, and television publicity requested.

NOTIFY HOMICIDE UNIT, DETECTIVE HEADQUARTERS, CITY HALL, PHILADELPHIA, at any time, day or night, in person or telephone, MUnicipal 6-6700, or submit information through your local Police Department.

March 8, 1957

THOMAS J. GIBBONS
Commissioner

Prepared by The Philadelphia Inquirer as a public service.

The "Boy in the Box" poster Philadelphians saw everywhere they looked in spring 1957. Authorities hoped it would generate leads to identify the little boy found dead in the Fox Chase area; the case remains unsolved today.

die or the murderer is caught. They just won't let the case go.

While the murder victim was being buried in a potter's field, Philly detectives worked feverishly to track down the killer. In the days before DNA and automated credit card tracking, it was no easy feat. Yet, they performed an incredible amount of investigative work. Unfortunately, at every step, they found themselves *clearing* suspects, not arresting them.

The Philly police didn't have much evidence to go on. First, they had the box, which had come from JCPenney and had been used to pack a baby bassinet. Cops were able to track down eleven of the twelve people who bought that bassinet model in Philadelphia. All of the boxes were accounted for, and every person cleared. Whoever owned the twelfth box was likely involved in the murder.

The second major piece of evidence was the blanket, which had almost certainly come from the killer's home. Police quickly found out where it was made, but too many were manufactured to connect this particular blanket to a particular person.

The third and last important object was a blue corduroy man's cap. Crime scene investigators found the cap about three yards from the victim, with footprints connecting the two. Again, the cops did their legwork. They located the maker, who said she had made only twelve of those

The Boy in the Box was dubbed "America's Unknown Child" by the Vidocq Society, a group of active and retired cops who work unsolved cases on their own time. The Society had the victim moved from the potter's field in which he was originally buried to Ivy Hill Cemetery near Philadephia. Visitors leave flowers and toys for the unidentified murder victim.

caps — and she remembered this specific one! The customer had asked her to stitch on an adjustable strap on the back. She described him to detectives, but, once again, the detectives ran into a dead end.

The LaSalle student was immediately cleared, having passed a lie detector test soon after he reported the crime. There was only one other witness to the crime scene, a man who said he was driving down Susquehanna Road when he saw a car parked at the spot where the body was found. He saw an adult woman with a child he described as a boy about twelve years old standing at the back of the car. The two were busying themselves with something in the trunk. He thought they might have a flat tire, so he pulled up to offer his help. The woman and child made a point of ignoring him and even shifted their bodies to block the witness's view of the car's license plate. The witness drove off.

So now cops had no evidence to connect the victim to the killer and no good witnesses to speak of. What they did have, though, were leads, tips, and calls from relatives of missing people. And *plenty.* The case was publicized so widely that police weren't surprised when the phone starting ringing and the letters poured in. A U.S. Marine private thought it might be his long-lost younger brother, a Long Island man believed it was his abducted son. One woman, an artist, said she had seen the boy on the bus with a man who looked like he could be his father; she even sketched a picture of the father.* A barber came forward and said he definitely cut the boy's hair the week before. Police followed up on all these tips and missing persons claims, but none of them led to an arrest.

About four years after the boy was discovered, Joseph Komarnicki, an ex-detective who had worked for the Philadelphia Police Department's missing persons unit, read a newspaper story about a woman who had confessed to tossing her dead three-year-old daughter into a garbage can. She was caught when neighbors called the police after seeing her son rummaging through a trash can looking for food. A connection with the malnourished Fox Chase boy, Komarnicki wondered? At his own expense and on his own time, he flew out to Colorado to investigate further.

The story got even more interesting: When the Colorado police arrived at Margaret Martinez's home, they asked where her boy was. She told them he was staying with relatives in Philadelphia. But when the cops

*Eerily enough, the picture she drew looked strikingly similar to a bust created by a forensic sculptor depicting what the boy's father could have looked like. See the photos at *http://www.americasunknownchild.net/Artists.html*.

searched her house, they found her underfed son hiding under a bed. Martinez, it turned out, had spent time in a hospital for the criminally insane and had relatives in the Fox Chase area of Philadelphia, and she apparently traveled frequently without her husband. Plus, she fit the description of the driver who witnessed the woman and "twelve-year-old-boy" on Susquehanna Road shortly before the boy's body was discovered.

But the whole thing turned out to be yet another waste of time. After questioning her, police didn't consider Martinez a possible suspect.

Not five months later, in February 1961, an even more disturbing story unfolded, this time involving a family of traveling carnival workers. The parents of ten, Kenneth and Irene Dudley were arrested in Lawrenceville, Virginia, when their seven-year-old daughter died of "malnutrition, exposure and neglect."[1] Like the Philly boy, her body was found in the woods covered by a cheap blanket, and she was wearing clothes purchased at JCPenney. The family had spent 1957 working for carnivals up and down the east coast. One of the Dudley's children, a four-year-old named Kenneth, had died in 1941. The father buried the child's body in the yard, for which he was arrested and sentenced to nine months in prison.

After the arrest, police discovered that four of the Dudley's other children were missing, and that they were similar in age to the Boy in the Box. When Philadelphia cops found out about this, they immediately headed down to Lawrenceville. "This lead is definitely worth checking," Chief Inspector John Kelly told a reporter for the *Philadelphia Bulletin.* "The family's mode of living is significant. It fits into what we've believed was that of the dead boy's family."[2]

During their interrogation, the mother and father revealed that the missing children were, in fact, dead. They had let the kids die of malnutrition and then disposed of the bodies during their travels. None, however, was the child from Fox Chase.

After four years, the police were precisely nowhere. But it wasn't from a lack of effort. Police were (and still are) obsessed with tracking down the boy's killer. Some cops have pursued the case into their retirement at their own expense — including Sam Weinstein and Elmer Palmer, the first cops at the scene in 1957. Another such man was Remington Bristow, who had worked as an investigator for the medical examiner's of-

Another Bad Lead,
Another Missing Child

The investigators working on the Boy in the Box case were plagued by one bad lead after another. In 1955, they got their hopes up once again when they learned about the abduction of a two-year-old boy in the town of East Meadow on Long Island, New York. On Halloween of that year, Steven Craig Damman's mother had left him outside a grocery store to keep an eye on his seven-month-old sister, who was in her carriage. When Ms. Damman came out of the grocery store, her children were gone. The daughter was quickly found, but Steven was nowhere to be seen.

Damman fit the description of the Boy in the Box, and he was born at about the same time. Philly detectives sent the dead child's footprints to Nassau County police, along with X-rays of the body. They didn't match. It was just one more painful moment for Philly investigators. And, sadly, the Steven Damman case was just one of many missing child cases with no answers. The boy was never seen again.

fice when the Boy in the Box case was opened. In 1960, with nothing of any substance left to work with, Bristow hired a psychic from New Jersey, hoping she could help dig up some new clues.

The psychic said that she needed something made of metal belonging to the victim in order to pinpoint her visions. Since the boy had no belongings, Bristow gave the psychic some staples from the JCPenney box.[3] Upon touching the staples, the woman said she saw a big house with a large group of children playing in the yard; there was also a log cabin on the property.

Bristow searched the Fox Chase area and eventually located a foster home about one-and-a-half miles from the crime scene. It matched the psychic's description perfectly, right down to the log cabin in the backyard. A year later, the family moved and all their belongings went up for sale. Bristow went to the tag sale and saw a bassinet much like the one sold by JCPenney, as well as plaid blankets similar to the one covering the victim.

Furthermore, Bristow learned that the foster father had a stepdaughter who had had a number of children out of wedlock, all of which were dead of natural causes or accidents. There were rumors that the girl was mentally retarded, and Bristow knew that the stigma of having a retarded daughter giving birth out of wedlock was something many people would not live with. He believed that the boy was the child of the stepdaughter and that the family kept him a secret, which would account for the fact that no one in the area recognized the boy.

Bristow was absolutely sure that he had found the killers. The Philadelphia Police Department, though, didn't agree. Bristow spent years trying to convince the department to investigate this angle. It wasn't until 1984 that two Philly detectives found the foster father and interviewed him. Nothing came of it; the detectives cleared him as a suspect.

After thirty-five years spent trying to catch the murderer, Remington Bristow died in 1993. He went to his grave convinced he had solved the Boy in the Box case.

In 1998, the TV show *America's Most Wanted* aired a segment about the case — and the Philadelphia Police Department was again deluged with tips, information, and general suggestions from fans of the program. Capitalizing on the newfound resurgence of public interest in the case, the department officially reopened the case. The decades-old murder mystery was given to Philly native Detective Thomas Augustine, a thirty-five-year veteran of the force. He remembered seeing the posters of the victim when he was growing up and always had a fascination with the case.

Augustine, along with members of the Vidocq Society,[*] a nonprofit organization dedicated to solving cold cases worldwide, pursued Bristow's foster home lead but, as with early investigators, found nothing there.

That same year, the Boy in the Box was exhumed from the potter's field where he had originally been buried, and DNA samples were taken in case investigators succeeded in tracking down a relative. The Vidocq Society footed the bill of giving the child a proper burial. His body is now in Ivy Hill Cemetery under a headstone with a picture of a lamb and the words "America's

[*]The Vidocq Society is named after a pioneer in the solving of cold cases, the Frenchman Eugène François Vidocq (1775–1857), a prolific criminal who in later life opened history's first private investigator's office. It's said he was so effective at solving cases because he had committed so many crimes and understood the criminal mind. The Vidocq Society meets annually in Philadelphia.

Unknown Child."

February 25, 2000, the forty-third anniversary of the discovery of the young victim, marked the most recent turning point in the investigation. An Ohio psychiatrist for an unnamed woman called the Philadelphia police saying his patient had firsthand knowledge of the victim's fate. She had asked the psychiatrist to contact the police on her behalf. The woman is usually referred to by the pseudonym "Mary."

What did the woman know, and how did she know it? Mary said she witnessed the murder and was forced to help dispose of the body. This pricked up the ears of Detective Augustine, but he wanted to hear more. Through her psychiatrist and over a span of two years, Mary related an incredible story. She had grown up near Philadelphia, in Lower Merion Township, the daughter of schoolteachers. One day when she was still a young child, her mother put her in the car and drove to a house she had never seen before. Her mother went to the door and handed over an envelope full of what Mary assumed was cash, and the woman of the home gave her a boy about two or three years of age. Mary said her mother drove her and her new "brother" home.

The little boy, according to Mary, lived in the basement and was never allowed out of the house. For a bathroom he had a drain in the middle of the basement floor, and he was kept undernourished. Some accounts of Mary's story say the boy was sexually assaulted. All of them claim he regularly received beatings, the last of which ended his life. Her mother had been giving the boy a bath one day when he vomited up the baked beans she had fed him a few hours earlier. In a rage, Mary's mother slammed his head into the bathtub, killing him. She put the boy's body in the JCPenney box and took Mary to the Fox Chase area to help dispose of the body. They stopped on Susquehanna Road and began pulling the boy's body out of the trunk when a passerby stopped to ask if they needed help. The girl's mother told her to ignore the man, and they moved to block the license plate. The man drove off and the two women dragged the box and the boy's body through the bramble and into the woods.

It certainly was a strange story, but the investigators — both paid and volunteer — did what they did best: they grabbed hold of the lead and followed it wherever it took them. Eventually, they met the mysterious "Mary." In 2002, Tom Augustine, along with retired fingerprint expert Bill Kelly and ex-investigator for the medical examiner's office Joe McGillen, drove to Ohio to interview the witness. Mary told them in a face-to-face interview about the killing of the boy she said was named Jonathan. Mary came across as a reputable enough witness for the three men to pursue the clues she provided. Her psychiatrist, who had been hearing about this story for the better part of a decade, said he believed she was fully sincere. The investigators located a college roommate of Mary who verified that Mary had told her about the murder.[4] But even though Mary knew a number of small details about the crime, they were details already related in newspaper reports. And since she was not a blood relative, the DNA of the Boy in the Box will remain in a lab somewhere, waiting for a positive match.

For the retired investigators, the case plods along at a snail's pace. Hunting down subjects from leads and tips is difficult enough when the trail is hot; fifty years later, it's next to impossible. Memories fade, witnesses die, trails go cold. Plus, these men are much older than they were when the case was fresh. Traveling and spending hours scrutinizing case files isn't what it used to be. The Vidocq Society has taken on the Boy in the Box case and vows to continue to aggressively pursue all leads, but no news has been made public in years.

Twelve

L&O SVU: ("Burned," Season 8) A woman accuses her husband of rape, but because he doesn't have a record of violence, he is released. The husband later sets his wife on fire.

TRUE STORY: A judge dismissed an order of protection Yvette Cade had taken out on her estranged husband Roger Hargrave. Two weeks later, Hargrave set Cade on fire at her job.

Yvette Cade was terrified. Her estranged husband, Roger Hargrave, had stepped up his campaign of harassment and intimidation against her and her twelve-year old daughter. He was stalking her — vandalizing her property, constantly phoning, and showing up at the house at all hours. In July 2005, Cade had been granted a restraining order against Hargrave; it did little to keep him away. Now the order was about to expire. Cade wanted the restraining order renewed and she wanted a divorce. She had loved Hargrave once but that love had been replaced by fear.

Cade was living in Ohio and attending college when a relative introduced her to Hargrave. At first Cade wasn't interested romantically in Hargrave, who lived in Maryland. Hargrave, however, was smitten with the pretty young woman. The two began corresponding as friends and eventually their relationship deepened. He was kind to her and tried to help her in any way he could. Cade knew Hargrave had a checkered past with convictions for assault and for burglary. He told her that he had put all that behind him; he swore he was a changed man. Cade believed everyone deserved a second chance. Like Cade, Hargrave had a child from a previous marriage. Cade was impressed by the way he doted on his son. She and her young daughter relocated to Maryland.

Cade and Hargrave married. Life was good in the beginning. Hargrave was attentive to his stepdaughter and seemed to be very much in love with his new wife. The family's happiness, though, would be short-lived. Hargrave became increasingly jealous and paranoid, spying on Cade and accusing her of cheating. He drank heavily and talked about sending their children to live with other relatives. The sweet man Yvette had married turned into a bully who began to verbally and physically abuse her. Cade wore long sleeves to hide the bruises on her arms. The abuse escalated and Cade began to fear for her life. Hargrave beat her on her legs with a hammer and threatened her with a knife. He blackened her eyes, busted her lip, left bruises on her arms and legs, and chipped away at her self-respect. "I thought that he loved me and I just thought that these were problems we could work through. I was blind," Cade would say later.[1]

Yvette's family caught on to what was happening and urged her to leave the marriage. She told her husband she wanted a divorce and Cade and her daughter moved out of the neighborhood. Hargrave tracked them down and began to show up at their new address; on several occasions, he tried to break into the house. Cade was frightened for her daughter and herself. Hargrave insisted she attend marriage counseling with him; Cade refused. No amount of counseling could make her fall back in love with a man who had savagely beaten her for most of their marriage. Getting the restraining order in July had been the first step to reclaiming her independence and her self-respect.

Two months after Cade got the restraining order against him, Hargrave petitioned the court and asked that the order be lifted so he and Cade could attend marriage counseling together. He neglected to mention that Cade had refused to go to counseling with him. "I still love my wife very much," he wrote. "I know that she's gotten a final protective order, but I think it should be modified, because I want to be with my family. And I think, if we got counseling, all of our problems could be solved, so I would like a modification hearing." A hearing was set for September 19. Hargrave did not show up in court. Cade did.

Cade told Judge Richard Palumbo that Hargrave had been violating the order of protection and that she feared for her life. She brought along photographs documenting the bruises Hargrave had given her. The judge wasn't interested in the photos; he seemed more interested in getting to the next case on his docket as the following transcript from the proceedings bears out.

Yvette Cade: Your honor, he's violating the

peace order. He's contacting my family. He's still contacting me. He's intimidating my daughter, and he's vandalizing other people's property. I want you to look at these pictures. . . . I want an immediate, absolute divorce.

Judge Palumbo: Well, I'd like to be six foot five but that's not what we do here. You have to go to divorce court for that.

Yvette Cade: OK. Well, I want you to look at these pictures because I don't want him to continue to think —

Judge Palumbo: Uh, this case is dismissed at the request of the petitioner [Hargrave].

Yvette: He was trying to force me into marriage counseling.

Palumbo: It might not be a bad idea, if you want to save the marriage.

Yvette: I don't want to, because —

Palumbo: Well, then you're in the wrong place. Get a lawyer and go to divorce court. This petition is denied, or dismissed. I mean it's silly! You have any children?

Yvette: No.

Palumbo: Just get a lawyer and get a divorce. That's all you got to do. Get a lawyer and go to family court and get a divorce.

Yvette: You told him that last time.

Palumbo: No, no, no, no! Ma'am, you can

get a lawyer and go. He doesn't have to go. You can go!

Yvette: He's like stalking me.

Palumbo: Look, do you work?

Yvette: I do, but I have a lot of bills.

Palumbo: Everybody's got bills! Go see a lawyer — a divorce lawyer.

Yvette: A lawyer costs a lot of money.

Palumbo: Madam, if you want a divorce . . .

Yvette: I do.

Palumbo: Go get a lawyer. I can't be your lawyer. I've got to be independent, you know like an umpire.

Although Hargrave had repeatedly violated the order of protection, Judge Palumbo did not issue an arrest warrant or ask police to look into the matter. Instead, he dismissed the order of protection and the case, writing "Dism. Prot. Order" on the paperwork. (Later, Palumbo would claim the dismissal was a clerical error.) Cade left the courtroom dejected and humiliated — and without a valid order of protection against the man who was threatening to harm her. She didn't know where to turn.

On October 10, Hargrave called Cade at 2:30 a.m. and threatened to burn her "like Crisco." She hung up. He called back fourteen times; Cade let the answering machine pick up. She got very little sleep that night. In the morning, she left for her job at the T-Mobile store in Clinton, Maryland. At 9:30 a.m. Hargrave marched into the store. Cade was surprised and frightened to see him. He approached her and told her he loved her. When she didn't reply, he poured gasoline over her head from a plastic soda bottle. Cade was confused, unsure of what Hargrave had poured on her but she was terrified by the look in his eyes. She ran toward the back door, Hargrave at her heels.

Outside, Hargrave grabbed Cade and stomped down hard on her foot, crushing her bones. She fell to the ground. By now, Cade realized she had been doused with gasoline. Hargrave had a book of matches in his hand. Cade pulled away from him and tried to run. "I love you. I love you," he said as he lit a match and tossed it onto her back, setting her on fire. Cade screamed as she felt her face catch fire. She ran back inside the T-Mobile store, her face and torso engulfed in flames. Hargrave followed her, retrieved his car keys from her desk and fled.

Cade ran to a sink in the backroom and hosed herself down, desperately trying to put out the fire. She was in agony; her face felt like it was melting. A coworker called 911 and two customers raced to help Cade, throwing a blanket over her to extinguish the flames. Another customer wrote down Hargrave's license plate number. Cade was airlifted to the hospital. On the way, emergency workers heard Cade mumble over and over through her burned lips, "He cannot take my joy. He cannot take my joy."

Hargrave was apprehended and charged with attempted murder. The brutal attack had been witnessed by a half-dozen people — and captured by the store's security camera.

Against all odds, Yvette Cade survived. She sustained third-degree burns over 60 percent of her body and was hospitalized for three months. Doctors had expected her to remain in the hospital for at least seven months but Cade made a miraculous recovery. Although she was permanently disfigured and in constant pain, she wasn't bitter; she remained positive and upbeat throughout her ordeal. Her courage and her attitude helped speed her recovery.

Cade underwent eighteen grueling surgeries and extensive grafts to repair her skin. She did not see her own face for sixty days after the attack. When she finally did look in the mirror, she discovered that her once smooth cocoa-colored skin was gone, replaced by bumpy patches and steaks of white. Her ears had melted in the attack; her right earlobe was gone. Her hair had been burned off. Cade's arms and chest were covered with burn marks. Her range of motion in her arms was limited.

While Roger Hargrave awaited his trial for the attempted murder of Yvette Cade, Judge Richard Palumbo reinstated Cade's order of protection. It was far too little, far too late. Fellow judges disputed that a clerical error had been made and pointed out that in Maryland, judges — not clerks — are responsible for filling out docket paperwork. Palumbo came under intense public scrutiny for his mishandling of the case.

"The problem with Judge Palumbo's conduct, in short, was not that someone checked the wrong box on a court form," stated an editorial in the *Washington Post*. "It was that the judge, faced with a woman who claimed — rightly, as it turned out — to be highly vulnerable to physical assault, could not take the time to figure out what was going on in the case. He treated her like a scammer trying to game the system for advantage in a divorce proceeding. Ms. Cade is grievously wounded; that might have happened even had the order, now belatedly restored, been in place. But at least a court wouldn't have made her more vulnerable."[2]

"He treated me less than human, like an annoyance. He wanted to get on to the next docket and was not interested in helping me. He was annoyed that I was back in front of him again," Cade said.[3] As it turns out, Yvette Cade wasn't the only victim of domestic abuse who had been mistreated by Palumbo.

A former county prosecutor and state delegate for Prince George, Maryland, Palumbo was appointed to the bench in 2001. He quickly earned a reputation for making disparaging comments against battered women. He compared three women who repeatedly appeared in his court seeking protective orders against their partners to "buses that come along every ten minutes." He also chastised a strangulation victim — whose voice box was broken by her abuser — for not speaking loudly enough in court. "I can't read your lips," he complained. "Speak up. Speak up."

Several weeks after Yvette Cade was set on fire, Palumbo was suspended from the bench and restricted to administrative duty. Plaintiffs who had appeared before him in court filed a complaint charging that the judge "demonstrated his insensitivity to the needs of the alleged victims and their families through his frequent inappropriate comments during the course of hearings on these cases."[4] The State of Maryland also brought misconduct charges against him alleging that he misused his power as a judge to avoid prosecution for a traffic accident he was involved in (he reportedly left the scene after slamming his Mercedes into the back of a shuttle bus).

In April 2006, Roger Hargrave was tried for first-degree attempted murder, and first- and second-degree assault. He pleaded not guilty, claiming that he intended only to harm Cade, not kill her. His attorney attempted to persuade the jury to convict Hargrave on the lesser charge of assault. Prince George County State's Attorney Glenn F. Ivey personally handled the prosecution. His first — and most powerful — witness was Yvette Cade, who recounted the day her husband set her on fire. She was composed and calm; speaking in an unbroken voice she told the court that hours before he attacked her, Hargrave had called and said "he wanted to fry me like Crisco grease." She glanced several times at Hargrave; he did not meet her gaze. At Ivey's request, Cade showed the jury her injuries, coming down from the witness stand to let them get a closer look.

The prosecutor next played the security tape of the attack. Frame by frame, the court watched the crime unfold. Hargrave, wearing a striped rugby shirt and baseball cap, was seen entering the T-Mobile store. Cade, dressed in a black pants suit, was at the printer. She returned to her workstation and handed the copy she just made to a customer. Hargrave came around the counter and splashed gasoline on Cade from a green plastic Sprite bottle. Cade jumped up and tried to escape Hargrave; he took off after her. The two of them were offscreen for a few seconds. Then Yvette, her face and torso ablaze, ran back into the frame. It was a horrifying sight that left some members of the jury and several courtroom spectators in tears. Hargrave watched impassively.

The jury deliberated for just under eight hours before finding Roger Hargrave guilty on all counts. Cade declined to give a victim's impact statement and asked the court to join her in a prayer. Before sentencing, Hargrave, however, asked to address the court. He said that he had recently become a Christian and hoped one day to counsel victims of abuse. "I still can't figure out what I thought I was doing. I'm sorry for the pain I've caused. I can only explain my actions as Dr. Jekyll and Mr. Hyde." Hargrave did not look at Cade.

The judge was disgusted. "You never once said 'I am sorry for what I did to my wife.' You said you were sorry for what happened to her. You're avoiding responsibility for what you did," he said before sentencing Hargrave to life in prison.

"With this sentence from the judge," Cade told reporters, "I finally feel safe from him."

Citing health reasons, Judge Richard Palumbo retired from the bench in July 2006. His sudden retirement saved him from facing a disciplinary hearing resulting from the traffic accident and the Cade case. Since Palumbo was no longer a sitting judge, the State dismissed the misconduct charges. "I think it sends a terrible message to domestic violence victims in general and the public at large," said Carol Alexander, executive director of the Maryland women's shelter House of Ruth. "For him to be able to resign and just wash his hands of this matter is just absurd."[5]

Yvette Cade divorced Roger Hargrave. She

The ID

In a study conducted by the American Psychological Association (APA), a subcommittee reviewed the first forty convictions to have been overturned using DNA evidence. It found that in thirty-six cases, a witness's false identification was the leading cause for the wrongful conviction.

The report cites a number of factors involved in misidentifying a suspect, including the "relative judgment process": a witness's tendency to "choose from a lineup the person who looks most like the culprit relative to the other members of the lineup." In other words, a lineup often provides a "close-enough" ID, not an absolute ID.

The APA's report, and others on the subject, provide recommendations for creating the most fair and accurate witness identification processes possible. Yet today there are no federal rules regulating procedure for conducting lineups.

("Eyewitness Identification Procedures: Recommendations for Lineups and Photospreads," Gary L. Wells, et al., 1998) continues to deal with the trauma inflicted on her that fateful October day. She has to wear a plastic mask for twenty-three hours a day to prevent scar tissue from developing on her face, and a protective bodysuit to keep her skin flat. She takes a dozen pills a day to ward off infections and make the pain more manageable. After the trial, she appeared on Oprah Winfrey's show without a mask or makeup. She showed Winfrey the scars on her arms and told her that she has come to terms with her appearance. "Beauty comes from within," she said. "I don't question God but maybe this is my calling. I was comfortable with it, and I have to continue my life." As for the pain, Cade admitted that "every day is a struggle."[6]

Today, Yvette Cade counsels victims of domestic violence. "Often I'm told my story has helped someone make changes in their own life," Cade says. "If my experience can help other people, then my tragedy is not in vain."[7]

THIRTEEN

L&O SVU: ("Scavenger," Season 6) A serial killer taunts investigators into finding him.

TRUE CRIME: Over a span of three decades, BTK killer Dennis Rader murdered ten people in Wichita, Kansas. He often communicated with the police about the murders, which led to his capture.

"I am BTK." Thirty-two hours of interrogation, and he finally said it. The man sitting across the table from detectives had begun killing people over thirty years ago, when some of the most hardened veteran cops on the Wichita PD were just pimple-faced high school kids wondering what they were going to do with their lives. Even though he had killed one of his own neighbors, the police never came close — they never knocked on his door, put him on surveillance, or spoke to other neighbors about him. Hell, they had never even heard his name until recently.

Depraved and cruel as this man was, the detectives probably expected to find a sign that they were in the room with a brilliant killer. After all, the guy taunted police for three decades, writing letters and poems describing each murder down to the last detail. He must have *something* going on in his head, some spark of intelligence. But no. There was no gleam in this man's eye. He wasn't even a thug. He was just a middle class man from Wichita who had watched enough cop shows on TV to know how to foil a murder investigation. He couldn't spell and even plagiarized some of the poems he sent to the police.[*] People who knew him socially described him as a nice guy, a family man — nothing more, nothing less; those who worked with him considered him an officious prick, a jackass — nothing more, nothing less. He wasn't smart, he wasn't even slightly interesting. Dennis Rader was so consumed with his desire to

[*]In his confession, Rader claimed that his wife poked fun at him one day by telling him his spelling was as bad as BTK's, which had become highly publicized.

236

bind, torture, and kill people that he could never passionately pursue any other interest. Killing people was simply his only passion.

It was the middle of winter in 1974 when Rader decided for the first time to act out the sexual depravity he had been bottling up since childhood.[†] For a couple of weeks, he had been casing out the home of Joseph and Julie Otero, who had moved to Wichita only two months previous. Joe was a retired air force mechanic who had recently found work maintaining planes at a local airport. Rader noticed that the husband drove one of the cars to work, and the wife took the station wagon on errands. On January 15, he drove by in the morning and saw just the station wagon in the driveway. He had with him what he called his "hit kit" — knives,

[†]Beginning at an early age, Dennis Rader had combined torture, sex, and death in his mind. Before (and during) his three-decade-long murderous rampage, he would go downstairs to his parents' basement, set up a camera, tie his legs up, cover his head with a hood, and stage his own hanging. And at least once, he dug his own grave, put a Halloween mask on, climbed into the hole, and took his own picture.

guns, electrical tape, plastic bags, and lengths of Venetian blind cords — and decided that this was the day.

Rader went around to the back of the house, cut the phone line, and entered the kitchen. He was surprised to see almost the entire family, including the husband. The killer told them he didn't want to hurt anyone, but he was a desperate man, a fugitive on the lam who needed money, food, and a car. He herded everyone upstairs — Joseph, Julie, nine-year-old Joseph, Jr., and eleven-year old Josie . . .

When the older Otero kids, Carmen, Danny, and Charlie — thirteen, fourteen, and fifteen years old, respectively — arrived home from school that afternoon, they found their parents in the bedroom, not moving. Their mother was on the bed with her ankles tied together. Her hands were tied, too, and there were bruises on her neck. Their father was on the floor at the end of the bed. He, too, had his hands tied. His head was covered in a plastic bag tied tightly with a brown belt and covered by a blue shirt. Frantic and confused, the kids began untying their parents' hands and trying to resuscitate them using CPR. One of them called the police. Where were Joe, Jr., and Josephine? And how were they going to

238

Dennis Rader, the BTK Killer, started killing in 1974 and wasn't caught until 2005. He bound, tortured, and murdered ten people, including two children.

tell them their parents were dead?

When police entered the Otero home, they immediately found Joe and Julie in the bedroom. They began searching the other bedrooms and located little Joe, tied up on the floor next to his bunk bed. A plastic bag covered his head. His hands were tied behind his back. Police noticed a chair in the middle of the room, facing Joey's body.

It was strangely out of place. Did the killer pull up a chair to watch the little boy suffocate?

If investigators had the slightest doubt that the murderer — or murderers — enjoyed what he was doing, those doubts were shattered the moment they ventured into the dark basement with their flashlights. Eleven-year-old Josie Otero was hanging by her neck from a pipe running across the ceiling, partially nude. She had been gagged, and every joint on her body was bound with cord. Her feet were just millimeters off the floor. Semen stains dotted the floor in front of her.

The Wichita PD was stunned. The killer or killers had left a couple of clues, including a knife on the ground by the back door, but investigators were stymied. Initially, they assumed it was a hit related to drugs. Whoever committed the crime had planned it and carried it out in an almost "professional" way. When detectives learned that Joseph Otero was an air force mechanic previously stationed in Central America, where he serviced the personal airplane of Omar Torrijos, Panama's dictator, the speculation was reinforced. A witness who saw someone driving the Otero's car described the perpetrator as foreign looking.

This sealed it for many cops on the case. It was drugs.

As they were pursuing this angle and looking into every fact they could find about Joe Otero's life, they found they had another, similar murder on their hands. On April 4, 1974, police received a bizarre call from a Wichita resident reporting that a young man, his head and shoulders covered in blood, was wandering around the neighborhood calling for help: "He's in there now doing a number on my sister. Please help me," he had said to the caller.

Police called to the scene found twenty-one-year-old Kathryn Bright lying in the hallway. She was clutching the telephone receiver, but she wasn't moving. She could speak, but just barely. "I can't breathe, help me," she said to the officer, barely able to push the words out. She had been strangled. Her face was turning blue. A thin cord had been tied tightly around her neck, and her ankles were tied together with a woman's stocking. She had been stabbed several times. Whether or not Kathryn Bright had been able to dial her phone for help is unknown. It's a moot point, anyway: the phone cord had been ripped from the wall.

Another officer found a nightgown saturated in blood in another bedroom, with two teeth on it. Tied in a knot to the bed were two pieces of clothing, and stockings were tied to a chair in the room; the chair was covered with blood. This was the room where Kathryn's nineteen-year-old brother Kevin had been. Kevin had stayed at his sister's house overnight. When they were confronted by the killer, Kevin fought back and received two gunshots in the face and head. He survived the horrific encounter, but his sister was pronounced dead at the hospital.

That night, as Dennis Rader made small talk with his wife at the dinner table, he was thinking about the attack on Kathryn Bright, and how that guy with her might have survived and was probably telling the cops all about their fight. If he hadn't been there, Rader could have enjoyed the whole thing much more. He would have to be extra careful next time.

But Rader had nothing to worry about. Eventually, Kevin Bright would describe his attacker as possibly Mexican, or maybe "Oriental."[1] Rader was lucky enough to have one of those faces that's hard to pinpoint. If he were an actor, he could play a Caucasian in one movie, a Hispanic in another, and an Arab in another. But the fact is, his multidimensional face wasn't his luckiest break. That would turn out to be the methods the Wichita PD used to investigate his murders. From the very beginning, law enforcement refused to share details of the crimes with the public. When it comes to serial murders, public vigilance is often the best tool the police have. When there are no leads to speak of, which is usually the case in these types of crimes, it's often some small detail noticed by someone close to the killer and reported to the police that results in an arrest: an ex-girlfriend who notices a familiar detail in the sexual deviance of the crime; a parent who knows her son owns a certain type of knife; a teacher who connects a student's writing quirk with something she saw on the news. Dennis Rader had left all sorts of clues attesting to what made him tick. But the police wanted to handle the investigation by themselves; they understandably wanted to keep certain details of the crime private in case they got someone to confess. It's a standard police tactic to ensure that only the real killer knows certain details. There are just too many nuts out there who want to take credit for crimes they didn't commit. However, there's always a middle ground. If investigators are careful, they can release certain details to prompt leads and tips while keeping others close to the vest in case they find someone who confesses to the crimes.[*]

Don Granger, a reporter for the *Wichita Eagle and Beacon* newspaper, was sitting at his desk on October 22, 1974, when he got a phone call. The BTK killer was on the other end, telling Granger that he would find an important message in the pages of a certain engineering textbook on the shelves of the Wichita Public Library. The reporter called the police, who quickly retrieved the note. The writer, who called himself "Rex," described every last detail of the Otero murders and crime scene. He advised the police that two men they had in custody for the killings were innocent: "I did it all by myself with no one's help," he proudly wrote.

This was the first of many communiqués Rader would initiate with the police. They came in the form of poems, stories, codes, and angry rants and, as it turned out, were

[*]In his in-depth book *The BTK Murders,* Carlton Smith makes a convincing case that the Wichita PD didn't release nearly enough details about the case, which seriously hampered its own investigation.

meant to be chapters in a book he was writing. Fraught with spelling mistakes, they seemed to be the work of a crazy child. One of the most chilling aspects of Rader's letters was how matter-of-fact he was. For instance, after describing how he killed Josie Otero by "hanging by the neck" and Joseph, Jr., with the "old bag trick," he added, "Otero's watch missing. I needed one so I took it. Runs good."[2]

"Runs good." Was Dennis Rader taunting police, or did he think he had some sort of relationship with them, that they might care that he got a decent watch? Subsequent events would show that it was probably a bit of both. Rader, it would turn out, was taking criminal justice classes at a local college at the same time he had begun his serial murder spree. He was drawn to positions of authority, and liked to believe the police were his peers. The most authoritative position Rader would ever land, though, was local dog catcher.

On March 17, 1977, Shirley Vian, a twenty-six-year-old mother of three, was feeling ill, and sent her six-year-old son Steve to get some soup from the market. As Steve was walking down the street, a man dressed in a tweed jacket approached him holding a photo of a woman and a young boy.* Pretending to be a detective, he asked the boy if he had ever seen these people. Steve said no, and the man went on his way. Steve went home to help take care of his mother. A few minutes later, there was a knock at the door. When Steve opened it, the "detective" was standing there with a gun. He forced his way into the house. Shirley came downstairs, and Rader made it clear that he wanted to rape her. Her first instinct was to get him away from the kids, so she let him lock them in a bathroom by pushing a bed against the door. She then begged him not to do it, but he simply responded, "Have to."[3]

Steve and his siblings, four-year-old Stephanie and eight-year-old Bud, heard their mother screaming. They tried to push the door open but couldn't. Steve began banging on the door shouting for the man to leave his mother alone. Stephanie was sitting on the floor crying. Rader opened the bathroom door a crack and threw some toys in for the kids.

As Rader continued strangling Shirley Vian, Bud broke the bathroom window and screamed for help. Rader tied a plastic bag

*The people in the picture were Rader's wife and son.

around Shirley Vian's head and masturbated. He later expressed his desire to hang Stephanie like he had done to Josie Otero, but because of all the racket, he knew he had to get out of there. By the time the kids got help, Rader was gone.

The scene had many of the earmarks of Rader's previous murders. Vian was found face down on the bed. Her arms and ankles had been bound with black tape, and a cord was wrapped around her neck five times. She had died of strangulation.

And still, the Wichita PD made no official announcement connecting this case to the others.

Nine months later, in early December 1977, the police received an anonymous call: "Yes, you will find a homicide at 843 South Pershing, Nancy Fox." The cops hoped it was a prank phone call, but when they arrived at Fox's home, they found the phone line outside had been cut. When they went inside, they saw the twenty-five-year-old facedown on the bed, with her hands and feet tied and a length of pantyhose tied around her neck. Again, the killer had masturbated on the floor.

Fox, a part-time jewelry store employee, had come home that night at about 9:30

p.m. She lived in one side of a duplex, which was located only about two miles from both the Otero and Vian homes. It had been an ordinary day for her. Little did she know when she entered her home that Dennis Rader was hiding in her bedroom closet. He had been there for about an hour. In fact, he had been stalking Nancy for weeks. Within an hour of arriving home, Nancy Fox was dead.

Two months later, the Wichita TV station KAKE received a document from an anonymous source, Rader's second communication with the media and the police. In the first line, he grumbles that he isn't getting the attention he deserves: "How many people do I have to Kill before a I get a name in the paper or some national attention." Alluding to the Shirley Vian murder, he wrote "SHIRLEYLOCKS SHIRLEYLOCKS WILT THOU BE MINE,"[*] followed by a seven-line poem about the murder. At the end of the letter, he writes, "7 down and many more to go," then asks that he be referred to as "BTK," an acronym for bind, torture, kill.

[*]The Shirleylocks poem was an altered version of the children's rhyme "Curly Locks."

■ ■ ■ ■

For over a year, Rader stayed out of people's homes. He was living his false "normal" life: husband, father, breadwinner, criminal justice student. On April 28, 1979, the urge struck him to murder once more. He had been keeping his eye on a sixty-three-year old woman by the name of Anna Williams. He broke into her house when she wasn't home and crawled into her closet. Anna was out later than Rader expected of a woman her age, and he eventually got tired of waiting and left. When Williams came home, she saw that her place had been ransacked. She was so frightened by what she thought was a basic burglary, she started staying at a relative's house. When her son-in-law retrieved her mail about two months later, he found a package containing a scarf and a piece of jewelry belonging to Williams, along with a drawing of a bound-up woman, and a poem titled "Oh, Anna, Why Didn't You Appear?"

On the bottom corner of the note, Rader drew his "BTK" symbol — the "B" made to look like a woman's breasts, with the "T" and "K" combined in one character and pushed up against it, forming a single symbol. He was marketing himself. In the rest of his communications, he would use this symbol and variations on it; it became his "logo." In cooperation with the police, the media kept the symbol secret, so police could use it to verify further communications from the killer.

Years went by. Wichita had its normal number of murders, but no one was coming home to find Dennis Rader emerging from their closet with a pistol in hand and promises not to harm anyone. Then, on April 27, 1985, six years almost to the day of his foray into Anna Williams's closet, Rader killed again — a widow named Marine Hedge who lived down the street from him. The small, fifty-three-year-old woman would return Rader's wave when they passed each other on the street. It was very easy for him to figure out when she was home alone. On the other hand, killing a neighbor was a dangerous prospect; the risk of getting caught increased exponentially.

At this point, Rader's son was a Boy Scout and Rader was a scoutmaster. They had a camping trip coming up, which he believed he could use to his advantage. The campground was pretty far away from Marina Hedge's home, but he figured it was close

Rader's BTK "logo." Police and the press kept its existence secret for years in order to ensure that messages from the killer were bona fide.

enough to be his alibi. On April 27, as the boys and other fathers were roasting marshmallows in the evening, Rader said he had a headache and retired to his tent. He was able to sneak out and drive off in his car without anyone noticing. When Rader got to Hedge's home, her car was in the driveway so he figured she was home. He cut the phone line and quietly broke into the house.

Marine was actually out with a friend and didn't come home until the early hours of morning. Rader waited patiently and when she got home, he strangled her. He found her car keys, carried her body outside, and drove to his church, which he had keys for. He brought Marine's body to the basement and spent about an hour tying his victim up and taking pictures of her. Then he dumped Marine in a culvert. When Rader got back to the campground, everyone was still asleep. No one knew anything.

The murder of Marine Hedge seems to have energized Rader. After his long hiatus, he was back to his old ways. On September 16, 1986, he arrived on the doorstep of Vicki Wegerle, a twenty-eight-year-old mother of two who was waiting for her husband, Gordon, to come home from work for lunch. Rader said he was from the telephone company and that he had to check her lines. Vicki let him in. After spending a few moments pretending to inspect her phone jack, he rushed Vicki upstairs. As Vicki's two-year-old boy sat in the living room downstairs, Rader tied Vicki's hands and feet, and strangled her with a nylon stocking.

He snatched the keys to the Wegerle's '78 Monte Carlo and drove off. As Gordon Wegerle approached his home for lunch, he passed Rader on his own street, noticing that the car was the exact same model and color as Vicki's, but he didn't think much of it. When he arrived home, he thought it odd that their son was by himself in the living room. He took a glance into the bedroom, but there was no sign of his wife. He probably wasn't happy that she had left their young son all alone, but Vicki was a responsible mother and there must have been a good reason. Anyway, he was home now, and she would surely be arriving soon. Gordon passed the time playing with his son. Before he knew it, forty-five minutes had elapsed. Gordon was getting worried. He went upstairs again, and this time took a better look. He found Vicki on the floor between the bed and the wall — a spot he couldn't see when he initially checked from the doorway.

Following the rule of investigation that says you begin with those closest to the victim and work outward, police initially considered Gordon Wegerle a good suspect in his wife's murder. When they outright accused Wegerle of killing his wife, he stormed out of the interrogation room. They didn't have enough evidence to arrest him, but they knew he did it. Even though the lab had skin samples from under Vicki's fingernails, they were never submitted for DNA testing. If they were, they might have been matched to DNA from Rader's other crimes.[4]

Dennis Rader spent the next four years attending to what he later referred to as his "social obligations" — earning money, going to church, raising his children. His wife had no clue that her husband was keeping records of his crimes and depravity hidden in secret spots around his house, as well as in his parents' basement and his file cabinet at work. Included in his stash were self-bondage photos, copies of every letter he sent to the media and police; sketches of the BTK logo in its various stages; a table of contents for his planned book, *The BTK Story;* newspaper articles; his own crime scene photos; and crude drawings of women on fantasy torture devices.

And if she ever saw her husband repeatedly squeezing a rubber ball, she might have thought he was trying to relieve tension. In reality, he was exercising to build up the muscles in his hand for a murder he had planned.

In the middle of the night, on January 19, 1991, Rader threw a cinder block through the sliding glass doors of Dolores Davis, a sixty-two-year-old woman who, Rader knew, lived alone. When Dolores ran downstairs in fear and confusion, the killer used the same story he told the Oteros — he was on the run and wanted her car, and he needed to tie her up to ensure she didn't call the police, but he would not harm her. Davis submitted, and he bound her hands and feet and then strangled her. He drove her body out of the neighborhood and dumped it under an overpass. In a disturbing flourish, Rader put a cheap plastic mask of a woman on her face. Two days later, he came back and took Davis's picture.

About two weeks after that, Dolores Davis's body was discovered by a fifteen-year-old-boy walking his dog. When he realized what he had found, he started running home. He was so distraught that he initially ran in the wrong direction.

Dolores Davis was Rader's tenth and final victim. By this point, police were slowly connecting some of Rader's murders, largely because he was sending them letters describing details. They had also connected DNA evidence from a few of the crimes. Plus, over the years, they had taken extra steps to share more details with the public, and the media had begun reporting on his letters and other communications. But during the nineties, Rader had slowly tapered off communicating with the police, and the serial killings began fading from the news. The identity of BTK was as much a mystery to Wichita law enforcement as ever, and it would remain so for another thirteen years.

In 2004, a man named Bob Beattie, a law professor with a background in psychology, decided he would attempt to lure BTK out of his lair. He had followed the BTK murders since the midseventies, and, based on the fact that in his letters BTK seemed obsessed with notoriety, as well as the fact that the killer was reportedly writing a book about his story, Beattie came up with a plan: he would begin writing his own book about the killings — the first of its kind. If his project drew enough publicity, he figured, BTK would be upset that someone else was enjoying the spotlight. The killer (if he was still in the area, or even still alive) would start up his correspondence again in order to co-opt media attention. It was a long shot, but over the years Beattie had taken such an interest in the case that he wanted to write a book about it anyway.

Beattie did end up landing a publishing deal and getting some press — and just like *that,* Rader began sending letters to the police. Beattie had read him like a book.[*]

By now, the police had become a little more adept at dealing with serial killers. They worked closely with the media outlets to string him along — releasing enough details of his communiqués to possibly spark a good tip, and holding back enough to easily rule out false confessions. This time around, though, investigators didn't need the public's help. Rader trapped himself. He had begun to think he had some sort of rapport with the police, that the hunted/hunter relationship of respect actually applied in his case. Worried that paper, handwriting, and the photocopy machine he occasionally used could be traced, Rader had become wary of writing letters. He started using dead drops, but they proved unreliable.

"Can I communicate with a Floppy [disk] and not be traced to a computer?" he wrote to the Wichita Police Department. "Be honest."[5]

The cops reading the letter smiled. They sent their message: *Sure, Rex, no problem.*

On February 3, 2005, KSAS-TV in Wichita received a package containing three

[*]Again, Smith covers this aspect of the case in great detail.

notes from the killer and a purple floppy disk labeled "Test Floppy for WPD." The station handed it over to the police, who eagerly uploaded the disk's contents. The words appeared on the screen: "This is a test. See 3×5 Card for details on Communication with me in the newspaper." A cursory search through the disk's Properties section contained the name "Dennis" and the owner of the computer: Christ Lutheran Church in Park City. Detectives performed an Internet search for the church. With one mouse click they saw the name of the congregational president: Dennis Rader.[6] They picked him up and he confessed to everything.

Kansas reinstated the death penalty in 1994, but since Rader committed his crimes previous to that, he received ten consecutive life sentences. He will be eligible for parole in 175 years.

At the sentencing hearing, Rader had to face his victims' families on an equal playing field. He listened to statements from Charlie and Carmen Otero; Kevin Bright; Steve Relford, Shirley Vian's son; Beverly Plapp, the sister of Nancy Fox; Stephanie Wegerle; and finally, Dolores Davis's son Jeff.

"From this point on, we declare our independence from the tyranny of your actions," Jeff Davis began. "While you begin your slow and painful descent into hell, we will choose to rise above our pain. While you sink into an emotional abyss of hopelessness and despair, we will channel our grief into positive endeavors, those life activities which would please the ones we've lost. While you agonize over the reality that your last victim was ironically your own family, we will embrace the new family we now have, with whom we will always share a common bond forged from the pain and adversity of loss. While your body wastes away in prison, we will renew ourselves by incorporating into our lives those characteristics modeled by our loved ones: humility, compassion, honor, integrity, kindness, selflessness, and love — traits which your twisted, cancerous mind cannot comprehend, I realize. While your wretched soul awaits pronouncements of the one true justice, your damnation to hell for eternity, we will thank God for every day he gives us, realizing as only we can just how precious life is."

He concluded: "Just as your days are now over, ours are just beginning. In the final analysis you have to live with the cold reality that while all of us here will overcome your depravity, you have now lost everything and you will forever remain nothing. May that thought torment you for the rest of your tortured existence."[7]

And, in a show of solidarity, each one of them walked out as Dennis Rader stood up to make his final statement.

260

Fourteen

L&O SVU: ("Game," Season 6) Teenagers take their obsession with video games to the point of murder.

TRUE STORY: Alabama teen Devin Moore killed two police officers and a dispatcher after being arrested for stealing a car. Moore claimed his addiction to the video game Grand Theft Auto led him to commit the crimes.

The man's goal was simple: steal as many cars as he could in as little time as possible. And kill anyone who got in his way. He turned left and spotted the vehicle he wanted — a silver Ferrari. Carjacking took seconds. He backed the car up and pulled out into the street. There were few people around, which made his job easier. The man drove through the city to a garage he used to store his hot cars. There was already another car in the bay — he was becoming a skilled car thief. He parked his newest acquisition and headed back onto the street. It was late but for him, the night was young. He figured he could jack a few more cars before the morning.

He was hyped up, ready for action. A guy on the street gave him the once over, which annoyed him. The man used his fists and a baseball bat to teach the guy a lesson. He left him bloodied and beaten on the sidewalk. Steps away he eyed his next challenge, a tricked-out Porsche 911. He was hardly inside the car when he saw them — two cops in blue uniforms. They ordered him to get out of the car and put his hands on his head. He pulled a gun instead and fired fours shots at the officers. He was a good marksman; he hit both of his targets. One officer was fatally wounded; the other managed to return fire as the man made off in the stolen car.

He had a hunch he was going to break his own record that night — making him the Grand Theft Auto champ in his neighborhood. His hands were starting to cramp up but he still had at least ten good minutes left before he had to turn the game off and go to bed.

■ ■ ■ ■

Released in 2002, Grand Theft Auto: Vice City transports players back to Miami circa 1980. The aim of the video game is to successfully complete criminal missions such as carjacking, drug trafficking, and felony murder. For fun, players can mug innocent citizens they encounter or pummel pedestrians with their fists. They can also solicit sex from prostitutes, streetwalkers whom the players can then beat to death if they so choose. Points are earned for successfully committed crimes. Killing a police officer earns players one thousand points. In one version of the game, a hidden Easter Egg (unpublicized game content players must find) offers players a huge bonus for running down a group of monks.

The game ignited a storm of controversy and game makers have been hauled to court for several civil suits. Critics contend that the game desensitizes children to violence and encourages antisocial behavior. Jack Thompson, a colorful Florida-based attorney and nemesis of the gaming industry, dubbed Grand Theft Auto a "murder simulator."

"Grand Theft Auto is a world governed

by the laws of depravity," *60 Minutes* correspondent Ed Bradley told viewers during a segment on the game. "See a car you like? Steal it. Someone you don't like? Stomp her. A cop in your way? Blow him away. There are cops at every turn, and endless opportunities to take them down. It is 360 degrees of murder and mayhem: slickly produced, technologically brilliant, and exceedingly violent."[1]

Repeated exposure to video game violence affects minors more than adults, insists child psychologist David Walsh, who is an expert on the subject. He told *60 Minutes* that, "[T]he teenage brain is different from the adult brain. The impulse control center of the brain, the part of the brain that enables us to think ahead and consider consequences, manage urges — that's the part of the brain right behind our forehead called the prefrontal cortex. That's under construction during the teenage years. In fact, the wiring of that is not complete until the early 20s."[2]

What's more, "when a young man with a developing brain, already angry, spends hours and hours and hours rehearsing violent acts, and then he's put into this situation of emotional stress, there's a likelihood that he will literally go to that familiar pattern that's been wired repeatedly, perhaps thousands and thousands of times."[3]

Grand Theft Auto has been blamed for crimes committed by young people around the country, from a drive-by shooting in Tennessee, to multiple homicides carried out by a gang in California. A teenager in Alabama claimed the game conditioned him to kill when he was tried for the murder of three police officers. There would be no bonus points for that young man, just hard time in a penitentiary.

Devin Moore had been playing Grand Theft Auto: Vice City obsessively during the spring of 2003. The eighteen-year-old lived with his family in Fayette, Alabama, a rural town with a population of 4,900. A handsome but troubled young man, Moore had recently graduated from high school. According to court testimony, Moore's father often beat and berated young Devin, and the child's mother was frequently drunk or high on drugs. Moore had lived in twenty different homes in his lifetime. For the eighteen-year-old, Grand Theft Auto was a means of escape. While playing the game, he could forget about the beatings and the way his mother looked when she passed out on the floor after a three-day drinking binge.

Moore had never been in trouble with the law; playing a thief in the video game gave him a chance to pretend to be someone else. In a few weeks, he would leave to serve in the U.S. Air Force; Moore was excited about starting a new life. But his life was about to change in a way he'd never anticipated.

In the early morning of June 6, 2003, Moore was arrested after police officer Arnold Strickland found him sleeping in a stolen car. Strickland took Moore to the Fayette Police Station to book him on suspicion of auto theft. Moore was docile and cooperated with the officer on the way to the station. But then, inside the station, the teenager snapped. He charged at Strickland and managed to get control of his .40 caliber automatic Glock. Moore shot Strickland twice in the head. Officer James Crump heard the shots from another part of the station and came running in. Before Crump could draw, Moore shot him three times, once in the head. On his way out of the station, Moore shot police dispatcher Ace Mealer five times, hitting him once in the head. All three men died at the scene. Moore ducked into the fire station next door and told them there had been a shooting. Then he fled the scene in a stolen patrol cruiser. The killings took less than a minute. His crime spree was eerily similar to scenarios found in Grand Theft Auto.

Moore was apprehended four hours later in Mississippi. He told the arresting officers, "Life is a video game. You've got to die sometime."

In his confession, Moore said he shot the three men because he didn't want to go to jail. He was indicted for the capital murders of Arnold Strickland, 55; James Crump, 40; and Leslie "Ace" Mealer, 38. He pleaded not guilty by reason of mental defect. Defense attorney Jim Standridge contended that Moore's crimes were caused by post-traumatic stress disorder (PTSD) — and Grand Theft Auto, which the teenager played excessively in the weeks before the murders. It was an interesting defense strategy; however, the judge barred the jury from hearing testimony connecting Moore's crime spree to the video game.

At trial, the defense introduced evidence that Moore had suffered mental and physical abuse as a child, leaving him psychologically damaged. At the time of the murders, Standridge said, Moore was suffering from PTSD brought on by the abuse. Several witnesses were called to the stand to describe the defendant's deeply dysfunctional home life for the jury. Moore's sister testified that her father, Kenneth Moore, regularly beat her and Devin and the rest of the family. She recalled the time he whipped her in front of the family as punishment for breaking her curfew when she was a teenager.

A relative who lived with the Moore family for a year said that Kenneth Moore beat Devin at least four times a week, making him strip before each beating. He said that Kenneth frequently called Devin "crazy" and "stupid." Other defense witnesses testified that Moore's mother was an alcoholic and cocaine addict who took drugs while she was pregnant with one of Devin's sisters (the infant had tested positive for cocaine and syphilis when she was born).

Psychiatrist Charles Nevels confirmed that Moore had PTSD. He said that Moore had been in a dreamlike dissociative state when he shot his three victims. "My opinion was that he was unaware of what he was doing, the wrongfulness of it. And there wasn't anything he could do about it," Nevels testified.[4]

Prosecutor Chris McCool vehemently disputed the defense's contention that childhood abuse and violent video games caused Moore to commit murder. "Three good men blown away for no other reason than that the defendant didn't want to go to jail," McCool told the court. He called psychiatrist Brent Willis to rebut Nevel's testimony.

Willis agreed that Moore suffered from PTSD but said tests indicated Moore was exaggerating his symptoms. He said he was convinced that Moore knew right from wrong. Willis maintained that Moore was able to recall in detail the events of the crime, proving that he was not in a dissociative state as the defense claimed.

Investigator Mark Allison had interviewed Moore after he was arrested in Mississippi. Allison told the court that during the interview Moore "had a blank look on his face. It was like it was business as usual for him." To Allison, Moore seemed unfazed that he had just taken three lives; he was more upset about how the event would affect his future. "He became teary-eyed when he realized his crimes would interfere with his plan to enlist in the military," Allison said.

McCool argued that the defendant had killed the three men not because he had PTSD but because he simply didn't want to go to jail. Moore had admitted he hatched a plan to evade punishment while he was being booked in the Fayette Police Department. McCool played the taped confession Moore gave detectives in Mississippi. "I started planning in my head how I was going to escape. But things didn't go as planned," he said on tape. "The reason I shot the officers was that I didn't want to go to jail." The tape recording was the strongest piece of evidence in the case; it effectively undermined the defense.

Jurors deliberated for an hour before finding Moore guilty of capital murder. They returned to the jury box to hear sentencing arguments. Their next task would be to recommend whether the defendant should be sentenced to death or given a life sentence. Judge James Moore (no relation to the defendant) had the power to accept or reject the jury's recommendation.

The defense had one last chance to convince the court to spare Moore. Standridge reminded jurors that his client had been suffering from PTSD when he committed the murders. He asked that they show leniency to Moore, who was only eighteen at the time of the crime. "You've already decided that Devin Moore will spend the rest of his life in an eight-by-ten cell," he said. "Now all you have to decide is if you want to kill him. Is it enough for him to spend the rest of his life in jail, or do you need to kill him, too?"

"If triple murder doesn't warrant the death penalty . . . nothing ever will," prosecutor McCool rebutted. The jury and the judge agreed. Devin Moore was sentenced to die by lethal injection.

Before his sentence was announced, Moore addressed the families of his victims, telling them, "I pray the Lord has touched your hearts and you can find it in your hearts to forgive me." The families were unimpressed. The defendant "never shed a tear through the course of this trial," Glen Strickland, the brother of victim Arnold Strickland, remarked afterward. "I'll forgive him the day he's injected."[5]

While Devin Moore was adjusting to life on death row, the families of his victims were busy preparing a civil suit against the makers and distributors of Grand Theft Auto. The plaintiffs hired Jack Thompson to represent them. Outspoken and controversial, Thompson is a tireless crusader against obscenity and violence in music and pop culture. He's waged war on such public figures as Janet Reno, shock jock Howard Stern, hip-hop producer Luther Campbell, and singer Madonna; and has sued producers of the Comedy Central animated series *South Park,* and video game makers. During a dispute with Sony, the attorney called the Japanese company's production of violent video games "Pearl Harbor 2."

In 2005, Thompson was allowed to file the lawsuit *Strickland v. Sony* in an Alabama court pro hac vice.* The civil suit contended that the makers and distributors of Grand Theft Auto were complicit in the triple homicide committed by Devin Moore. "Not one of the families is saying that Devin Moore is not responsible, in every sense, for what he did," Thompson told reporters.[6] "What we're saying is that Devin Moore was, in effect, trained to do what he did. He was given a murder simulator . . . The video game industry gave him a cranial menu that popped up in the blink of an eye in that police station. And that menu offered him the split-second decision to kill the officers, shoot them in the head, flee in a police car, just as the game itself trained [him] to do."[7]

Thompson's words were music to Devin Moore's ears, affirming the defense strategy Moore had been unable to introduce at his criminal trial. He wrote Thompson and of-

---

* Pro hac vice is a temporary license for an attorney to practice in a jurisdiction for which he is not licensed.

fered his assistance with the civil suit. However, Moore warned him that he'd have a tough time getting a judge to hear arguments that Grand Theft Auto had played a part in his crimes. "If I couldn't use [evidence that the game caused him to kill] as a defense while facing capital punishment, my life, how can any lawyer do so or victims of the family for money?" Moore wrote.[8] He complained that his trial had been unfair because the judge prohibited his attorney from linking the crimes to video games. He was appealing the verdict because of the ban, and because his case was heard by an all-white jury; Moore is black, as was one of his victims.

An earlier civil suit against the makers of the video games Doom, Quake, and Resident Evil had been dismissed in 1997. So far, a case has yet to be heard against the gaming industry. In 2005, the Alabama Supreme Court rejected an appeal by the defendants to dismiss the *Strickland v. Sony* suit. "No one has ever before survived a motion to dismiss, so we're excited," Thompson said.[9] His excitement would be short-lived: months later his pro hac vice status was revoked after he violated a court-imposed gag order and allegedly sent dozens of harassing e-mails to the defense and to the judge. *Strickland v. Sony* continues to chug through the legal system, without Jack Thompson.

FIFTEEN

L&O SVU: ("Taboo," Season 7) A young woman charged with killing her newborn claims she didn't know she was pregnant.

TRUE STORY: College student Holly Ashcraft was accused of murdering her newborn baby after hiding the pregnancy.

Michael Walker was down on his luck. Homeless and hungry, the Californian routinely hit the Dumpsters looking for recyclable bottles he could cash in for a few bucks. Just after midnight on October 5, 2005, he stopped by the alley behind the Two Nine Café on South Hoover Street in Los Angeles. It was his second visit to the alley that day. Walker was rooting through the Dumpster when he noticed a white cardboard box on the ground that hadn't been there earlier. The box was taped shut, leading him to believe it might contain

275

Holly Ashcraft (middle), her sister, and attorney Mark Geragos leave court after a hearing. Charged with infanticide, Ashcraft contended the baby was stillborn.

Ed Ou/Daily Trojan

something valuable. It took him a few minutes to peel off all the layers of tape to get the box open. It was dark in the alley and Walker wasn't sure exactly what he had found. There was a bundled towel inside the box. He unwrapped it and saw what he thought at first was an animal. He looked closer and realized he was staring at a baby — a dead baby. Walker put the box down and ran to a nearby supermarket to call the police.

Several minutes later, officers responded to the scene. Walker, who had refused to give the police operator his name, had already fled the area. The officers found a dead newborn male of Caucasian or Latino ethnicity; the baby was small but appeared to be full-term. The umbilical cord was still attached, indicating the birth most likely occurred outside of a hospital. The baby's body was taken to the coroner's office for an autopsy. For identification purposes, he was named Baby John Doe 171. The cardboard box that served as his coffin was booked into evidence and dusted for fingerprints. Along with the towel, the box had also contained paper trash, including some envelopes addressed to a Holly Ashcraft.

The Los Angeles Police Department was desperate to find the baby's mother. At a news conference the next day, Detective Moses Castillo encouraged the woman to come forward and promised counseling services would be provided to her. "I can't imagine what's she's going through. I know it's a very difficult situation," Castillo told reporters. "The best thing, right now, to do is get medical attention for herself. Call us."

Castillo also urged the anonymous caller to come forward, explaining that he was being sought as a possible witness, not a suspect. Castillo released a recording of the phone call. One of Michael Walker's relatives recognized his voice. She contacted him and convinced him to cooperate with the police. Based on what Walker told them, the detectives were able to determine that the baby had been left in the alley sometime after dark on October 4.

Baby John Doe 171 was one of four newborns abandoned in public areas in Los Angeles in 2005. None of the four survived. Another eight infants were dropped off at designated Safe Surrender sites that year. National statistics for abandoned newborns are unknown. What is known is that each year dozens of babies across the country are abandoned; the lucky ones are those that are left behind in hospitals by mothers who skip out on them. These newborns are called "boarders" and are cared for by the hospital until they are old enough to be put up for adoption. The unlucky ones, the unidentified Baby John and Jane Does, are discarded and left in public spaces like parks, alleys, and trashcans. Most of them do not survive.

There's no common profile for mothers who abandon their newborns. The women hail from different socioeconomic classes, ages, and races. The one thing they do have in common is secrecy, says Deanne Tilton Durfee, executive director of the LA County

Inter-Agency Council on Child Abuse and Neglect. "The expectant mother has hidden the pregnancy," she explains. "In some cases, they've denied its existence, haven't prepared for it, or they haven't told anyone."[1]

In an attempt to decrease the mortality rate of abandoned newborns, California enacted the Safe Surrender law in 2001. The law allows parents of newborns to drop off their unwanted babies at fire stations, hospitals, and other officially designated sites with no questions asked and no risk of legal repercussions. (The Two Nine Café where Baby John Doe 171 was found was located two blocks away from a designated Safe Surrender site.) Leaving a baby at any other nonapproved site is a prosecutable crime. There is a two-week grace period during which a parent may reclaim the baby. Advertisements for Safe Surrender feature the slogan "No shame, no blame." As of 2007, forty-six states have similar laws.

The Los Angeles Police Department canvassed the neighborhood where the unidentified infant was discovered hoping to find witnesses or, even better, the baby's mother. Holly Ashcraft was one of the people they spoke to. She was a twenty-one-year-old junior at the University of Southern California who lived above the Two Nine Café. Her apartment was just a flight of stairs and a few feet away from the Dumpster that served as Baby John Doe 171's grave. Ashcraft denied being the baby's mother or having any information about the case except what she had read in the college paper. Despite her denials, detectives remained suspicious of Ashcraft. Not only did she live in close proximity to the location where the baby's body was found, her mail had been found inside the cardboard box holding him.

The detectives returned to Ashcraft's apartment accompanied by members from USC's Student Affairs; they believed she was the abandoned baby's mother and were concerned for her health. Ashcraft agreed to let them take her to the hospital. There, a medical nurse determined she had recently given birth. Based on this new information, Ashcraft was arrested.

Holly Ashcraft was charged with murder and felony child abuse, charges that carried a sentence of twenty-five years to life in prison. She pleaded not guilty and was held on two million dollars bail. Ashcraft's attorney Paul Wallin complained that the bail was excessive, pointing out "that bail amount is normally reserved for mass murderers." Deputy District Attorney Efrain Aceves argued, "She's from Montana, and from our understanding, there were no ties to the community, so we're concerned that she would be a flight risk." Unable to post bail, Ashcraft was remanded to county jail.

Accused of infanticide, Ashcraft was vilified by the public. Paul Wallin tried to quell the growing outrage. "The public knows an extremely small amount of the facts," he told reporters. "When all of the facts come out, I believe the public will understand what happened and not believe our client committed any criminal offenses."[2]

Wallin's attempts at damage control were in vain — the public soon learned that Holly had been linked to *another* abandoned baby case a year earlier. In 2004, she had sought treatment at a local hospital after giving birth at home to what she claimed was a stillborn baby. She told doctors that she had disposed of the baby's body. The hospital contacted the police. Despite a thorough search of the area, police were unable to locate the baby's body. Without the body, it was impossible to tell if a crime had occurred; no charges were filed against Ashcraft. As it turned out, Wallin had also represented Ashcraft in that case. Now he struggled to convince the public his client was innocent in both cases, and that both babies had been stillborn. In the 2004 "incident," Wallin said, Holly was "not prosecuted for any crime, she wasn't even arrested for any crime. And no crime was committed."[3]

Holly Ashcraft had become major news, with national and local media reporting on her case. One of the reasons the media latched onto her story was that Holly didn't fit the perceived notion of what society expects a baby killer to look like. Instead, she was the picture of innocence — a college kid with a bright smile and a bright future, who had been raised in a middle class Midwestern family.

Ashcraft grew up in the small town of Billings, Montana. A pretty, fresh-faced sandy blonde, Ashcraft looked like she had been sent from central casting to play the stereotypical all-American girl. Friends described her as outgoing, energetic, and blessed with a good sense of humor. On a college webpage, Ashcraft listed her interests as music, art, and architecture.

She didn't have a steady boyfriend and none of her fellow students recall her dating much at all. No one who knew Ashcraft had suspected she was pregnant. Her attorneys contended that Holly herself hadn't even known. Just a few weeks before Ashcraft's arrest, her sister noticed she had gained weight and was vomiting. Holly attributed the weight gain to birth control pills she said she was taking; the vomiting, she said, was caused by food poisoning.

Ashcraft's friends and neighbors were flabbergasted to learn she was suspected of discarding two newborns in as many years. "I'm just shocked by this. It's totally out of character for her," a former dorm mate told reporters.[4] Many, like Ashcraft's landlord Ann Dorr, defended her in the press. Dorr described Holly as a model tenant and a sweet girl. "I feel like I need to protect her," she told reporters. "I'm not justifying what she's done, but I also don't like her to be judged. I think she was plain scared."[5]

Was it fear that caused the otherwise sensible, intelligent young woman to throw her baby away? Or was it ignorance? Did a lack of proper sex education leave Holly ill-equipped to deal with her own sexuality? As a student of Montana's Billings West High School, Ashcraft received abstinence-only education. Montana is just one of dozens of states that have agreed to implement abstinence-only programs in its schools in order to qualify for federal funding.

Each year, the federal government doles out fifty million dollars to states that replace traditional sex-ed classes with abstinence-only education. As part of the deal, states must refrain from teaching students about alternatives to celibacy or about contraceptives. Instead, students are taught that any sexual activity outside of the context of marriage is likely to have harmful psychological and physical effects; and abstinence is the only certain way to avoid out-of-wedlock pregnancy, sexually transmitted diseases, and other associated health problems. In 2005, Montana received $172,303 for enforcing abstinence-only teaching in its schools.

Louis Marie Roth, a sociology professor at the University of Arizona, suspects students "who receive strict abstinence-only messages and no other messages about sexuality feel that they have no social resources to turn to if they get pregnant." She believes that Holly may have found the act of abandoning her infant "more morally acceptable" than admitting that she had sex before marriage."[6]

Small towns are often more conservative than big cities; and Holly may have been afraid of being ostracized for having a child out of wedlock. "Coming from a small town like we did, things were kept very quiet because rumors or truths tended to spread easily," explains Kate Hamersley, who attended high school with Ashcraft. "Although there may have been other options than what Holly turned to, I would say that she was most likely frightened and was probably unaware of the rule of turning over a baby with no questions asked."[7]

Publicly, Ashcraft was not admitting to giving birth to Baby John Doe 171. However, DNA testing concluded that there was a 99.93 percent probability that she was the infant's mother. Los Angeles County Medical Examiner David Whiteman determined that the infant had been born alive after a thirty-two-week pregnancy. He was six weeks premature; medical experts said that with proper care, Baby John Doe 171 would have had a 99 percent chance of survival. In the official autopsy report, Whiteman attributed the infant's death to "caretaker neglect" and "prematurity and other undetermined factors." He noted that there was no evidence of trauma or internal injuries. He also noted that "intentional asphyxia cannot be excluded."

Ashcraft's attorney viewed the autopsy findings as favorable to Ashcraft. As for the medical examiner's decision not to rule out asphyxia, Wallin said that only meant that "anything is possible. That's not like they're saying they're making any findings that anything like that happened."

As far as Jane Robinson, the spokesperson for the LA County DA's office, was concerned, the autopsy report matched the DA's preliminary findings and "doesn't really change anything as far as the case goes."

Several weeks after her arrest, the judge agreed to reduce Holly's bail to $200,000. After posting bail, Ashcraft was released into the care of a relative who lived in Los Angeles. She was fitted with an electronic monitoring device and placed under house arrest while the case was pending. As part of her release, she was prohibited from coming into contact with any child under sixteen without another adult present. Several months later, Ashcraft dropped Paul Wallin as her counsel and hired Mark Geragos, the high-profile attorney who had defended wife killer Scott Peterson, actress Winona Ryder, and pop star Michael Jackson.

Almost a year after he found Baby John Doe 171 dead in an alley, Michael Walker came face-to-face with the woman who allegedly discarded the newborn. Walker was one of a handful of witnesses summoned to testify at a preliminary hearing on Holly Ashcraft's case in Los Angeles County Court. The hearing was being held to determine if the prosecution had sufficient evidence to bring Ashcraft to trial.

At Deputy District Attorney Franco Barrata's request, Walker recounted the night he found the dead baby tucked inside an ordinary cardboard box. Walker thought he had found an animal at first. "I touched the little feet, then I saw the baby's head in the corner," he said. When he realized what he was looking at, he "backed up and hollered."

Another prosecution witness, Detective Moses Castillo, testified that the officers who investigated Ashcraft in the first abandoned baby case she had been linked to had told her about the Safe Surrender law back in 2004.

David Whiteman, the medical examiner who performed the autopsy on Baby John Doe 171 told the court that he had found air in the baby's lungs, which indicated that the baby had been born alive. Whiteman said he believed "the child lived for a period of time" and had not been fed.

On cross-examination, Mark Geragos

disputed Whiteman's findings. He insisted that Ashcraft's baby had been stillborn and said that there was medical evidence that stillborn babies can have air in their lungs. Then, hedging his bets, Geragos argued that even if the baby *had* been born alive Holly still could not be tried for murder because the baby's death was not intentional. Baratta scoffed at the logic, responding, "If I take my son, my newborn, and refuse to feed him because I want him to die and I just sit there and watch him, watch him die, that is an intentional act."

Superior Court Commissioner Ronald Rose denied Geragos's request to dismiss the charges. He ruled that that the law "requires a parent to provide treatment and care" to newborns and that failure to do so can be grounds for criminal charges. Rose also noted with sadness that Holly's apartment was "less than a half mile away from a fire station. A phone call could have been made, the baby could have been taken to the fire station. Aid could have been provided." He ordered Ashcraft stand trial for murder.

In order to win a murder conviction, the prosecution had to prove that Holly's baby was born alive. That burden of proof was about to get a lot heavier. Four months after the preliminary hearing Mark Geragos filed a motion to dismiss the charges against Holly based on new medical evidence that, contrary to the coroner's official ruling, Baby John Doe 171 may very well have been stillborn.

"There is no incontrovertible evidence that this infant was born alive," stated Dr. Joan E. Hodgman, a professor of pediatrics in the Keck School of Medicine with more than forty years experience examining newborn deaths. "My opinion is clear that the murder of the infant on the part of the mother is unlikely and in no way proven by the evidence provided."[8] Additionally, if Holly had given birth to a stillborn in 2004, it was "more likely" that her second child was also stillborn, she said. "If the mother had one [late term] stillborn . . . that's bad news for future pregnancies."

Hodgman decried the Ashcraft case as a "miscarriage of justice" because "there's no specific evidence that she did the baby in." However, she did admit that Holly "easily could have smothered [the baby] and it wouldn't have shown up in an autopsy."[9]

In his motion, Geragos noted Hodgman's findings and argued that there was no evidence "that the fetus died by criminal means." He noted the coroner's original

DNA II

There's no doubt that DNA testing is the most important scientific break-through for police to appear in the last century. But everything comes with a price. Some jurors have become so used to seeing DNA solve a case on TV, they won't deem a defendant guilty *without* DNA evidence.

Unfortunately, it's not always possible for police to get enough good DNA to perform an adequate test. A piece of hair, for instance, is very difficult to get a good DNA reading from, and is therefore not nearly as useful to investigators as saliva, semen, or blood. DNA samples are also notoriously susceptible to contamination. If someone close by coughs when a DNA sample is collected, the sample may be contaminated. This makes securing and maintaining a crime scene more critical than ever.

testimony that the cause of death was "peri-partum demise due to prematurity and other undetermined factors."

Furthermore, "[t]he evidence showed that Ms. Ashcraft did not know she was pregnant prior to the stillborn birth, nor did witnesses who observed her one week before the incident," Geragos wrote. Holly, he insisted "unexpectedly gave birth to a stillborn baby while alone in her apartment" on October 9, 2005.

"More importantly," he added, "there was no evidence introduced as to what Ms. Ashcraft could have even done within minutes of the unassisted birth to resuscitate or save the fetus."

Judge David Wesley dismissed the murder charge against Ashcraft and replaced it with the lesser charge of involuntary manslaughter. The prosecution was not pleased. Rather than try Ashcraft for manslaughter, which carries a substantially shorter prison sentence than murder, Deputy DA Barrata moved to dismiss the charges "without prejudice" and reserved the right to refile. Barrata then immediately refiled the original charges of murder and felony child abuse. Geragos called the refiling a "last-ditch effort" by the prosecutor.

The new case was assigned to Commissioner Catherine Pratt; Pratt would be the fourth judge to oversee the Ashcraft legal saga. Barrata told Pratt that the prosecution had new medical evidence that Baby John Doe 171 was born alive. The medical examiner had found blood in the baby's umbilical cord, indicating that his heart had been beating when the umbilical cord was cut. The new evidence supported the prosecution's charge that Ashcraft was guilty of murder.

In response, the defense filed another motion to dismiss the charges. The dogged efforts paid off: On June 13, 2007, Los Angeles Superior Court Judge Samuel Mayerson threw out the charges. The judge ruled that the state could not prosecute Ashcraft because the charges against her had been previously dismissed twice; the limit under California law.

Sixteen

L&O SVU: ("Monogamy," Season 3) A pregnant woman is found unconscious and bleeding in a parking lot; her unborn baby has been cut out of her and stolen.

TRUE STORY: In Missouri, Lisa Montgomery is accused of strangling Bobbie Jo Stinnett and cutting her unborn child out of her body.

Bobbie Jo typed out the directions to her house and e-mailed them to Darlene Fischer. The two women had never met face to face, but they shared an interest in dogs and had begun communicating online in a chat room for rat terrier breeders and buyers. Twenty-three-year-old Bobbie Jo had recently begun a breeding business, Happy Haven Rat Terriers, and ran it from her home in Skidmore, Missouri, a tiny town in the northwest corner of the state, near the

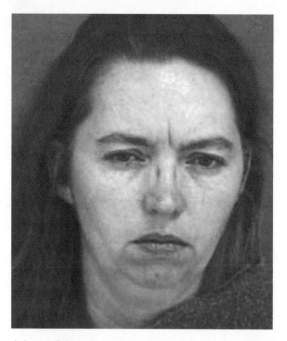

Lisa Montgomery is accused of stalking and murdering Bobbie Jo Stinnett, eight months pregnant, and then removing the fetus from Stinnett's body. Miraculously, the baby was recovered in fine health.

border of Kansas. Darlene was interested in purchasing one of Bobbie Jo's rat terriers. She lived in Melvern, Kansas, about two hundred miles from Skidmore. She told Bobbie Jo that she wanted to come to her house to check out one of the dogs.

Bobbie Jo was excited to make a sale. She had married Zeb Stinnett, her high school sweetheart, a year ago, and she was eight months pregnant. She had a job at Kawasaki Manufacturing in the nearby town of Maryville, but with a first-born on the way, she and Zeb would need all the cash they could get. And in the dog-breeding business, reputation is everything. If Fischer was satisfied with her purchase she might mention Happy Haven Rat Terriers to some friends. There was no telling where it could lead. Bobbie Jo finished typing the directions to her house and hit "Send." Darlene Fischer replied that she was really looking forward to meeting Bobbie Jo. She would be there on Thursday afternoon, December 16.

Darlene Fischer wasn't who she claimed to be. She *was* interested in rat terriers, but that was the only thing she told the truth about. Her name wasn't really Darlene Fischer, it was Lisa Montgomery. She and Stinnett had become fast friends online based on their mutual pregnancies. They traded e-mails in the rat terrier chat room about the details of their pregnancies and their future plans. But in reality, Montgomery wasn't pregnant. She had somehow, though, convinced her husband Kevin that she was. Kevin was Lisa's second husband; she had had four children with her first husband. This would be the first with Kevin.

Lisa told all her friends and neighbors about how happy she was to be having this new child with Kevin.* People noted that she didn't look pregnant, to which Lisa responded that she didn't "show" too much when she was pregnant with her other kids. That's just how her body worked.

Lisa Montgomery kept the ruse going with whomever she communicated. She'd write at length about her pregnancy in chat rooms and tell everyone who would listen about all the details. With her fellow rat terrier fans, she would lament that she didn't have any pictures of her dogs to share because it was so difficult to bend down to their level to snap a picture when you're pregnant. One day, she even showed her ex-husband, Carl Boman, an ultrasound photo of the baby that was allegedly growing in her stomach — an image she had downloaded from the Internet.[1]

Even Lisa's request for directions to Bobbie Jo Stinnett's house was a lie. She had already done a MapQuest search for Bobbie Jo's address and had no intention whatsoever of purchasing a dog from Happy

*A testament to the power of suggestion: Kevin Montgomery was reportedly convinced that he could feel the baby kick.

296

Haven Rat Terriers. After the MapQuest search, Montgomery's next stop on the Web was an online video of doctors performing a cesarean section . . .

Becky Harper, Bobbie Jo's mother, picked up the phone at 2:30 on the afternoon of December 16, 2004. She was calling her daughter to ask if she could come pick her up from work. Bobbie Jo answered, but said that she couldn't leave the house at the moment. There was a woman coming to look at one of the dogs. As Harper tried to think of another way home, her daughter looked out the window and saw a red Toyota Corolla pull up to the house. "Oh, she's here now. I have to go," Bobbie Jo told her mother and hung up the phone. Becky Harper found a way home, and about an hour after she spoke with her daughter, she stopped by the house.

When Harper walked inside, her life was destroyed on the spot. The description of the scene from an FBI agent's affidavit is chillingly objective: "The victim had been strangled in her own home, her abdomen had been cut open and the fetus removed."[2] Becky described it differently. She told the sheriff it looked like her daughter's "stomach had exploded."

As police cars pulled up in front of the Stinnett home to investigate the crime scene and interview neighbors, Lisa Montgomery was driving back toward her home in Kansas with Bobbie Jo and Zeb Stinnett's infant. When she got to Topeka, the closest large town to Melvern, she called her husband with some great news. She had been shopping in Topeka when she went into labor prematurely. She rushed herself to the Women's Birthing Center in town and delivered a beautiful, healthy baby girl. Lisa told her husband that she was in the parking lot of Long John Silver's and that he should come right away. After giving birth, of course, she was in no condition to drive. She needed Kevin to bring one of the kids to drive her car home. Kevin Montgomery and two of his stepchildren jumped in the car and sped down to Topeka. Pulling into the Long John Silver's parking lot, they saw Lisa holding the baby. She was beaming.

Back in Skidmore, Missouri, police contacted the FBI. With no evidence that the baby had been harmed, and given the fact that the crime scene was near borders with multiple states, they assumed this was a murder-kidnapping and that it would probably fall under federal jurisdiction.

Nodaway County Sheriff Ben Espy, meanwhile, requested an Amber Alert from state authorities. His request was initially declined, however, because he couldn't supply a description of the kidnapped baby. Espy argued his case, and the alert was finally sent, but not until after midnight.

Because there were no signs of forced entry, investigators concluded that Bobbie Jo Stinnett knew her murderer. Zeb was at work during the crime and was never considered a suspect. A neighbor had noticed a dirty red foreign car parked outside Zeb and Bobbie Jo's house for at least an hour. The best suspect they had was the person who had made the appointment with Bobbie Jo to check out her dogs.

Expediency was critical. Who knew how long this baby would live without proper medical care, or what exactly the killer was planning to do with it. A team of detectives and a computer forensics expert hacked into Bobbie Jo's computer and found a number of Bobbie Jo's recent message board chats with rat terrier enthusiasts. One of the messages was from a user whose e-mail address was fischer4kids@hotmail.com. They read the e-mails between Bobbie Jo and this user, including the exchange involving directions to the Stinnett's house. The prospective dog buyer claimed to live in Fairfax, Missouri, so investigators tried to locate a Diane Fischer from that town. No luck. So the computer was transferred to the Kansas City Regional Computer Forensic Laboratory for a more thorough investigation on who Bobbie Jo Stinnett's contact was.

The day after the murder, investigators were contacted by a dog breeder in North Carolina who had heard about the murder and had seen some communiqués between the two women involved. She provided both the site's URL and the IP address of Darlene Fischer's messages. An IP address is a number that is unique to each computer in a network, much like a street address is to a person's home. Although it was extraordinarily helpful to the agents in determining the location of the perpetrator's computer, it wasn't a simple matter of looking up the number in a databank; there are no IP "phone books."

Upon learning that the IP address belonged to Qwest Communications in Virginia, FBI agents contacted the company. They were put in touch with a security specialist who confirmed the address belonged to Qwest and informed them that the server it used was located in Topeka, Kansas. Investigating even further into the matter, the security specialist was able to supply the agents with the e-mail to which the IP address was assigned, as well as the phone number it used to access the Internet connection. *Now* it was just a matter of using a phone book. The messages had been sent from the home of Kevin Montgomery in Melvern, Kansas.*

FBI agents were dispatched to the Montgomery home. Outside, they saw the dirty red Toyota Corolla; inside, they found Lisa and Kevin Montgomery with their newborn daughter.

It would be difficult to imagine emotions more conflicting than the ones Zeb Stinnett must have experienced in that twenty-four-hour period. On what should have been just a normal day, he found out that his wife had been mercilessly slaughtered in their own home for her unborn baby — and yet, the baby was miraculously tracked down

---

*About a month after the resolution of the Bobbie Jo Stinnett murder, U.S. Attorney General John Ashcroft cited this investigation in speeches supporting the Patriot Act. Law enforcement agents could not have tracked down Lisa Montgomery so efficiently without provisions put in place by the Patriot Act, Ashcroft contended.

and recovered, alive and well. Zeb would be raising his daughter, whom he named Victoria Jo, alone. He must have known even then that every time he looked at his precious child, he would be reminded of Bobbie Jo's cruel end.

Lisa Montgomery was charged with kidnapping an infant, resulting in the death of its mother. She was indicted on January 12, 2005, and sent to Leavenworth prison to await trial. Her trial was initially scheduled for March 15, 2005, but when the DA's office announced that it would be seeking the death penalty, the defense began issuing one motion after another for continuance. As of this writing, Montgomery has yet to face a jury.

Interviewed about his wife's alleged crime, Kevin Montgomery thanked all his friends, neighbors, and parishioners at his church for their support, adding that he hoped Zeb Stinnett and Bobbie Jo's family were getting the same kind of support. The towns of Skidmore and Melvern were, of course, shocked by the murder of Bobbie Jo Stinnett and the kidnapping of her child. "This is something none of us can begin to understand," said Reverend Harold Hamon at Bobbie Jo's funeral. "I've been a preacher for fifty years, and I've seen some terrible

The Arrest

Technically, a person can be arrested for a sex crime based solely on the accusation of the alleged victim, but it's not the preferred course of action.

Only 20 percent of sex crimes are committed by strangers — that is, someone the victim has never seen and had no contact with. The rest are committed by acquaintances — anyone ranging from the victim's spouse to someone he or she recognizes from the neighborhood.

Police are more likely to take a chance on arresting a stranger, the idea being that this person is likely a violent predator; they want to get him off the street as quickly as possible.

In the case of an acquaintance, the police and DA will attempt to build a case before the arrest. One of the most useful tactics for cases involving an attacker who is known by the victim is to record a phone conversation between them in which the victim refers to the specific crime. By listening to the suspect's reaction, investigators can get a good picture of the nature of the crime — or whether it even occurred inthe first place.

things. But this has got to be the apex."[3]

A café owner in Lisa Montgomery's town of Melvern had this to say about the gruesome crime: "This stuff is supposed to be in New York City or Los Angeles . . . [It] blows you away when it's here."[4]

If this man had opened up a newspaper during the past decade, he might have chosen his words more carefully. More and more crime headlines are being generated from actions in his neck of the woods — rural America — and have been for some time. "This stuff" is simply not supposed to happen at all, whether your town is dominated by skyscrapers or the sky itself, whether you drive a subway for a living or a tractor. It might surprise him, but "big city" people are blown away by crimes like this, too. The murder of Bobbie Jo Stinnett and the abduction of her baby was an unspeakable act.

SEVENTEEN

L&O SVU: ("Counterfeit," Season 3) A woman is found raped and murdered in her car. The investigation points to a police officer who is accused of raping the woman during a traffic stop.

TRUE STORY: In 1986, California Highway Patrol officer Craig Peyer murdered college student Cara Knott during a phony traffic stop. Peyer had been stopping and harassing women motorists for some time.

Cheryl Johnson looked in her rearview mirror and saw every driver's nightmare: flashing red lights and that pitiless silhouette behind the wheel of a patrol car. The pretty, blonde-haired nurse had no idea why she was being pulled over, but she dutifully slowed down her car and came to a stop on the shoulder of the freeway. The cop turned on his car's speaker and told her to back the car up to the Mercy Road exit and pull off the freeway. This seemed pretty odd to Johnson, but she knew that California Highway Patrolmen are deadly serious about their job, so she put the car in reverse and did as she was told.

The area around I-15's Mercy Road exit was a no-man's land, a dead-end road beyond which was a bridge spanning a dried-out creek bed, overgrown weeds, and trash. At night, the entire area was pitch black. When they were safely off the freeway, the officer told Johnson to get out and approach his car. He motioned for her to get into the passenger seat, which she did. The cop, Johnson noticed, was spit-and-polish. For someone who spends the entire day sitting in his car and driving around, the CHP officer kept his car immaculate. He was a somewhat stocky guy, his hair parted neatly and not a strand out of place. He wasn't necessarily good-looking, but he had a nice face. Up close, he seemed like a pleasant enough guy. He began lecturing her about the importance of safe driving and pointed out that one of her headlights was loose. He didn't enjoy writing up tickets, but he had seen some pretty bad accidents and a lot of blood in his time — one of the worst crashes resulting from faulty headlights.

Then the cop changed the subject to more personal matters. As he turned off his police radio, he started asking Cheryl Johnson about her personal life. Where did she grow up? Did she have a boyfriend? What did she do for a living? Cheryl answered his questions. Although she made small talk with him and didn't feel overtly threatened — the cop's questions stopped just short of inappropriate — she was getting the willies. To be sitting here with a CHP officer, the very symbol of order and structure, in a context that simply didn't make sense — it was just way too much of a dichotomy, it was surreal.

Then he started talking about how dangerous the area was. "Somebody could get raped or murdered here, and nobody would ever know," the police officer said. "At least I'm with you."[1] *Is he trying to tell me something?* Johnson must have wondered. *Is he really concerned about my safety or is this some sort of veiled threat? And if it's a real warning, why did he make me come down here in the first place?*

Finally, after ninety minutes of chatting with the CHP officer, Cheryl finally got the courage to make it clear that she needed to leave. She got out of the patrol car and into hers. *What was that all about?* Johnson

California Highway Patrolman Craig Peyer in court with his lawyers. Peyer pulled over and strangled college student Cara Knott as she was driving to her parents' house on Christmas break.

Don Kohlbaver/San Diego Union Tribune/Zuma

thought as she hit the freeway.

As it would turn out, Johnson was only one of many women pulled over by Craig Peyer for questionable purposes. A by-the-book cop in every way but one, Peyer had a penchant for pulling women over at the Mercy Avenue exit under the ruse of offering them a lesson on highway safety. His real intent was to . . . talk. That's all. When he saw a good-looking woman drive past, he'd floor his car and pull her over. Of course, when someone flies past at seventy miles per hour, mistakes can be made. Once, when he stopped a brunette that had caught his eye, she turned out to be a long-haired he. On another occasion, Peyer made the right choice — the woman was indeed good-looking — but her husband was lying in the fully reclined passenger seat taking a nap. When Officer Peyer saw the man, he curtly gave them a speeding ticket and took off down the freeway.

Peyer's highway stops were so out of the ordinary that the CHP occasionally received a phone call from an irate driver who didn't think too much of Peyer's little highway safety seminars. Apparently, though, the cop's bosses were old-school: *These people may not like it now, but they'll thank us later.* They even praised the officer for his diligence and enjoined him to keep up the good work.

But Craig Peyer's strange habit, and the CHP's incurious attitude about it, would come to a head one cold night in December 1986.

The Knott family had just celebrated Christmas and was planning to spend the next week relaxing. Sam and Joyce Knott were the proud parents of four great children: Cynthia and Cheryl were older and living on their own; Cara was a student at San Diego State University, and John was the youngest. Sam ran a tight ship, wanting to know where his younger ones were at all times and demanding they call if their plans had changed or if they were going to be home late. It wasn't a control issue as much as it was Sam's best trait: affection for his family. Joyce and Sam Knott knew what great kids they had, and they wanted to protect them at all costs. At the urging of Sam, Cara and her mother even took a self-defense course together. You never know when you're going to need to protect yourself, Sam said. It's best to be prepared. In the class, Cara and Joyce learned that the minute you feel threatened, you should explode: kick with your feet and scratch with your hands. The perpetrator will most likely flee.

Two nights after Christmas, as the Knotts were watching TV, the phone rang. It was Cara calling from her boyfriend, Wayne Bautista's, house. She had been taking care of Wayne, who had come down with the flu. The rest of his family was visiting relatives in another part of the state, and Cara had been caring for him since Christmas. She was on her way home, she told her father.

She wanted to see her parents and siblings; Wayne would be okay one night on his own. The Knotts were looking forward to seeing Cara. She hadn't been home for a couple of days and Christmas just wasn't quite the same without her.

Everyone got involved in a movie and it wasn't until about two hours after Cara had called that they realized how much time had passed. She should have been home an hour ago. They assumed she got held up taking care of Wayne, and that she was probably on her way home now. Just to make sure, Sam called Wayne who said Cara had left his house at 8:30 p.m., right after she called. The Knotts knew something was not right. It wasn't like Cara to deviate from the plan without letting someone know. Instantly, everyone had the same thought. They got into their cars and began driving different routes to Wayne's house. Cara's parents, siblings, and brother-in-law Bill, Cynthia's husband, drove all night and found no sign of Cara or her white Volkswagen Bug. Wayne, flu and all, searched as well.

As the hours passed, everyone involved became more and more convinced that something awful had happened to Cara. They drove in shifts; someone would be home to man the phone, while others searched I–15, the side roads, and gas stations. Then, when someone came home, the other person would get in the car and join the search.[2] They would flag down police when they saw them, but got no help. First of all, a person had to be missing at least twenty-four hours before an official report could be filed. Second, a twenty-year-old girl a few hours late coming home? Please.

At about 7:00 a.m., Cynthia and Bill pulled off I–15 at the Mercy Road exit. They drove around the desolate area and saw nothing but scrub, grass, weeds, and garbage. The desolate area gave them the creeps. They couldn't imagine what Cara would be doing down there, but when Bill saw some barriers set up blocking vehicles from a bike path, something told him to explore the area. There was just enough room to pull the car through. They didn't have to drive very far before they saw Cara's car. Cynthia jumped from the car before Bill had even stopped it.[3]

Cara's pocketbook was in the car, the keys were in the ignition, and the driver's side window was rolled partly down, but Cynthia saw no other sign of her sister. Bill and Cynthia rushed to the nearest phone. First they called the police, then the house. Soon, the Knotts and the police officers were milling around the lone VW Bug.

Craig Peyer finished his shift that night and went home. He lived with his third wife, Karen, who thought as highly of Craig as his fellow cops did. Peyer was a stand-up guy who took his job seriously, as evidenced by the fact that he consistently gave out more tickets than anyone. And, of course, when he wasn't handing out speeding tickets, he was educating drivers on the hazards of highway travel. His peers even noticed that his badge was always newly polished. He might have been a little too gung-ho for some guys, but he always greeted people with a sincere smile and a willingness to chat about any subject under the sun.

There was, however, another side to Officer Peyer, and only those who knew him intimately had ever seen it. His first wife, for instance, would tell you that he never polished his own badge, that he made a point of making her do it, and that he openly flirted with other women in front of her, and that when she confronted him about it, he would get violent. And his second wife would tell you that Craig constantly stalked her after their divorce.[4]

Craig Peyer, it turned out, was a "guy's

guy" in a bad way. Once, after giving one of his wives an expensive-looking necklace, he told the fellas that the stones were fake, but she couldn't tell. He liked that. Another time, the safety-first highway patrolman put used tires on his wife's car, but told her they were new. And just to make sure he fit in well with the guys, he told stories about how he operated behind enemy lines in 'Nam with Special Forces troops. In reality, he fixed helicopters while serving in Vietnam.[5]

Karen must have noticed the scratches on Craig's face when he came home from his shift on December 28. If she asked what happened, he probably told her the same story he wrote on an injury report at work — that he slipped on some gasoline when he was filling his tank at the station and fell face first into a chain-link fence. Better to be considered a spaz than a killer.

Cara's family remained congregated around the VW on the brisk morning of December 28. It was a tangible sign of Cara, and they didn't want to leave it. None of the Knotts had slept, but they weren't tired. Deep down, every one of them was assuming the worst.

One of the police who arrived on the scene took a walk down the bike path. When

314

he reached the bridge, he looked down into the gulley sixty-five feet below. There was Cara Knott, dressed in sweats and her favorite white leather boots. The officer looked over toward the Knotts and back down to Cara. He'd have to call homicide.

The Knott family's emotions alternated from fuming anger at the police for not taking their panic seriously during the hours Cara was missing to overwhelming shock and anguish that the last moments of this beautiful girl's promising life were spent in sheer terror, probably crying for her family, and that she had been dumped over the bridge like a piece of refuse. No, this was not happening. No way.

Teams of detectives, uniformed officers, and crime scene units scoured the area. They measured a set of distinct, extra-wide tire tracks near Cara's car, scanned the entire area for clues, took fingerprints from the VW, and picked up tiny fiber samples from Cara's clothing. She had clearly been choked, but medical experts couldn't determine whether it was the cause of death.

Everyone was a suspect — especially Wayne's father, Jaime, who was taking a particularly keen interest in the case. Rumors spread that this was the work of a serial murderer from Washington, the Green River Killer, who was believed to have been in the area at the time. Some people who had been driving down I-15 at the time of the murder came forth and told police about a strange hitchhiker near Mercy Road waving money at cars trying to flag them down.

The newspapers grabbed the story and held on. As the police went about their business as quietly as possible, tracking down every lead and tip no matter how goofy it sounded, a local television reporter decided to use Cara's murder as a springboard for a story. She contacted the California Highway Patrol and asked if she and her cameraman could ride with an officer on patrol for a segment on highway safety. No problem, they would be happy to accommodate her. And they knew just the man for the job: Craig Peyer, the resident expert on highway safety. And so, on the evening news, one day after the murder of Cara Knott, there was CHP Officer Craig Peyer, looking into the camera, comfortable as could be, offering sage advice to women about how to keep themselves safe when confronted by a stranger on the highway.

Then one day soon after the news segment, it hit CHP Sergeant John McDonald:

316

the complaints about Craig Peyer from drivers pulled over at Mercy Road, the wide tire tracks at the crime scene, the scratches on Peyer's face. A hunch would have been something to mull over, but with the pieces fitting so perfectly together, McDonald didn't hesitate to call detectives. The last thing he ever thought he'd be doing was phoning homicide with a tip about a fellow cop. Homicide felt the same way when they got the call. *A cop? A cop murdered Cara Knott?* Nevertheless, they searched Peyer's patrol car. Initially, they found nothing, but when they dug down into the trunk, there under the spare tire was a length of yellow nylon rope. CHP cars were equipped with two ropes; this third was definitely not CHP standard issue. They called the highway patrolman in for questioning.

When Peyer came in, detectives didn't waste any time. They wanted to put him on the spot to see what his reaction would be. They told him that the tire tracks matched those of his car and that they knew about the complaints from female drivers he pulled over at Mercy Road. They had to be honest, from their side of the table it looked really bad for him. Peyer protested his innocence, but began to get panicky — and his interrogators exploited it. They got in

317

his face, shouting that they knew he did it, that he had killed a beautiful young woman and that he was going down, it was only a matter of time.[6]

Peyer struggled but succeeded in maintaining his cool. He didn't break down against the interrogators' onslaught. But he made a fatal slipup. When the detectives asked him about the ropes, Peyer replied, "Those are the only two ropes, I don't know about any other rope."[7] That was it. They had never mentioned the third rope. How did Peyer know about it if he hadn't put it there? Their question about the rope had been purposefully vague — a classic interrogator's trick — and Peyer had fallen right into the trap.

Craig Peyer's murder trial began the following May. The prosecution couldn't determine a motive or declare the rope in the trunk as the murder weapon (investigators found no skin or blood on it), but they had mountains of circumstantial evidence. It turned out that Peyer had written a traffic ticket at 10:20 p.m. on the night of the murder but suspiciously crossed out the time and penned in 9:20 to give himself an alibi for his whereabouts. He also seemed to have an obsession with the Mercy Road exit. Once, he brought a rookie down there to show her the ropes and commented that if a person happened to have killed someone, it would be the perfect place to dump the body.

The prosecution then paraded twenty women to the stand, who, one after another, chronicled their run-ins with Officer Peyer. Each one had been pulled over and brought down to Mercy Road, where Peyer talked to them about everything from the weather to relationships.

Witnesses included a gas station attendant who saw Peyer pull up and fill his car not long after the murder took place. The attendant said that Peyer commented that he'd had a terrible night. He then took out his nightstick from the trunk and cleaned it off with a rag.

In addition to the physical evidence of the tire tracks and scratches on Peyer's face (documented in the injury report), the prosecution showed the jury proof that blood samples taken from Cara's boots were the same type as Peyer's. They also presented six pieces of thread: three gold fibers on the victim's clothing, which matched those of a patch on Peyer's uniform, and three purple fibers taken from Peyer's clothing matching those from the sweatpants

The Polygraph

Polygraph machines are notoriously inaccurate and fairly easy to defeat if you know how. Drugs, alcohol, hunger, and a person's natural or reactive level of anxiety are all factors in a polygraph's accuracy. For these reasons, lie detector results are rarely allowed as evidence in a trial. Still, to someone unused to the inside of a precinct house, the prospect of taking a polygraph can be daunting, indeed.

How does a polygraph work? Since telling a lie causes stress, and stress, in turn, causes certain physical reactions, polygraph machines measure and quantify such reactions as sweating, blood pressure, breathing rate, and pulse.

An important new breakthrough in brain wave technology, however, will eventually make the polygraph look like something out of the Middle Ages. Scientists are making great strides in learning how to, basically, read minds. It's been proven that certain brain waves surge when people are confronted with something recognizable.

So, for instance, if a suspect says he didn't know the victim, a detective can show him a picture of the victim. It would be virtually impossible for the suspect to control the reaction of his brain to the picture. Experiments are also being conducted with MRIs, which actually display nerve-ending activity in the brain.

Cara wore that night.

Pretty damning evidence. But Robert Grimes, Peyer's defense attorney, had a habit of pulling rabbits out of his hat when he needed to. And he needed to here. Grimes was particularly skilled at cross-examination, and when he got hold of the prosecution's expert witnesses, he had their heads spinning — and the jurors'.

The prosecution had lots of evidence, but their case wasn't buttoned up as tightly as they would have preferred. Grimes built the smallest investigative mistakes and most minuscule chances of inaccuracy into gigantic mountains. By the time he got through with the deputy coroner, the jurors were wondering if the guy even had a college degree in science. And Grimes got the state's fiber expert to admit that there was no way to be absolutely sure where the fibers came from.

Grimes's strategy was to make it seem that the homicide detectives and the DA were convinced early on that Peyer was guilty, and that they ignored evidence that steered them away from the CHP officer. For instance, he pointed out that police found fingerprints in Cara Knott's car that didn't belong to her, her family, or Craig Peyer. Even now, with Peyer on trial, they still didn't know whose prints those were! And what about that hitchhiker? Did the police even *try* to locate him?

It worked. The jurors couldn't come to a consensus. A hung jury was declared. Peyer walked.

District attorneys will occasionally decide that a retrial in the case of a hung jury isn't worth it. Craig Peyer could only have been so lucky. This time the DA chose to go with a new kid on the block — Paul Pfingst, an aggressive lawyer from New York, who had just made the move to the left coast.

Pfingst approached the case from a different angle than his predecessor. He learned from the previous prosecutor's mistakes, and from watching the first trial he knew the defense tactics and strategy backward and forward. Sure, there was plenty of circumstantial evidence, and he planned to make full use of it. But, more importantly, he wanted to disarm his foe before the trial even started. In hearing after hearing, Pfingst went for Grimes's throat.

Joe Cantalupe and Lisa Petrillo provide a comprehensive outline of events in their book about the Peyer case, *Badge of Betrayal*. First, Pfingst successfully argued that the mention of the so-called mystery hitchhiker should be banned. This person, Pfinsgt said, was not a suspect and was never interrogated or even seen, for that matter, by the police.

Pfingst also blocked the use of defense witnesses testifying that Peyer had actually scratched his face on the chain link fence. In the first trial, Grimes skillfully used these witnesses to cast a shadow of doubt in the jurors' minds. These people were simply repeating what Peyer had told them; none of them saw Peyer take his spill. Their testimony was hearsay, Pfingst contended.

It might be said that the DA's office won the trial in the judge's chambers. In the end, the jury handed in their verdict: guilty of murder in the second degree. Craig Peyer was sentenced to twenty-five to life.

For over two decades, Craig Peyer has maintained his innocence from behind the bars of California's Men's Colony medium-security prison. In 2004, he had a chance to prove that innocence. California prosecutors approached him with an offer they thought he couldn't refuse. DNA technology had come a long way in the past twenty years, and they wanted to test his DNA to see if it was an exact match to the blood found on Cara Knott's boots (not just the same type). Peyer refused to take the test. When asked why by his parole board, he stood mute.

Today, Joyce Knott lives alone. Fifteen years after losing her daughter, she lost her husband. Sam Knott died of a heart attack while driving in his car in 2001, a few hundred feet from the spot where Cara was murdered. He had just been picking up trash at a memorial park set up in Cara's honor. He was only sixty-three years old.

EIGHTEEN

L&O: SVU: ("Web," Season 7) A teenager sells photos of himself, naked, to pedophiles on the Internet.

TRUE STORY: Teenager Justin Berry set up his own pornographic website featuring erotic images and video of himself. Pedophiles paid for Berry to perform sex acts on a live webcam.

Justin Berry was nervous. He'd been in the spotlight before but this audience was different. The men and women before him were some of Washington's most influential power brokers. They were here in the House Subcommittee on Oversight and Investigations for a panel entitled "Sexual Exploitation of Children Over the Internet." Justin Berry was the star attraction. The nineteen-year-old had come forward to share his own sordid, terrible tale of sexual exploitation.

He leaned in toward the microphone and in a soft voice recounted the five years he spent performing sex acts online for money. A hushed silence fell over the room as Justin spoke about his customers — online pedophiles who manipulated and seduced children into stripping and performing sex acts in front of webcams around the country. Justin said there were many children who were currently being preyed on. "My experience is not as isolated as you might hope," he said.[1]

Justin told the panel he was frustrated that the government was not doing more to stop child exploitation. He had given the government a list of 1,500 alleged pedophiles — former subscribers of his various websites. Yet only two men had been arrested. Justin felt the government was dragging its feet. His testimony had been emotionally draining. He was grateful that his benefactor, Kurt Eichenwald, was there to support him.

Just a year earlier, in 2005, Justin Berry's life had been spiraling out of control. He was eighteen, addicted to cocaine, and starring in his own online porno show. For a monthly fee of thirty-five dollars, subscribers to mexicofriends.com could log on and watch Justin having sex, in real time, with a number of Mexican prostitutes. Subscribers with more money and more specific tastes had the option of requesting special performances. For the right price, Justin would do just about anything — as long as it was on camera that is. He liked to think of the men who paid to watch him as fans, not johns. In the past year, Justin had expanded his business to include webcam feeds of other young men.

Justin was leery about a stranger who contacted him and asked a lot of questions. The man claimed to be a music producer; Justin suspected he might be a cop trying to set him up. Still, when the man asked if they could meet, Justin agreed. As it turned out, Justin's new friend wasn't a producer or a policeman; he was a reporter for the *New York Times* named Kurt Eichenwald who had been investigating a story on Internet pornography fraud when he came across mexicofriends.com. Eichenwald found the sexual content disturbing but he was most concerned about the models featured on the site. They looked young, very young. Eichenwald believed he had uncovered a cache of child pornography.

The reporter and the online porn star met in California and struck up a friendship. Justin was candid with Eichenwald, answering all of the reporter's questions about his life and his Web business. Justin said he had been seduced into the world of online pornography when he was thirteen years old. At the time, he was living in Bakersfield, California, with his mother and sister; his father — who Justin claimed had once bashed his head into a wall — had moved to Mexico. Justin was something of a loner, a shy boy who preferred computers to the surfboards preferred by his peers. When he learned that the Internet service provider Earthlink was offering free webcams to new customers, Justin eagerly signed up for the freebie.

He quickly hooked the webcam up to his computer and joined a social networking site online. Justin made friends immediately — but they weren't the friends he had expected. The first e-mail he received was from an older man who complimented him on his looks. Justin shrugged it off. Then one day, another man offered him fifty dollars to take his shirt off in front of the webcam. Justin felt strange but obliged. It was easy money.

He was amazed that men were willing to pay to watch him strip online. Justin's online popularity grew; soon, he was fielding requests from dozens of fans. They would log on to the site and ask him to perform sexual acts in front of the camera. In lieu of cash, the men promised to purchase items from a "wish list" Justin set up on Amazon-.com.

By the time he was sixteen, Justin was running his own profitable Internet porn site with himself as the star attraction. He accepted credit card payments for his online performances; a live, on-command masturbation session cost several hundred dollars. He had a few different business partners — men who offered advice on running a profitable website, and who also molested him in various hotel rooms around the country. One of Justin's business partners set the teen up in an apartment close to the Berry home so Justin could carry on his Web business in private.

The teenager spent his profits on drugs and a new hobby, street racing. Business was booming. But it was only a matter of time before his secret was revealed. Then one day, a classmate found photos of a very nimble Justin performing fellatio on himself. The photos made the rounds at school and Justin became a pariah. He left California and went to live with his father in Mexico.

With his father as a business partner, Justin opened up a new website: mexico friends.com. The site featured videos of Justin having sex with prostitutes procured by his father. It was this site that had caught reporter Kurt Eichenwald's attention.

Kurt Eichenwald had inadvertently stumbled upon a great story — one every reporter dreams of. But he was conflicted. As a reporter, he had a responsibility to remain objective and aloof from his subjects. As a human being, Eichenwald felt he had a moral responsibility to do what he could to save a troubled young man from self-destructing. Eichenwald knew that Justin was "supposed to be a porn star." In the end, the reporter split the difference — writing the story and befriending his subject. It was a decision for which he would be both lauded and criticized.

At Eichenwald's request, Justin gave him a crash course in running an Internet porn site. He showed him computer logs, web-cam footage, e-mail exchanges with customers, and credit card receipts. Justin told Eichenwald that the Internet was populated by pedophiles trolling for innocent children. What's more, Justin said he wasn't the only kid who'd been lured into the world of pornography. There were many other young-sters peddling sex online for money. Sheepishly, he also admitted that he had harassed a few of his competitors and ran at least one out of business by threatening to tell the boy's parents what their son was doing in his spare time.

Eichenwald urged Justin to cooperate with the government to help rescue these exploited children, and catch the pedophiles who preyed on them. The reporter relocated Justin to Washington, DC, and put him in touch with an attorney who would facilitate the young man's dealings with the Justice Department. Justin was given immunity in exchange for his cooperation with the government. He would be free from prosecution for any illegal activities associated with the running of his websites. Justin gave federal agents a list of 1,500 names, alleged pedophiles who subscribed to his website. He also offered up information about the children he said were currently running websites of their own.

On December 19, 2006, the *New York Times* ran Eichenwald's story about Justin Berry. In the article, "Through His Webcam, a Boy Joins a Sordid Online World," Justin is portrayed as an innocent led astray by adult predators. His downfall is attributed to the men who paid to watch him undress and perform for the camera. Readers get a disturbing glimpse into the child pornography industry. We follow Justin as he matures from a naive thirteen-year-old into a savvy businessman who runs his own profitable pay-for-view website and refers to himself as a "cam-whore."

It's a disturbing story, made all the more so by the fact that young Justin grows up to become a predator himself, encouraging other minors to perform for his website, and eventually molesting a minor. Yet Eichenwald's friendship with Justin appears to have affected his objectivity about the young man's transformation; he devotes just a few sentences of his feature-length article to it: "Justin created a new Web site, justinfriends .com, featuring performances by him and other boys he helped recruit. But as videos featuring other minors appeared on his site, Justin felt torn, knowing that these adolescents were on the path that had hurt him so badly. Justin was now 18, a legal adult. He had crossed the line from underage victim to adult perpetrator."[2]

Eichenwald goes on to paint a frightening image of the Internet. "Justin's dark coming-of-age story is a collateral effect of recent technological advances," he writes. "Minors, often under the online tutelage of adults, are opening for-pay pornography services featuring their own images sent onto the Internet by inexpensive Webcams. And they perform in the privacy of home, while parents are nearby, beyond their children's closed bedroom doors."[3]

The webcam, states Eichenwald, "transformed online pornography the way the automobile changed transportation. Not long ago, adults who were sexually attracted to children were largely isolated from one another. But the Internet has created a virtual community where they can readily communicate and reinforce their feelings."[4]

The response to the article was overwhelming. The public was outraged to learn that pedophiles had found a new way to victimize children. Eichenwald received accolades for his reporting as well as a Payne Award for Ethics in Journalism. "The *New York Times* saved Justin as well as telling his story," Alex Jones declared on National Public Radio. Jones, the director of Harvard's Shorenstein Center on the Press, Politics and Public Policy praised Eichenwald for saving "a lot of other Justins by telling that story. The *Times* did its journalistic duty with distinction, but in this special situation, Eichenwald and the *Times* also had a human responsibility and they met that too."[5]

But not everyone was applauding the efforts of Eichenwald and the *Times.* Columnist Jack Shafer had mixed feelings about the story. "While I admire Eichenwald's journalistic enterprise and thoroughness, I'm astonished at how he loses control of his 6,500-word investigation when he appears two-thirds through it to serve not as a reporter but as the legal advocate and protector of the now 19-year-old Berry," Shafer wrote on Slate.com.[6]

Justin and Eichenwald appeared on the Oprah Winfrey and Larry King shows. Justin's story was recounted in numerous newspapers and magazines and he became something of a tragic media darling. But was Justin's story what it appeared to be? Was he a victim or a skilled teenage opportunist?

Numerous discrepancies in Justin's story were uncovered after the *Times* article was published, most concerning his chronology of the events he described. Justin claimed to have set up an online PayPal account to accept credit card payments when he was thirteen but records show that he was actually sixteen. His first subscriber signed up when Justin was seventeen, not thirteen as he claimed. These discrepancies shed doubt on Justin's official story. A thirteen-year-old is generally more vulnerable than a sixteen-year-old.

Called to testify against a man accused of molesting him, Justin was unable to recall specific events, or how old he had been during the alleged crimes. Justin turned to the judge at one point and asked him quizzically, "How old was I?"

"Justin Berry had his first day in front of a court today and it seems the whole thing got him confused . . . We have repeatedly questioned the veracity of Berry's allegations and the many inconsistencies in his timelines, but it seems that he is having trouble remembering now too," reported the online webzine GenerationQ.net. "Age is the biggest factor in this case and one that affects Justin Berry the most. Was he underage? Was he legal age? That seems to change depending on what he is talking about."[7]

Not surprisingly, the 1,500 alleged pedophiles who had subscribed to Justin's website cried foul. They claimed that they had paid for a legal, albeit pornographic, service. As it turns out, the site even featured a disclaimer stating, "This site contains no child pornography or any other illegal content. This site contains nudity and gay erotica, all models are eighteen years of age or older."[8] What's more, federal agents found that just one minor had appeared on mexicofriends.com. That boy was the thirteen-year-old that Justin had molested online.

And what of Kurt Eichenwald? Was he a hero? Or was he a dupe who'd been taken for a ride by a streetwise teenager? Eichenwald was criticized for accepting most of what Justin Berry told him at face value, and for becoming part of the story. In a letter to the reporter, Jack Shafer contends, "Berry gets off fairly free in your account. The way you skate over the last two years of his life makes me think something important has been left out. Also, he appears to have known enough about right and wrong to exit the child-porn trade for a year before re-entering as an adult participant on the business side. Is he really deserving of his immunity?"[9]

Reporter Jim D'Entremont was Eichenwald's harshest critic, labeling the article as "broadsheet journalism marinated in tabloid ideas." He asked, "How credible are Justin's sometimes unverifiable statements? To what extent was Justin, who had made a career out of catering to men's fantasies, cravings, and projections, telling Eichenwald just what he wanted to hear? Did Justin, confronted with an authority figure who had cast himself in the dual role of savior and cop, cooperate mainly out of fear of prosecution? Was Justin, as the brother of a man he turned over to the FBI has suggested, simply looking for a 'get out of jail free card'?"[10]

Based on Justin's information, the feds arrested two of his former business partners: Greg Mitchel, a thirty-eight-year-old from Virginia, and a twenty-four-year-old Nashville resident named Tim Richards. Dozens more men were investigated. Mitchel pleaded guilty to child pornography charges. Richards maintains his innocence and of this writing is awaiting trial. Agents were unable to locate the children Justin said were being exploited.

Experts report that 20,000 images of child pornography are posted on the Internet every week. The proliferation of home computers and cheap Internet access has made child pornography a $3 million dollar industry.

NINETEEN

<u>L&O: SVU:</u> ("Uncivilized," Season 1) A known pedophile is suspected of killing a young boy in the park. The real killers turn out to be two young men who killed for the thrill of it.

TRUE STORY: The famous Leopold and Loeb case. Two privileged young men murdered a child simply to see if they could get away with the "perfect crime."

In 1924, fourteen-year-old Bobby Franks was abducted and murdered on his way home from school. The killing was heinous but it was the motive behind it and the identities of the perpetrators that led the press to dub the case the crime of the twentieth century. The perpetrators were represented by Clarence Darrow, the brilliant lawyer who one year later would defend teacher John Scopes in the famous

Scopes Monkey Trial.

Nathan Leopold and Richard Loeb were the scions of two wealthy, prominent Chicago families. Both men led lives of privilege, with chauffeurs, servants, and assistants catering to their every need. "Babe," as Leopold was known, was nineteen and attending law school at the University of Chicago. He possessed a brilliant mind, and was fluent in five languages. He was also an avid bird watcher and recognized expert on American songbirds. Loeb, whom everyone called "Dickie," was eighteen years old, a gifted student, and the youngest person ever to have graduated from the University of Michigan.

Leopold and Loeb were fifteen and fourteen, respectively, when they first met. For the next few years, the two were nearly inseparable. That all changed when they went away to college in Ann Arbor and rumors circulated on campus that they were lovers. Homosexuality was scandalous in Chicago in the 1920s; to dispel the rumors, the pair made a point of always bringing along another friend when they were out in public together. Leopold and Loeb arranged clandestine meetings after hours. Free from prying eyes, they would drink and talk for hours about their favorite topics: morality, crime, and philosophy. Babe was fascinated by the philosophy of Friedrich Nietzsche. He was particularly drawn to Nietzsche's concept of the "superman." An intellectually and physically superior being, the superman lives by his own code of ethics. This being is above reproach and not beholden to conventional morality. The superman "has an obligation only to his equals," Nietzsche wrote. What's more, "he may act to all of lower rank and all that are foreign as he pleases." Leopold found this notion very appealing. An egotist, he had long viewed himself as special and believed his superior intellect elevated him above the rest of society. He thought of himself as a superior being, but considered the beautiful, charming, fiercely loyal Loeb to be the real embodiment of Nietzsche's superman.

Loeb had mixed feelings about being put on such a pedestal. Although he came across as cocky and arrogant, he was secretly insecure about his intellect and self-worth. He was also more interested in detective stories and crime than in any philosophy. Loeb had been committing petty crimes since he was a child. Breaking the law was thrilling for him; he felt no remorse. Eventually, he recruited his best friend Nathan to join him in his criminal escapades. For Le-

Best friends and sons of privilege, Nathan Leopold and Richard Loeb dreamed of committing "the perfect murder."

opold, the crimes were a way to get closer to Loeb, with whom he was deeply in love. The two reached an agreement they called the "compact." In exchange for aiding and abetting Loeb in his illegal activities, Leopold would be allowed to take sexual liberties with his usually reticent, heterosexual-leaning friend.

At first, the crimes were relatively minor; the duo made harassing phone calls to their college professors and vandalized property. But soon, Loeb seduced Leopold into committing arson and burglary. They found their secret life thrilling. "If only our friends knew we had done this," Loeb often said.

The two became increasingly preoccupied with planning and committing crimes. One of their favorite hobbies was planning the hypothetical "perfect crime." They spent months talking about what that crime would be, finally settling on kidnapping for ransom. To avoid getting caught, they would kill the victim. Loeb grew bored with talking — he wanted to put the plan into action. Leopold was less anxious to go through with it but he knew that the reward for his participation would be sex of some sort with Loeb. Once he acquiesced, Leopold devoted all his energies to the project. The brilliant mind that had earned him so many accolades in the past was now occupied with the minutia of comitting murder. The killing was the least complicated part of their plan; the real challenge was in the details — composing the ransom note, establishing a fake identity to rent a car, scouting locations for the ransom to be dropped off, purchasing rope and hydrochloric acid, choosing an appropriate place to dispose of the body, perfecting their alibis. The only thing they left up to chance was the victim. They planned to bring him to Wolf Lake, an area Leopold used for bird watching. There,

Victim Bobby Franks lived near the Loeb family. The fourteen-year-old was a classmate of Richard's younger brother and had been to the Loeb's mansion.

they would strangle him with the rope; Leopold would pull on one end, Loeb would pull on the other so that they would both be equally culpable for the murder.

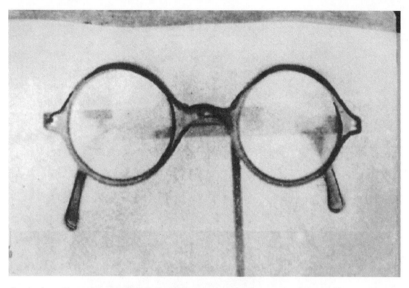

Ironically, Leopold had stopped wearing glasses a few months before the murder. He had stashed the glasses in his suit pocket and forgotten about them. They were found at the crime scene and traced back to him.

On the afternoon of May 21, 1924, Leopold and Loeb went trolling for a victim. They drove the rental car to a local boys' school. Using Nathan's bird watching binoculars, they scanned the grounds for an appropriate victim. Loeb's younger brother attended the all-boys school and Loeb recognized a few familiar faces. A boy named John caught his eye but slipped away before they could make contact with him. The next boy they spotted was Bobby Franks. Fourteen-year-old Franks lived

Legendary attorney Clarence Darrow was hired to represent Leopold and Loeb. A fierce opponent of the death penalty, Darrow was determined to save his clients from the gallows.

across the street from the Loeb family and occasionally played tennis on their court. Loeb lured Franks into the car by telling him he wanted to talk to him about a tennis racquet he was considering buying. Franks got into the passenger seat; Loeb sat behind the boy in the backseat, Leopold was in the driver's seat. The three chatted as Leopold drove around the block. Without warning, Franks was hit over the head with a chisel. To stop him from crying out, a rag was stuffed into his mouth.

They pulled Bobby Franks into the backseat and covered him with a blanket. The

Their lives spared, Nathan Leopold and Richard Loeb were sentenced to life plus ninety-nine years in prison. The judge recommended that they not be considered for parole.

duo planned to get rid of the boy after the sun set. To pass the time, they stopped at a roadside stand for sandwiches and root beer. After their meal, they drove to the culvert. Franks, they discovered, was already dead, thwarting their plan to strangle him and share in his murder. They stripped the body and poured acid on the face and genitals to prevent identification (Franks, like his killers, was Jewish and circumcised;

at the time circumcision was uncommon among gentiles). The chisel and the victim's shoes and belt were tossed out onto a deserted road. They burned the rest of Franks's clothing.

From a pay phone, Loeb called the Franks house posing as "George Johnson." He informed Mrs. Franks that he had kidnapped her son and would contact her the next day with his ransom demands. The Franks family received the ransom note the next morning. It read, in part:

Dear Sir:
As you no doubt know by this time, your son has been kidnapped. Allow us to assure you that he is at present well and safe. You need fear no physical harm for him, provided you live up carefully to the following instructions and to such others as you will receive by future communications. Should you, however, disobey any of our instructions, even slightly, his death will be the penalty.

Bobby's father, Jacob Franks, was ordered to place $10,000 in old bills in a cigar box and await further instructions. Several hours later George Johnson — this time Leopold — called to tell Franks he was sending a yellow cab to pick him up. Franks was to have the cab driver take him to the drugstore on 1465 East Sixty-third Street. Johnson promised to phone Franks there with information on where to drop off the ransom. Franks was flustered, and in the heat of the moment, forgot the address of the drugstore. As the cab pulled up outside, another call came in for the Franks. It was a family friend calling to report that a boy had been found dead near the lake.

The news traveled fast. By afternoon, the local papers had reported on the story. Leopold and Loeb began to fear their plan had gone awry. They decided to phone the drugstore anyway, just in case Jacob Franks was there. He was not. They didn't know it yet, but the body had already been identified as Bobby Franks.

The city coroner determined that Bobby died from suffocation. He had also been struck on the head with a blunt instrument. Defense wounds on the body indicated that he struggled with his killer. His face and genitals had been disfigured by some kind of acid. There was no evidence of sexual abuse.

Police experts examined the ransom note. It had been written in perfect English, signifying intelligence — "a dangerous attribute in a criminal," declared the coroner.[1] Suspicion fell first on Bobby's schoolteachers. However, they were cleared after providing airtight alibis.

Loeb talked incessantly about the murder to anyone who would listen. Two days after Bobby's body was found, Loeb recruited a few of his fraternity brothers to join him on a hunt to find the unnamed drugstore the killer had instructed Jacob Franks to go to. They visited several stores in the area before settling on the Van de Bogert & Ross drugstore. When questioned, the druggist confirmed that a call had, in fact, come in for a Mr. Franks on May 21. Loeb was barely able to contain his excitement. Someone asked him if he knew who killed the Franks boy. Loeb jokingly replied that he was the killer. "If I were going to murder anybody, I would murder just such a cocky little son of a bitch as Bobby Franks," he said.[2]

The police launched an intensive investigation into Franks's murder. At the crime scene, they found a pair of horn-rimmed glasses. The glasses were commonplace but sported a rare spring hinge that had been sold to just three people in the area. Nathan Leopold was one of them.

Initially, police did not consider Leopold a suspect. A game warden at Wolf Lake told them that Leopold often visited the area to observe the local birds. The police visited Leopold at his house to inquire about the glasses, and to ask if he noticed anything out of the ordinary the last time he was at Wolf Lake. Leopold denied having lost his glasses but when he could not produce them, admitted that the glasses were probably his. He told police that he had fallen down the last time he was bird watching in that area; the glasses must have inadvertently slipped out of his pocket. They asked him to demonstrate how he fell. Leopold put the glasses in his pocket and attempted to recreate his fall. He tried several times and each time, the glasses stayed put in his pocket. This aroused the officers' suspicion. They questioned Leopold about his whereabouts the day Bobby Franks was murdered. He told them he had spent the day with his friend Richard Loeb. Leopold granted them permission to search the house. The officers hoped to find the typewriter used to draft the ransom note. They found a typewriter but it was not the one they were looking for.

The police began to strongly suspect Nathan Leopold was involved in the Franks murder. They wanted to see if Richard Loeb would confirm his alibi. Because of Leopold and Loeb's social standing in the community, the police handled the two young men with kid gloves. They were taken to the La Salle Hotel to be interviewed separately. Their stories were similar: they both claimed to have spent the day of the murder cruising around in Leopold's car, having dinner, and later, hanging out with two girls. State's Attorney Robert Crowe, who was handling the case, believed the duo was innocent. The next day, he treated them to dinner.

Armchair detectives and reporters alike scrambled to solve the case and collect the $5,000 reward offered by the Franks family. Reporters tracked the ransom typewriter down; it belonged to Leopold's college study group. Members of the group revealed that Leopold recently took the portable typewriter home with him. Thinking he was helping the duo, Leopold's chauffeur contacted the police and told them that Leopold's car had been in the garage all day. Without a car, he insisted, the young men could not have committed the crime. Leopold and Loeb had both said they had been out in Leopold's car; their alibi was blown. They were questioned again. Faced with the new evidence against them, the duo confessed.

In their confessions, each young man

blamed the other for the actual murder. The two friends who dreamed about carrying out the perfect crime quickly became the perfect witnesses — for the prosecution. They helped the police retrieve the chisel and Bobby Franks's shoes. "We have the most conclusive evidence I've ever seen in a criminal case," prosecutor Crowe announced to the press.[3]

Leopold and Loeb seemed oblivious to the dire situation they were in, chatting nonchalantly about the crime to police, prosecutors, and the press. Neither young man expressed remorse; their arrogance and lack of affect shocked the public. The murder "was just an experiment" Leopold told a reporter. "It is as easy for us to justify as an entomologist in impaling a beetle on a pin."[4] Loeb informed the police chief, "This thing will be the making of me. I'll spend a few years in jail and I'll be released. I'll come out to a new life."[5]

The two friends were indicted for multiple counts of murder and kidnapping. State's Attorney Crowe announced that he would seek the death penalty for both men. The defendants' families hired Clarence Darrow to represent them. Crowe and the public assumed Darrow would try to win an acquittal by pleading the boys not guilty by reason of insanity. They were wrong. He had Leopold and Loeb plead guilty. Given the public sentiment for the defendants, Darrow wanted to avoid a jury trial. He knew a jury would be more likely than a judge to send the defendants to the gallows. Since the defendants admitted their guilt, the case would be heard and decided by a judge.

Some three hundred people attended the sentencing hearing. The hearing was similar to a trial, except that the defendants' guilt had already been established. In spite of that fact, State's Attorney Crowe proceeded as if Leopold and Loeb had pleaded not guilty, calling more than one hundred witnesses to the stand to prove their guilt.

The crux of the defense's strategy was that the defendants, although sane, were mentally diseased. Darrow had three prominent forensic psychiatrists (known as alienists at the time) testify about the mental development and psychological makeup of the defendants. He hoped that their testimony would mitigate the heinousness of the crime and convince the judge to spare the defendants' lives.

The hearing was the first time psychiatric testimony formed the basis of a defense. Believing the defense was pulling a fast one and trying to admit evidence that the defendants were insane, Crowe objected. "Any suggestions of insanity with a plea of guilty is just as out of order as an alibi," he complained. "They pleaded guilty. Now they can't come around and say, 'But we're really insane.' If they are, a jury must decide." Darrow countered, "I don't believe there is a judge in Cook County that would not take into consideration the mental status of any man before they sentence him to death." The psychiatric testimony was admitted.

The three defense psychiatrists had spent many days interviewing Nathan Leopold and Richard Loeb. All three had been impressed by the defendants' high intellects and shocked by their apparent lack of affect. (By today's standards, both Leopold and Loeb would be categorized as sociopaths.) The psychiatrists testified at length about their peculiar relationship — a relationship Darrow described as "weird and impossible." The young men were drawn to one another, and yet each confessed to having had, on occasion, considered killing the other.

Jointly, they were a case of *folie a deux* — the insanity of two. According to Dr. William White, Loeb "needed an audience," and Leopold was that audience. White believed that on his own, each defendant was incapable of murder. Together, they were explosive. Dr. Gluck testified that the Franks murder was "the inevitable outcome of this curious coming together of two pathologically disordered personalities, each of whom brought into the relationship a phase of their personality which made their contemplation and the execution of this crime possible."[6]

The doctors said that Loeb "showed no remorse, no regret, no compassion for the people involved in the situation." As for Leopold, he had told one of the psychiatrists, "making up my mind about whether or not to commit murder was practically the same as making up my mind whether or not I should eat pie for supper, whether it would give me pleasure or not."[7] Darrow contended that this lack of compassion was evidence of the defendants' diseased and disturbed minds. For Crowe, it was more proof that they deserved to hang.

Both Darrow and Crowe delivered impassioned, extended summations. Darrow's closing argument lasted twelve hours and would go down in history as one of the most moving speeches ever delivered in a courtroom. He blamed the murder on nature, on the defendants' youth and mental disease.

"Why did they kill Bobby Franks? Not for money. Not for spite. Not for hate. They killed him as they might kill a spider or a fly, for the experience. They killed him because they were made that way. Because somewhere in the infinite processes that go into the making up of the boy or the man something slipped, and those unfortunate lads sit here hated, despised outcasts, with the community shouting for their blood," Darrow said.

"[W]hatever madness and hate and frenzy must do to the human mind, there is not a single person who reasons who can believe that one of these acts was the act of men, of brains that were not diseased. There is no other explanation for it. And had it not been for the wealth and the weirdness and the notoriety, they would have been taken care of, instead of the statement demanding that this court take the last pound of flesh and the last drop of blood from two irresponsible lads . . . Your honor, if these boys hang, you must do it. There can be no division of responsibility here. You can never explain that the rest overpowered you. It must be by your deliberate, cool, premeditated act, without a chance to shift responsibility. It was not a kindness to you. We placed this responsibility on your shoulders because we were mindful of the rights of our clients, and were mindful of the unhappy families who have done no wrong."

Crowe argued that the defendants should be put to death. He criticized Darrow for sympathizing with the killers and not the victim. "When we get all through, Mr. Darrow says that Your Honor ought to be merciful and finally, and that is his concluding defense, he appeals to your heart and your sympathy and not to your mind or your conscience. Robert Franks had a right to live. He had a right to the society of his family and his friends and they had a right to his society," he said. "I believe that the facts and circumstances proved in this case demonstrate that a crime has been committed by these two defendants, and that no other punishment except the extreme penalty of the law will fit it; and I leave the case with you on behalf of the State of Illinois, and I ask Your Honor in the language of Holy Writ to 'Execute justice and righteousness in the land.' "

Judge John Caverly had a reputation for being lenient on youthful offenders. The age of the defendants weighed heavily in his decision. The public and prosecution wanted the young men hanged. Nevertheless, the judge declined to send Leopold and

The NYPD Movie/TV Unit

Talk to any NYPD cop and he'll tell you that the job is not as glamorous as it appears to be on TV — that is, if he doesn't work in the NYPD Movie/TV Unit. In 1966, the New York City Police Department established the world's first such unit to help directors film on the city streets while ensuring the public is inconvenienced as little as possible. In a city as bustling as New York, even a three-second take of a building's exterior requires traffic control. The Movie/TV Unit even allows directors to use uniformed cops assigned to the scene to be used as "atmosphere," free of charge. Officers also oversee stunts, the use of child actors, prop weapons, and staged criminal acts.

Movie and TV producers bring an estimated $5 billion per year into the city, so it pays to have such a unit. And yes, the men and women in the Movie/TV unit are real cops.

Loeb to the gallows. He sentenced them each to life plus ninety-nine years in prison and recommended that they not be considered for parole. "To the offenders, particularly of the type they are, the prolonged years of confinement may well be the severest form of retribution and expiation," Caverly said.[8]

Richard Loeb and Nathan Leopold were housed in Joliet Prison. Loeb died in 1936 after being attacked with a razor by another inmate. Leopold remained by Loeb's bedside as he lay dying and later washed the blood from Loeb's body. "[A]s strange as it sounds, he had been my best pal," Leopold wrote in his autobiography *Life Plus 99 Years.* "In one sense, he was also the greatest enemy I ever had. For my friendship with him cost me — my life. It was he who had originated the idea of committing the crime, he who had planned it, he who had largely carried it out." Leopold was released in 1958 and moved to Puerto Rico. He died from a heart attack in 1971.

TWENTY

L&O SVU: ("Fault," Season 7) A released sex offender kidnaps two kids and murders their parents.

TRUE STORY: Class III pedophile Joseph Duncan is accused of stalking and murdering members of the Groene family to abduct eight-year-old Shasta and nine-year-old Dylan. He allegedly killed Dylan soon after, and brought Shasta back to her hometown.

Many people would consider the home of Brenda Groene to be "in the middle of nowhere." The closest city, Coeur d'Alene, Idaho, is about ten miles to the north. With a population of about fifty thousand, Coeur d'Alene is the biggest city in Northern Idaho. To the west is Coeur d'Alene Lake, and to the east and south stretch hundreds of square miles of wilderness. The entire region of Northern Idaho is 80 percent forested — sheer heaven for outdoorsmen. The forest is filled with elk, caribou, cougars, bears, and just about any other mammal you can point a gun at and shoot. The area is so pristine, it's a favorite winter nesting ground of bald eagles migrating south from Alaska and Canada.

Like most guys in Northern Idaho, Brenda's boyfriend Mark McKenzie was an avid hunter and fisherman. When he wasn't at Spokane Stainless Products, where he had worked his way up from stainless sink installer to manager, Mark liked to bring Brenda's younger children, Dylan and Shasta, to nearby streams and catch crawfish. After school and on weekends, he would take her older son, thirteen-year-old Slade, into the forest and teach him the art of hunting elk and deer — tracking, stalking, and shooting.

But Brenda Groene and her family didn't quite live in the middle of nowhere. Her small gray cinderblock house was situated on Frontage Road, near Interstate 90, trafficked by people commuting to their jobs in Coeur d'Alene or heading east to Montana. The house was so close to the Interstate that drivers could easily see it from the road. Shasta and Dylan liked to stand at the side of the road and pump their arms up and down to make passing truck drivers blow their horns.

The house was also easy to get to. Brenda and Mark had lots of friends and family members, who would often pull off the Interstate for a quick visit. On the night of May 15, 2005, a Sunday, they had a small party, a barbecue in the backyard. Brenda, who was forty years old, and Mark, thirty-seven, liked to drink with their friends and occasionally smoke some pot. The party wasn't exactly a gathering of angels. At least one of their friends, Robert Roy Lutner, had a criminal record that included drug possession and domestic battery, and he had just served a second sentence for fraud: he had lied about his unemployment status and got caught. Brenda herself once served time for possession of marijuana paraphernalia, and one of her older sons was arrested for grand theft auto (which was later dismissed in a plea deal.)[1] But in the world of criminal justice, it was all fairly innocuous stuff. None of these people were violent criminals by any stretch of the imagination. They just wanted to extend the weekend as long as they could by drinking some beer and laughing with friends.

As it got later and everyone accepted the

fact that the workweek was upon them, people got into their cars or onto their motorcycles and pulled out of the driveway, taking the back roads toward the town of Wolf Lodge or getting on the Interstate heading in the direction of Coeur d'Alene. The small house was peaceful and still, as Brenda and Mark kicked back and relaxed. The only sound was the occasional car or truck speeding by on the freeway.

The next day, the Groene's neighbor Bob Hollingsworth stopped by the house. He owed Slade ten dollars for mowing his lawn and he wanted to pay him. He pulled up in his car and honked his horn. No one came out. That's strange, Hollingsworth thought. They always come outside when they hear the horn. He got out of the car and walked to the rear of the house. The back door was open, and there was blood all over it. The Groene's dog was barking inside the house. Hollingsworth stood there for a moment, frozen in horror. Then he ran to his car, drove home, and called the police.

Hours later, the property was sealed off and Kootenai County police were investigating one of the most ghastly murder scenes they had ever witnessed. The bodies of Brenda and Slade Groene were lying in the

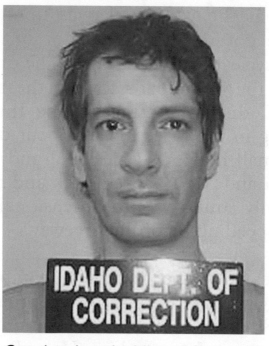

Convicted pedophile, vicious murderer, and wily manipulator of the legal system, Joseph Duncan killed three people in order to abduct and rape two children, Shasta and Dylan Groene. He later killed Dylan and then brought Shasta back to her hometown of Coeur d' Alene, Idaho.

kitchen in pools of blood with their hands tied behind their backs and tape covering their mouths. Mark McKenzie was dead in the living room, also with his hands tied. Each of them had been killed by repeated blows to the head.

Shasta and Dylan were gone.

Investigators had to simultaneously find out who committed the murders and locate the children who, they believed, were still alive. Learning the identity of the killer would surely help them find the kids, but murder investigations are often painfully slow processes. And considering that they had no leads at all, they just didn't have time. The FBI, Idaho State Police, and Kootenai County investigators began working double overtime on the case. The Groene children's father, Steve Groene, who had joint custody of the kids, went on television and implored the abductor to drop Shasta and Dylan off at a highway rest area. At this point, he didn't care about the kidnapper, he just wanted his kids back.

For the police, the case was a dead end. They had to consider any possibility, including the company Brenda and Mark kept. Autopsies revealed the presence of drugs in their blood. Rumors spread that the Mexican Mafia was involved. Was this a gang murder? Could it have been a drug-related hit? Not likely, thought the police. "We've busted a lot of drug labs," said Kootenai County Sheriff Rocky Watson. "They don't mow their lawns and plant flowers, and [Brenda Groene] did."[2]

Fingerprints

In the mid-nineteenth century, it was proven that fingerprints are unique to every person and that they don't change with age. The first fingerprint classification and identification systems were developed later in the century. There are only three main patterns of fingerprints: loops, series of curves that fold back on themselves; whorls, concentric circles; and arches, which look like sine waves stacked upon each other. So it's not the general patterns that discern one fingerprint from another, but rather the points where a line in the pattern ends (ridge ending) or splits into two (bifurcation).

Until relatively recently, the standard fingerprinting technique was to ink each finger and make an impression on paper. When they needed to find a match, fingerprint experts would compare two fingerprints to find identical ridge endings and bifurcations. However, more and more police precincts are trading in their ink pads for digital scanners. Suspects' fingers are scanned by a computer, automatically entered into a database, and sent through the system to be paired with similar prints. Experts will then take a closer look to make exact matches.

Hopes were temporarily raised when police began questioning a "person of interest": Robert Roy Lutner, who had visited the house that day and had gone upstairs alone with Brenda for a few minutes.[3] But after seven hours of interrogation, he was dropped as a possible suspect. Police were back where they started.

An army of law enforcement personnel and local volunteers searched the back woods near the Groene home. They knew the kids would be familiar with every nook and cranny of the woods, and it would make sense that they would have run off to hide if they had witnessed the murder of their family. That's what they hoped, anyway. The worst case scenario was that the killer or killers had taken the children.

The name Joseph Duncan is forgettable enough. It's nothing like Ted Bundy or John Wayne Gacy. But when his crimes were brought to light, the mere mention of Joseph Duncan would send chills down the spines of everyone from the northwestern segment of the United States. Either that or it would trigger spasms of rage. Or both. Like the devil himself, Joseph Duncan inspires both deathly fear and burning hatred.

A Class III pedophile, Duncan spent more of his life inside prison than out. According to him, he showed the first signs of being a sexual predator at the age of twelve, when he made a five-year-old perform oral sex on him. He never looked back. At the age of seventeen, his violent sexual deviancy landed him in prison. In Tacoma, Washington, he forced a fourteen-year-old at gunpoint to perform oral sex on him and then beat the boy with a stick and burned him with a cigarette. Duncan was sentenced to twenty years for that crime, but instead of prison he was sent to Western State Hospital for rehabilitation, where he was diagnosed as a sexual psychopath. After two years, though, doctors saw no change in Duncan, and their young patient refused to take part in the hospital's programs. Duncan was sent to prison to serve the rest of his sentence.[*]

[*]Duncan wasn't the only family member doing

At some point in the early nineties, Duncan hooked up with a pen pal — a man by the name of David Woelfert — who was quickly impressed by the young man. Woelfert wrote multiple letters to the parole board vouching for Duncan's character and asserting that Duncan was fully rehabilitated. "It is my intention to back him, support him, and help him in any way possible upon his release," he wrote in one letter. "I will 'be there' for him. I believe him. I believe *in* him."[4] Duncan also wrote to the parole board, arguing that he was a stupid kid when he committed his crime but that he had since grown up. "I am a positive person. I like me. I trust me . . . I am already a new person."[5] His mother jumped into the third ring, writing that her son had had a hard time growing up. He was spoiled by his father, wet his bed, and suffered from paratyphoid.[6]

The parole board didn't show much interest in these letters for a few years, but in 1994 Duncan was paroled. Woelfert paid Duncan's rent at a halfway house in Seattle, Duncan got a job in telemarketing, and the

---

time for rape. His stepgrandfather Earl Erskine was a convicted pedophile serving a twenty-year sentence at the same prison.

two men became close friends, according to parole records. Duncan also began seeing a married woman. He told his parole officers about the relationship, saying it was an attempt to explore his feminine traits and that she was "helping him with his transsexual fantasies."[7] It might not have been exactly what his parole officers wanted to hear, but as long as he was staying away from kids for now, they were content. The next month, Duncan stopped showing up for his parole meetings. He took off in his girlfriend's car, but was quickly caught at his sister's house in Kansas City, Missouri.[*]

Duncan was sent back to prison to serve

[*]In 1996, two siblings, eleven-year-old Sammiejo White and nine-year-old Carmen Cubias, disappeared from a Seattle motel close to where Duncan was living. Their bodies were found in 1997. Police didn't connect the murders to Duncan at the time, but he would later become a suspect. Another murder that Duncan may yet be implicated for is the case of Anthony Martinez, a ten-year-old whose body was discovered in Riverside, California. Again, the police didn't initially connect it to Duncan, but subsequent events would lead to the discovery of a partial fingerprint belonging to Duncan on the duct tape used to bind Martinez. It's believed that Duncan was in

the rest of his sentence for violating his parole. During this time he made another friend through the mail. He and a man named Dr. Richard Wacksman traded letters. Like Woelfert, Wacksman was easily taken in by Duncan. He wrote to the parole board and called Duncan's parole officer attesting to the inmate's high moral character. At first, he used his credentials as a physician, saying he was willing to take a risk for the sake of the young man. He offered to let Duncan stay at his house — with his wife and two children, eight and nine years old. Angered by the parole board's refusal, he resorted to the old "taxpayer" angle: "Why, as a taxpayer of Washington State, must I be forced to pay for this shabby service?" He accused the parole board of wasting money and controlling the lives of possible parolees just to keep their jobs.[8]

In 2000, Duncan was released from prison. He had served his entire twenty-year sentence and walked out of prison labeled a Level III sex offender. It didn't take long for him to prove that sex offenders don't often change their ways, and that prison is

---

the area at the time of the murder. (In January 2007, Duncan confessed to all three murders.)

decidedly *not* a deterrent for future crimes.

Duncan moved to Fargo and began taking computer classes at North Dakota State University. He impressed his professors with his natural penchant for computer programming. They were all shocked when their star pupil was arrested in the summer of 2004 for molesting a six-year-old boy in a school-yard.

Duncan's old friends held fast in their conviction that the Level III sex offender was fully rehabilitated. One of the prison pen pals paid for his lawyer, and another friend paid the $13,000 bail.[*] Prosecutors asked that bail be raised to $25,000, but the judge disagreed. Most likely, it wouldn't have mattered. Duncan's friends would still have covered bail, and Duncan wasn't at all concerned about saving his friends some money. The following spring, while awaiting

[*]When the news broke that Joseph Duncan had been not only released on bail but that the bail was a measly $13,000, people were outraged. But it should be noted that the judge who set the bail said that when he did, he wasn't aware of Duncan's past crimes. He said that if he were aware of Duncan's status as a Class III sex offender, he would have set bail high enough to keep him behind bars while he awaited trial.

trial, he rented a Jeep and headed west. At some point, Duncan decided to put his computer skills to work. He started an anonymous blog called the Fifth Nail. On it, he posted his thoughts about society, sex offenders, and his own inner torment. Sex offenders, he wrote, are mistreated by society. "Despite my actions, I'm not a bad person," he wrote. "I just have a disease from society, and it hurts a lot." He viewed the locking up of sex offenders as unfair and, in the long run, inefficient: "We should offer . . . amnesty for certain types of offenses if the offender agrees to treatment. That would be a very practical and effective way to reduce sex crimes dramatically."[9]

Personal messages posted under the pseudonym "Joe" describe how he is controlled by demons. "If [the demons] win then a lot of people will be badly hurt, and they've had their way before, so I know what they can do." As the days go by, he gives up hope: "[L]ast night I was on my knees begging [God], crying out loud to him, to help me. He didn't answer, again."[10]

His final blog entry was posted on May 13, 2005, two days before the murders: "I wish I could be more honest about my feelings, but those demons made sure I'd never be able to do that. I might not know if it matters, but just in case, I am working on an encrypted journal that is hundreds of times more frank than this blog could ever be (that's why I keep it encrypted). I figure in 30 years or more we will have the technology to easily crack the encryption (currently very un-crackable, PGP) and then the world will know who I really was, and what I really did, and what I really thought."[11]

It was at this point that Duncan began driving his Jeep around the countryside looking for a child to kidnap. He happened to be heading down Interstate 90 when Shasta was in the yard playing with Dylan. After seeing her, Duncan went to a sporting goods store and purchased night-vision binoculars. He spent the next three days and nights stalking the little girl and her family as if he were a hunter and they were wild game. He gathered all the information he could in order to make sure his plan would go off without a hitch. Duncan's plan, though, was not to steal the girl away in the middle of the night. The bloodbath he left behind was all part of the plan.

On that May night, he drove his rented Jeep and parked it out of sight, on Bob Hollingsworth's property. He entered the house with a shotgun and used zip ties to bind everyone in the house. He was most likely able to do this by telling everyone they would be all right if they didn't struggle. He brought Dylan and Shasta out to the backyard and told them to stay near the swing set, and then went back into the house and began bludgeoning Brenda, Slade, and Mark with a claw hammer. The children could hear Mark screaming. Then they saw Slade stumble out of the house, bleeding terribly. Shasta called him over to untie them, but he didn't seem to even hear her; Shasta would later describe Slade as appearing to be "retarded."

After ruthlessly murdering three people, Duncan calmly walked outside to the swing set. He picked up the bound children and put them in the family's truck, drove to his Jeep, and transferred them into it. He told the kids his name was "Jet."

Duncan and the children drove east to Montana. They sped down the back roads, heading deep into the forest. While dozens of people searched the woods of the Wolf Lodge area, Duncan and his two young, confused, and terrified captives were one hundred miles away, living in a makeshift camp at the end of an abandoned logging road in the Bitterroot Mountains of western Montana. Duncan built fires and cooked for Shasta and Dylan, no doubt attempting to gain their trust.

Few details are known about what exactly occurred during the period of Shasta and Dylan's six-week-long abduction. But what is known is that Duncan raped the children and made movies of it with his digital video camera. At some point, he murdered Dylan, dismembered him, and burned him. Duncan then headed back to Northern Idaho with Shasta.

On Saturday night, July 2, Nick Chapman and Chris Donlan went for some late-night coffees at Denny's in Coeur d'Alene with their girlfriends. It was about 1:40 a.m., when Chapman and Donlan went outside for a smoke. They stood under the restaurant's bright lights talking about nothing in particular when a red Jeep pulled up. Chapman saw a man and a little girl getting out of the truck. It struck Chapman as odd that a little girl would be out this late at night. When the pair walked past, Chapman knew instantly that the girl was Shasta Groene. For the past month, he had seen her face on posters and billboards everywhere. With no idea whether the man was armed and violent, or even if he had accomplices, Chapman bode his time.

Inside Denny's, Duncan and Shasta sat down in a booth. The local bars had yet to close for the night; the late-night rush wouldn't happen for a while. It was just the wait staff, the manager, and a few patrons.

Suddenly, Nick Chapman's girlfriend, Tessa Syth, got a call on her cell phone. It was a text message from Chapman. Figuring he was joking around, she was shocked by his message: "Teddybear, that little girl looks like Shasta Groene." She looked over. Nick was right. It was difficult for the gals to look inconspicuous, but they didn't want to scare Shasta's captor off.

Waitress Amber Deahn walked to Duncan's table to take their order. She and the rest of the staff had already identified the girl as Shasta Groene. As Duncan ordered onion rings and cheese fries, Deahn gave Shasta a promotional movie character mask and crayons. Shasta said "thank you" but was looking down at the table the whole time. As this was happening, the police received a call from Deahn's manager. Four minutes later, they got a call from Nick Chapman.

Within a few minutes three police cars quietly pulled into Denny's. They didn't use their sirens; they wanted no fanfare so they could take the perpetrator by surprise.

When the police entered the restaurant and approached him, Duncan didn't even try to look innocent. He was cooked.[12]

Everyone wanted a piece of Joseph Duncan. Both federal and state law enforcement officials, not to mention local and county, had spent the past six weeks pouring vast amounts of manpower and money into catching this murderer, kidnapper, and pedophile. The catalog of Duncan's crimes was so extensive that state and federal prosecutors had to decide who would try Duncan for which crimes.

It was agreed that the State of Idaho would prosecute Duncan for the murders of Mark McKenzie, Brenda Groene, and Slade Groene. Federal prosecutors would handle the kidnapping of Shasta and Dylan Groene and the subsequent murder of Dylan.

The state went first. Duncan was assigned public defender John Adams. The Class III pedophile had lived out his nine lives long ago and found precisely zero wealthy benefactors willing to hand over a fat check for attorney fees. Given the amount of evidence stacked up against Duncan, Adams's only choice was to use an insanity defense. The only problem was, it was banned in Idaho courts in 1982. Juries are forbidden to consider a defendant's mental state when judging his or her guilt or innocence. Still, Adams filed a motion to the court to repeal the ban, arguing Idaho is nearly alone in the United States[*] and first-world nations in preventing a jury from weighing insanity as a mitigating circumstance.

Adams, as he expected, got nowhere with the motion. But he made it clear that he wasn't going to go down without a fight, no matter how heinous his client may be. He had a strong reputation for working hard for his public defender's salary.

Adams's next move involved the suppression of self-incriminating statements Duncan made to police, the jail chaplain, and a social worker. He filed a motion claiming that Duncan had not been informed of his Miranda rights, and that he had asked for his attorney a number of times during an interrogation by FBI agents. Adams said he didn't get the message until later that night; when he did, he phoned the jail and provided his cell phone number, with instructions to give it to Duncan. When his client

[*]Three other states don't allow an insanity defense: Kansas, Utah, and Montana.

requested to speak to him again, Adams argued, the police told him that Adams's office was closed and then continued the interrogation, during which Duncan incriminated himself. Furthermore, Adams claimed, the admissions Duncan made to the chaplain and social worker were privileged.

The judge ruled against Adams. The chaplain had clearly informed Duncan that three subjects were not privileged — child abuse, murder, and suicide — and that Duncan spoke about them nonetheless. The social worker, too, had followed the book, telling Duncan that certain subjects were not privileged.

The statements to the police, the judge ruled, were admissible, too. Duncan had repeatedly said during his interrogations that he didn't care what the courts heard or that Adams had told him not to talk to anyone; he wanted to tell what happened.

Prosecutors wanted dearly to see Duncan executed. In order to achieve this, however, they had to do something no one should be asked to do: view the digital movies Duncan made while on the run with the Groene children. A total of five videos were pulled off of Duncan's laptop computer, totaling sixty minutes. "Three of these segments contain vile, horrific, shocking images depicting child pornography," lead prosecutor Bill Douglas said.[13]

In order to do his job as a defense lawyer, unfortunately, Adams had to view them, too. He had to see all the evidence if he were to competently defend Duncan; he couldn't just take the prosecutor at his word that the digital files contained child pornography. He argued that words like "horrific" had "absolutely no legal value whatsoever."[14]

Adams asked for a copy of the files. The prosecution refused the request, saying that the possibility of the videos leaking out and ending up on the Internet outweighed the defendant's right to possess evidence against him. They added that the videos weren't essential to Duncan's defense anyway, because the prosecution didn't plan to use them as evidence. They were trying him for murder, not soliciting child pornography.

Still, Adams insisted that the prosecution provide the copies. The federal case against Duncan would likely include child pornography, and he filed a motion to make the prosecutor's office hand over copies. More important to Adams was the possibility that the movies would be introduced to the jury during the sentencing phase, which, in the case of guilt, would likely come down to life imprisonment or death. As the defendant's attorney, he had a constitutional *right* to copies of the tapes. His client's life hung in the balance.

After weeks of arguments, motions, and court hearings, a compromise was reached. "Any place in the world, at any time, we will provide access to that material," Douglas announced.[15] Copies would not be made, but the prosecution would not introduce the movies at all, even in the sentencing phase.

Finally, the state was ready to try Joseph Duncan. A jury was chosen . . . and then the two sides agreed on a plea. Why, given the staggering amount of evidence against Duncan, would the prosecution agree to a plea? First off, the police never found the murder weapon, and crime scene personnel didn't locate any physical evidence that Duncan had ever been inside the Groene house. Shasta was the only living witness to the fact, and no one really wanted to put her on the stand.

But the most important issue involved Duncan's computer. On it was information about not only the murders of the Groenes and Mark McKenzie, but possibly other crimes Duncan committed. It turned out that Duncan was an even better whiz with computers than his professors knew. He had encrypted the copy so thoroughly that no one could break the code — not state officials, FBI computer experts, or anyone else. Duncan had the state over a barrel. Take the death penalty off the table and he'd cooperate. Douglas refused, and provided a counteroffer.

The final plea agreed to required Duncan to supply the codes to his defense attorney. The state would not sentence him until the federal case was over. The state could still request the death penalty. But the fact that Duncan had to give the codes only to his attorney (as opposed to the first plea offer, in which he would give the codes to law enforcement) meant that the defense could use the codes as leverage in the federal case. In the end, Duncan would have to cooperate with state investigators, not federal.

As we write, the case proceeds, with both the prosecution and defense requesting and receiving various postponements. In April 2007, the defense requested another postponement. Steve Groene asked the judge to consider the fact that he is dying of throat cancer and feared that he might not live to attend the trial and support Shasta through it. Nevertheless, the judge granted the defense's request. Duncan's trial is scheduled for January 2008.

TWENTY-ONE

L&O: SVU: ("Perfect," Season 4) When a fourteen-year-old Pennsylvania girl goes missing, police suspect she's been kidnapped. Eight months later, she turns up dead in New York.

TRUE STORY: Fourteen-year-old Elizabeth Smart was kidnapped from her Utah home by two Mormon fundamentalists. She was found alive nine months later.

Most prisoners make an effort to look presentable when they get up in front of a judge. If possible, they'll trade in their orange jumpsuits for jackets and ties. At the very least, they will wash their faces and comb their hair. Sometimes, though, a judge will get a suspect who's plain annoyed by the whole proceeding — and says so with his body language. He'll enter the court clearly perturbed. When the judge speaks,

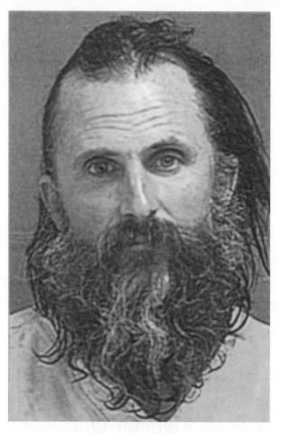

Brian David Mitchell, a Mormon fundamentalist drifter, snatched young Elizabeth Smart from her bedroom on the night of June 5, 2002, and held her captive for nine months. He was deemed unfit to stand trial in 2005.

the prisoner looks away bored, eyes half-closed, a model of passive-aggression.

Then, every once in a while, a judge is honored with a guest who makes a point *not* to make a good impression on the court. The suspect considers the court his own personal threepenny opera, a place to grandstand, shout obscenities, insult the judge, and even sing. Brian David Mitchell is one of these guys. He shows up disheveled and filthy, with a rat's nest on top of his head and a beard that doesn't look much better, and on cue, he likes to belt out his favorite medieval Christmas carol: "O Come, O Come, Emmanuel." And he never passes up the opportunity to lecture the court on the finer points of theology. "Arise and shed thyself loose of all filth and excrement and vomit!" he shouted from beneath his foot-long beard as he entered the courtroom in December 2006 for a court hearing.

Mitchell may be crazy and he may not be, but he definitely considers himself a prophet assigned by God to clean up the Mormon Church. According to him, it isn't fundamentalist enough. What makes Brian David Mitchell stand out from most other prophets roaming America's highways and byways, however, is his willingness to take extreme action in order to fulfill his prophecies, which came to a head after his abduction of a fourteen-year-old Salt Lake City girl, Elizabeth Smart.

■ ■ ■ ■

Brian David Mitchell entered the Smart family's life when Ed and Lois Smart hired him to do some odd jobs around the house. They had first seen the forty-nine-year-old preaching on a local street corner. He was ragged, dirty, and looked like he was down on his luck, so the Smarts asked him if they could pay him to do some work around the house. Mitchell said sure. He showed up one day and helped Ed repair the roof.

There was definitely something wrong with Mitchell, Ed could tell, but the preacher was polite enough and seemed to have some experience with carpentry. Ed Smart was glad he could help him out. But Mitchell was much further gone than Ed and Lois realized. They thought he was just an eccentric member of the Church of Latter Day Saints (LDS). The Smarts were LDS, too, and had seen plenty of people like Mitchell — fanatical fundamentalists who wanted to bring the church back to the nineteenth century and the days of its founder Joseph Smith, when real men had multiple wives, black people were banned from the priesthood, and everyone lived in mortal fear for their soul. At some point,

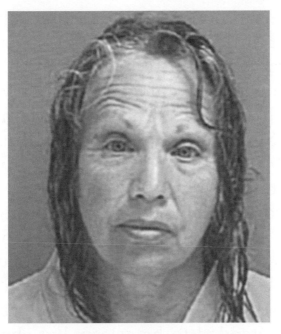

Wanda Barzee, Mitchell's accomplice, wife, and fellow fundamentalist. She too was considered incompetent to stand trial and resides at a Utah mental institution at the time of publication.

when Mitchell was helping with the roof, he must have caught a glimpse of Elizabeth and seen where her bedroom was.

On the night of June 4, 2002, Elizabeth and her family attended a ceremony at her middle school, where the teenager received two awards — one for athletics and one for academics. It was a great night. The Smarts were very proud of their daughter. They got home a little later than they expected to, and everyone went to bed. Elizabeth shared a room with her younger sister Mary Katherine; their brother Charles slept in his own room. Sometime after midnight, Brian David Mitchell (who called himself Emmanuel) arrived at the Smarts' house. Dressed all in black, he cut through the screen of the girls' bedroom window and approached Elizabeth's bed. Threatening her with a knife, he forced Elizabeth to get up. Mary Katherine, her blood running cold, pretended to be asleep, but she heard everything. She told police that the man was quiet and even polite as he led Elizabeth out of the room and out of the house. His voice sounded familiar to her, but she wasn't sure whose it sounded like. So terrified was Mary Katherine, that she stayed in bed silent until 4:00 a.m. Then she ran into her parents' room and told them what happened. Within an hour, the entire neighborhood was out searching for Elizabeth.

Mitchell and his wife Wanda Barzee, a like-minded loon who called herself "God Adorneth,"* had set up camps in the hills above Salt Lake City. There they planned to

*Wanda Barzee's personal history is as whacky as

390

live in an LDS paradise — Emmanuel with his harem, and no one around to interfere. Right now he had only two wives, but he and Barzee planned to expand the number and bide their time, waiting for God to inform them when the Apocalypse was kicking off.

The abduction was huge news nationwide, partly because the press is always interested in late-night abductions of well-off blonde-haired youngsters, and partly because Ed and Lois Smart were smart. Savvy enough to know that cases like this can get cold pretty quickly, they made sure to keep it in the spotlight. The more people who were informed about Elizabeth and knew what she looked like, the more chance there was for her safe return home.

Months went by with no sign of Elizabeth or her captors. Mary Katherine's story was understandably vague or inaccurate, and police soon discounted much of her account of the kidnapping. Then one day, it popped into her head out of nowhere: the kidnapper's voice was the same as that of the man who had helped fix the roof of their house.

Mitchell's. Due to space considerations, though, we don't cover it in detail here.

As far as the police were concerned, this lead was shaky at best. For the Smarts, though, it was a godsend. Elizabeth's parents hired a sketch artist to draw Brian David Mitchell and got the drawing into the hands of John Walsh, host of the television program *America's Most Wanted;* whose own son had been abducted and murdered. In an interview on *Larry King Live,* Walsh unveiled the sketch; he also aired it on his own show. Mitchell's estranged family saw the photo on TV and heard the description of the man. It was Brian, all right. They called the police.

Meanwhile, Elizabeth was living in the wilderness of Emigration Canyon with her captors. Mitchell and Barzee had built lean-tos and dug deep hidey-holes throughout the woods. They told the girl that God had commanded them to kidnap her and that her role was to be Mitchell's second wife. They gave her rags like theirs to wear as clothes and held a wedding ceremony. Mitchell then raped Elizabeth.

When she wasn't being raped, verbally assaulted, or listening to the madman threaten the lives of her parents and siblings, Elizabeth was tied up to a tree or shoved into a

The Lineup

If a suspect is questioned by police, he may be asked to stand voluntarily in a lineup. He might choose to do so, believing that the failure of the crime victim to pick him out will result in the police backing off him as a suspect. The opposite can occur, of course, and whether he's innocent or not, his status as a suspect will be furthered and he may very well be arrested.

Prior to arrest, the suspect's attorney (if he has one yet) does not have the right to witness the lineup viewing. After arrest, though, when the suspect's status progresses to defendant, the attorney will be present at any further police lineups.

hole in the ground with a weighed-down board on top to prevent her from escaping. Once, when Mitchell and Barzee weren't watching, Elizabeth attempted to escape. She was caught and severely punished, and she didn't try again. Soon after, Mitchell brought his "wives" to California and lived there for a short time. God then told him to return to Salt Lake City and get on with his mission of redeeming the Church of Latter Day Saints.[*]

After enough time had passed, Mitchell was convinced that Elizabeth was securely under his control. He would occasionally take her into Salt Lake City, making her wear a veil over her face so no one would recognize her. On a number of occasions, Elizabeth Smart was close to being rescued. One man recalled seeing a girl behind a veil trying to make eye contact with him in the parking lot of a buffet restaurant. And Elizabeth herself reported that at one point, in Emigration Canyon, she could hear her uncle's voice calling out to her, but she dared not call back for fear of Mitchell's wrath. Searchers sometimes came across Elizabeth's captor in the woods, in fact. Mitchell, however, could see them coming and stashed Elizabeth away long before they arrived. The fact that he walked away from

[*]Among Mitchell and Barzee's many strange acts of faith was building a covered wagon and pulling it from Utah to Idaho in 1998. The next year, they constructed another, larger one that they considered the Ark of the Covenant and spent Christmas Day hauling it down random Utah roads.

so many close calls must have reinforced Mitchell's belief that God was controlling events from above.

Nine months after Elizabeth's abduction, the trio was walking down the street in the town of Sandy, Utah. This time, Mitchell and Barzee made Elizabeth wear a wig and big sunglasses to hide her face. Mitchell should have disguised himself, too, since he was by now the most wanted man in the state. He was spotted, and the three were dragged into the police precinct for questioning. During the questioning, Elizabeth was recognized. She was reunited with her family, and the two prophets were arrested on kidnapping charges

Mitchell's courtroom antics got him a hearing as to whether or not he was sane enough to stand trial. According to Utah law, a defendant must possess a clear understanding of the charges brought against him, and he must have the ability to aid his lawyer in his defense. If he can't communicate adequately with his attorneys, providing his side of the story (that is, if his thinking is considered "delusional") and he's put on trial, his rights will be considered violated and an appeal will likely follow a conviction.

The Third Judicial District Court of Salt Lake City's decision on this matter explicitly states, however, that a defendant's inability (or refusal) to help out his lawyers "cannot in and of itself constitute incompetence."[1] It also points out that while courtroom behavior such as Mitchell's might show a certain eccentricity at the very least, it's not enough to necessarily qualify him for a long hospital visit in lieu of prison. Finally, the court stipulates that just because a delusional person might act rationally within his particular delusional system of thought (e.g., a defendant might believe it is totally rational to throw a pitcher of water at a judge, so he throws a pitcher of water at the judge) doesn't necessarily make him nondelusional. All of which means it's not very easy for a sane person to get himself a long visit to a hospital instead of a prison cell.

The main issue for the court was whether or not Mitchell was delusional or just radical in his religious beliefs. To that end, it sought the advice of a psychologist and a psychiatrist. The defense, as well, hired a psychologist to determine Mitchell's capacity to stand trial.

The two psychologists agreed that Mitchell was unfit for trial, saying he suffered from delusional thinking brought about by a psychotic disorder. Like David Koresh, the founder of the Branch Davidians (see chapter 7), Mitchell believed he was the Davidic King, a messiah for modern times. He said that God told him what to do, and he believed that certain people (like the prosecution) were sent by Satan to thwart him. The Antichrist was lurking about in the form of the United Nations and World Bank, waiting for him to get out of prison, upon which they would fight the mother of all battles. Mitchell/Emmanuel, of course, would be triumphant and then rule at the right hand of God. Because this was all in the cards, he was willing to be put in prison, just as Jesus willingly took the Cross.

The defense's psychologist, Dr. Jennifer Skeem, said that Mitchell suffered from "false personal belief[s] based upon incorrect inferences about external reality . . . in spite of what constitutes incontrovertible evidence to the contrary."[2] While acknowledging that Mitchell showed no outward signs of psychosis (hallucinations, incomprehensible speech), Skeem came to the conclusion that Mitchell's beliefs were those of a delusional person, not simply a person who holds radical religious views: He acted in antisocial, self-destructive ways *because* of his all-consuming beliefs; this, according to Skeem, was what put Mitchell over the brink of simply having extreme religious beliefs and into a downward spiral of delusion.

The psychologist retained by the court, Dr. Stephen Golding, concluded that Mitchell was psychotic, delusional, paranoid, and possibly schizophrenic. The defendant, he said, believed his thoughts and actions were controlled by an outside force (God), communicated through "revelations." Golding said that Mitchell's decisions about his case were not "the product of 'free choice,' but result from delusional compulsion."[3]

Dr. Noel Gardner, the court-appointed psychiatrist, was raised by fundamentalists and had an extensive education in religion, including a degree in Bible languages. Mitchell, he said, did not suffer from the mental disease termed "delusional disorder," was not psychotic, and was fit to stand trial. In his opinion, Mitchell did fit into the DSM-IV-TR definition for "delusional disorder," but, Gardner said, the defendant's problem was behavioral, not medical. Mitchell's first problem was his narcissistic personality, not delusional disorder. Gardner said that when he examined Mitchell's religious beliefs on their own, apart from

Mitchell's behavior, they were not all that uncommon among LDS fundamentalists. It was his personality that made them *seem* uncommon.

Mitchell was beyond self-absorbed, Gardner wrote. He considered himself the single most important person in the world, which made him unwilling to entertain any other thoughts about truth, existence, and reality. Because of this he became paranoid and lacked the ability to empathize with others. Gardner totally discounted his counterpart's conclusion that the intensity of Mitchell's beliefs proved delusional thinking: plenty of people feel religion with great intensity, but we don't call them crazy, Gardner pointed out. What about the great martyrs in history? The public doesn't generally regard the Catholic saints who died for their religion as suffering from "delusional disorder." Martydom is the height of self-destructive behavior as a result of extreme religious beliefs, yet we look up to the saints. Having had personal experience with religious fanaticism, the psychiatrist even said that Mitchell's beliefs, "while extreme and to some appearing to be delusional, are in fact quite conventional, ordinary and directly related to his immediate culture and subculture environment."[4]

Finally, Gardner contended, Mitchell's marriage to Wanda Barzee was instrumental in Mitchell's topple over the edge. He had been married before, to a more normally functioning person, and it ended in divorce. Gardner figured that the relationship soured largely because the first wife, in essence, didn't put up with Mitchell's self-glory. "[N]arcissism pursues as much grandiosity as its environment allows, and is either restrained by the requirements of relationships . . . or requires withdrawal and isolation as protection."[5] Barzee, Gardner believed, had been as "narcissistically wounded" in her previous marriage as Mitchell had been, and together they attempted to build themselves back up again by reinforcing one another's grandiosity.

Upon hearing both sides of the argument, the court pointed out that all parties were in agreement that Mitchell's decisions and actions were based solely on his religious beliefs. Therefore, the answer to the question "Are his beliefs delusional?" would determine whether the defendant would face a jury or not. In other words, the court had to answer a nearly impossible question: What is the difference between *extreme* religious beliefs and *delusional* religious beliefs?

The court acknowledged that Mitchell's personality was narcissistic but pointed out that narcissists can function perfectly well in society. "For this reason," the judge wrote, "narcissistic personality disorder fails to adequately explain the level and duration of [Mitchell's] . . . impairment of social functioning that has resulted from his religious belief system."[6] Mitchell was beyond narcissistic because his grandiosity "[found] expression in such colossal beliefs as he is the most important or most powerful person in the world."[7] Mitchell, the court determined, was not fit to stand trial.

The story is far from over. The courts are flexible, lawyers are wily, and the system moves at a snail's pace. The prosecution convinced the courts that given medication, Mitchell would be fit for trial. The court agreed. So what did Mitchell do? He refused to take the medication, of course.

At the time of publication, the issue as to whether or not the state can force Mitchell to take his meds is tied up in court.

TWENTY-TWO

L&O: SVU: ("Repression," Season 3) A teenager recovers memories of sexual abuse and fears her father is abusing her younger sister. The father ends up murdered.

TRUE STORY: Long Island teen Cheryl Pierson hired classmate Sean Pica to kill her father in order to prevent him from sexually abusing her little sister. Cheryl claimed she herself was subjected to sexual abuse for years.

It was a case of he said, she said — except in this case, the he wasn't around to tell his side of the story. As sixteen-year-old Cheryl Pierson told it, her father had been sexually abusing her for years. And recently, James Pierson had been spending a lot of time with his youngest daughter, eight-year-old Joann. Cheryl feared he was abusing the girl

— so she hired a classmate to kill him.

Sean Pica had sat next to Cheryl Pierson for years. Their last names cast them together in homeroom class and the two would often chat to pass the time. They'd talk about music, what they'd watched on TV, assignments they were given by teachers. Cheryl was a pretty and popular cheerleader. Sean was a quiet boy who wore braces and aspired to become an Eagle Scout.

Sean harbored a secret crush on Cheryl but realized nothing could come of it. He had a girlfriend and Cheryl was dating an older guy named Rob Cuccio. Plus, they ran with different crowds at Newfield High School. Cheryl was really into school spirit and cheering at their high school games. When she wasn't at school Cheryl was at home, managing the Pierson household. Her mother, Cathleen, had succumbed to kidney disease a year earlier. Sixteen-year-old Cheryl was charged with caring for her younger sister and keeping up with the household chores. Still, she didn't complain much and she seemed upbeat most of the time.

Sean was a talented carpenter and had plans to represent the school at a state woodworking competition. Lately though, he'd been hanging out with druggies, and doing a lot of coke. His weekly drug bill had ballooned to almost $300. To support his habit, he and a friend started burglarizing houses. Sean hid his habit from his family. His parents were divorced and Sean lived with his mother and her second husband before they split up.

One day in homeroom class, Sean told Cheryl about a newspaper article he'd read about a Long Island woman who had been arrested for hiring a hitman to kill her husband.

"Who would do that? That's crazy," Cheryl said.

"I would," Pica replied. "If the money was right."[1]

Cheryl thought for a moment. She told Pica she knew someone who would pay $1,000 to have someone killed. Pica was game.

A few days later, Cheryl confessed that she was the person who wanted someone killed, and that that someone was her father, forty-two-year-old engineer James Pierson. Sean listened wide-eyed as Cheryl explained how her father was abusing her. She even showed him the bruises on her arm to prove it. This struck a chord with Sean. According to Sean, as a child he had watched helplessly as his stepfather beat his mother. Now Sean was older and stronger. He promised Cheryl he would take care of the problem for her.

During lunch period, Sean accompanied Cheryl and her boyfriend Rob to the Pierson house on Magnolia Road in Selden, a suburban town in Long Island, New York. Cheryl wanted Sean to know where she lived so he could carry out the hit on her father. While Rob waited outside in his car, Cheryl gave Sean a quick tour of the house, stopping to point out James Pierson's gun collection. The teens discussed using one of the guns for the hit but decided against it, fearing the weapon would easily be traced back to Pierson. Sean had a friend who could probably get him a weapon. Failing that, he said he could always try to buy one in Manhattan, about an hour's drive away from Selden.

Weeks passed. James Pierson went about his business as usual, alive and well. Around Thanksgiving 1985, Sean called Cheryl and told her he had a plan. He knew that Pierson owned a rental house across the street from the family home. The rental unit was currently empty. Pica planned on breaking in, setting off the alarm, and ambushing Pierson when the older man came to investigate. Cheryl had a game that night and spent the evening cheering for her school's team.

It turned out that Pica had tossed a brick through the window of the rental house but the alarm didn't go off, and his plan to kill Pierson was thwarted. The holidays came and went without incident. Cheryl would later claim she had forgotten all about the plan to kill her father.

February 5 began as a bitingly cold morning. James Pierson rose early, as was his habit. He checked on Cheryl and Joann before leaving for work, exiting through the side door.

Sean Pica was hiding behind a tree outside the Pierson home. He shivered as he waited for his target to emerge. When Pierson finally came out, Sean shot him once in the head with a .22-caliber rifle he had stolen from a neighbor's house. Pierson fell to the ice-covered ground. Sean rushed toward him and shot him four more times in the back. Then he ran away.

Shortly afterward, Cheryl discovered her father's body and ran screaming to a neighbor's house. The neighbors phoned the police. Initially, police suspected the murder was a professional hit, possibly related to drugs or the mob. They investigated Pierson's background but found nothing to indicate anyone wanted him dead. Neighbors told police that Pierson was a coarse but caring family man, a strict father who showered his daughters with gifts and attention.

One of those daughters caught the attention of Suffolk County Detective Lieutenant Robert Dunn. He sensed there was something "off" about Cheryl and the Pierson family in general. Cheryl's role in the family seemed more like a caretaker than a child. Dunn found her behavior both odd and inappropriate — just an hour after her father was slain, she seemed relaxed and even complimented the detective on his cologne. Her demeanor did not gibe with that of someone who had just lost a parent. Back at the police station, Dunn confided to a colleague that he suspected Cheryl had been involved in an incestuous relationship with her father. He did some research on the subject; the more he learned, the more he became convinced that Cheryl was a victim of sexual abuse.

Following the murder, Sean asked Cheryl to meet him at a local pizzeria. She had only given him $400 of the promised $1,000 fee for killing her father. Sean had some demands: he wanted the rest of the money and he also wanted her to buy him a motorcycle and let him move into the rental house. Cheryl turned down all three requests.

A week later, the police received an anonymous tip from a teenager who claimed to have overheard Cheryl talking about having her father killed. Acting on this information, detectives arrested Cheryl. In custody, she broke down and confessed to having paid Sean Pica to kill her father. She did so, she said, to stop her father from sexually abusing her and her sister. Cheryl was pregnant. Tests determined that Rob Cuccio — not James Pierson as Cheryl believed — was the father. Five weeks after her arrest, Cheryl had a miscarriage.

Police picked up Sean and Rob, who they learned had delivered the money for the hit to Sean. The teenagers quickly copped to their involvement in the crime. Rob Cuccio pleaded guilty to felony solicitation and was given probation for his part in the murder-for-hire scheme. Sean and Cheryl were charged with second-degree murder and second-degree conspiracy to commit murder. In an arrangement with the DA, they agreed to plead guilty to the lesser charge of first-degree manslaughter.

The plea arrangements nullified any need

for a jury trial. Instead, a sentencing hearing would be held to determine the extent of the defendants' guilt and uncover any mitigating factors related to the crime. A sentencing hearing is similar to a jury trial in that the prosecution and defense both call and question witnesses and offer summations of the facts. It would be up to Judge Sherman to decide how much, if any, prison time to give Cheryl and Sean.

Sean's sentencing hearing was held first. His attorney Martin Effman asked that the judge show leniency in his sentencing decision because, "Sean Pica would not be here were it not for Cheryl Pierson." Effman also asked that Sean be tried as a youthful offender, a request the judge denied.

Effman explained to the Court that Sean was susceptible to Cheryl's plea "because Cheryl was a girl who had a problem with a father and Sean had witnessed physical abuse in his own home. He watched his mother abused by his second father."

Prosecutor Jablonski had his own take on Sean, painting the teenager as an opportunist who "did it for the money." Sean wasn't a hero or a loyal friend; he was a lying sociopath who needed the money to support his cocaine habit, Jablonski said.

Judge Sherman found the prosecution's

theory to be the most credible. He sentenced Sean Pica to twenty-four years in prison — just one year short of the twenty-five-year maximum allowed by law. Sean would be required to serve eight years before he could be considered for parole.

"I have no message to send society," Sherman said. "However, Sean, I do have a message for you: Your time in jail will be more bearable if you understand why you are there. You are not there for keeping a promise or for being loyal to a friend, but you are there for asking for $1,000 to murder a man you did not know."

Cheryl's sentencing hearing was scheduled for late September 1987. Judge Sherman had agreed to allow Cheryl to be sentenced as a youthful offender; the classification would all but guarantee Cheryl a lighter sentence than if she had been considered an adult.

While awaiting her hearing, Cheryl wrote an essay about her life entitled "House of Hell." She wrote, "Imagine being punished for four years and after your monster has finally gone away, you think all your problems are gone, but then you find out you still might be punished for the rest of your life. Why, I ask again . . . That question always seems to come up in my life. No one has any answer for me. Haven't I been punished enough?"[2]

Many people believed that Cheryl had, in fact, been punished enough. The public response to the case was overwhelming. Judge Sherman was deluged with letters asking him to set Cheryl free. Some of these letters were from fellow incest survivors, one of whom wrote, "Incest destroys your life. The daily emotional confusion between shame, love, pain, humiliation and fear are feelings that are impossible to describe to someone to whom this did not happen. It ends up for many of us in constant feelings of suicide and thoughts of murder."[3] As a result of Cheryl's case, then-mayor Ed Koch founded the Incest Helpline. Posters promoting the service featured the tagline "Daddy's little girl has a secret."

Was Cheryl lying about the sexual abuse? Cheryl's detractors claimed that she had killed her father for the insurance money, and to be free of the man who was a strict disciplinarian. Others insisted that she had killed him because she feared what Pierson would do when he found out she was pregnant. James Pierson's mother, Virginia Pierson, and his sister, Marilyn Adams, vehemently disputed Cheryl's allegations. They called Cheryl a liar, a "great actress."

In an ironic twist, Joann — the sister Cheryl claimed to have been protecting — sided against her. The little girl insisted that James Pierson had never been inappropriate with her or with Cheryl. Yet, neighbors would testify that a year earlier Joann had blurted excitedly to them that "Cheryl slept in daddy's bed last night."

Jay Fleckstein was incensed that Virginia Pierson and Marilyn Adams were refuting Cheryl's claims. Fleckstein, Cheryl's stepuncle, flew into New York to testify that Cathleen Pierson had confided in him about the incest. He told the court that his stepsister made him promise not to tell anyone. He also said that she told him that when she confronted her husband about the abuse he beat her.

All told, twenty-three witnesses came forward to support Cheryl's claims. They testified that James Pierson was a brute and that they suspected he was sexually abusing his daughter. Many of the witnesses were wracked by guilt for not having come to Cheryl's aid sooner. A remorseful neighbor admitted that he had been alarmed by the attention Pierson paid his older daughter. "He was always pinching, pulling her hair, fondling her . . . rubbing her bottom," the neighbor said. Why hadn't he contacted the authorities? Because, he said, "I thought I had an evil mind."

One person who did try to help Cheryl was a classmate. The girl told the school guidance counselor that she had witnessed James Pierson grab Cheryl by the arm and drag her back into the car. Since Cheryl didn't come in herself, the counselor told the girl, no action could be taken. The matter was dropped.

Prosecutor Jablonski didn't dispute Cheryl's motive. He believed she "fit the stereotype for an abused child," he said. But, he added, Cheryl "had no right to take the law into her own hands."

During Cheryl's sentencing hearing, Jablonski argued that Cheryl's was not an act of spontaneous rage but a premeditated murder. Cheryl was not in imminent danger when Pierson was murdered, the prosecutor pointed out. What's more, her behavior in the days leading up to and proceeding the murder was not that of someone who feared for her life.

Why *did* Cheryl act the way she did? Why was she able to laugh and carry on normally hours after the murder? Kathleen Otizinger, a psychotherapist who examined Cheryl after her arrest, testified that, "In many ways [children of incest] die inside. In order to survive they . . . develop an inner emptiness and an outer self that presents itself to the public as if nothing is wrong. There is a psychic numbing. They feel nothing."[4]

The psychotherapist went on to testify that despite the outward appearances of a "normal, average" family, the Piersons fit the profile of an incestuous family. Further, she was convinced that before his death, Pierson had begun sexually abusing his youngest daughter Joann.

She also said that Cheryl had been able to deny the abuse to herself and pretend it wasn't real until she confided in her boyfriend. After the secret was out, she explained, it became reality — a reality that suddenly demanded an immediate solution. Pierson had told Cuccio about the abuse around Christmas 1985, just two months before the murder.

According to Cheryl, the incest started when Cathleen Pierson fell ill. At first, James Pierson simply began paying more attention to her, she explained. "I thought it was just affection," she said. Her father told her that he "would touch me and stuff because he loved me and that I shouldn't let anybody else touch me like that, no other boys." But after a while, Cheryl realized that her father was behaving inappropriately.

414

And the sexual contact escalated as she grew older.

"The more close we got, the more possessive he got . . . just to make him happy I would do what he wanted me to do." The times that Cheryl resisted his advances were hellish on the family as he would yell and take out his anger on the rest of the family, she claimed. At fourteen, her father had sexual intercourse with her. Crying, she told the court, "When he was on top of me . . . I put a pillow over my face to block it out until it was over." Once when she refused him he smacked her across the face.

Cheryl felt her mother suspected what was going on and after Cathleen died in 1985, Cheryl felt guilty. She claimed that her father became more sexually demanding when she began dating Rob and sometimes demanded sex as many as three times a day. It was as if her father "had to prove he was the one I liked," Cheryl told the court.

Cheryl began to stay away from the house as much as possible, spending time with Rob. One day she returned home to find her sister cuddling with her father, much the way she had done when he first became inappropriate with her. On another occasion, Cheryl said, she came home to find her father and sister wrestling on the floor.

She feared that her father was going to begin sexually abusing young Joann.

Cheryl told the court that she hired Sean Pica to kill her father because "I thought that my father wouldn't have sex with me anymore . . . I'd live a normal life."

In a nine-page memorandum, Judge Sherman noted that the evidence supported Cheryl's claim of sexual abuse by her father. However, Sherman was not willing to give her a complete walk. "This Court must encourage victims of domestic violence to seek other alternatives than the path taken by Cheryl Pierson," he said. "More and more, complaints in this area have been received, believed and prosecuted by law enforcement agencies and sex offenders have been punished after plea or conviction after trial . . . This Court cannot countenance a planned homicide, albeit planned and carried out by teenagers suffering emotional stress; society has the right to condemn and the duty to punish such conduct and a term of incarceration is warranted."

Cheryl was sentenced to six months in prison to be followed by probation. When the sentence was read, Cheryl fainted. Jablonski was asked why Cheryl was given such leniency over Sean Pica. "Her motivation was certainly different. She wanted to have the abuse stopped. He did it for the money."[5]

Cheryl Pierson served three months of her six-month sentence before being paroled in 1988. She and Rob Cuccio married and now live on Long Island.

Sean Pica was incarcerated for sixteen years. He earned his GED, bachelor's, and master's degrees. He currently works as a social worker on Long Island.

Statute of Limitations for Rape

If you see an episode of *L&O: SVU* in which detectives can't arrest a rape suspect because the statute of limitations has expired, you're probably watching an older episode. Or the scriptwriters are taking liberties.

In June 2006, New York lifted its five-year statute of limitation on first-degree rape, criminal sexual act, aggravated sexual abuse, and sexual conduct against a child. District attorneys can now prosecute any of these crimes indefinitely.

Previously, the only crimes without statutes of limitation were "Class A" felonies: first-degree kidnapping and arson, and first- and second-degree murder, criminal sale of controlled substances, and criminal possession of controlled substances. Rape and other sex crimes were considered "Class B" felonies.

Until this law was passed, New York had the fourth shortest limit to prosecute such crimes, behind Utah, Florida, and North Dakota. In some other states, such as Delaware, Rhode Island, and New Jersey, only misdemeanors carry a statute of limitation.

Regarding civil cases, New York law previously required the victim to file suit within one year against the offender. Under the new law, victims have five years to file.

Twenty-Three

L&O: SVU: ("Pure," Season 6) A married couple rapes and kills a number of women.

TRUE STORY: Canadian couple Karla Homolka and Paul Bernardo raped and killed several young women, including Karla's younger sister Tammy.

Canada's Twelve-Mile Creek Watershed System is a massive system of lakes, rivers, and ponds in the Niagara Falls region, between Lakes Ontario and Erie. The great Niagara Falls sits on the eastern edge of the area. While thousands of tourists (and lots of honeymooners) visit the majestic Niagara Falls every day, local nature lovers prefer the peace and quiet of the small lakes that dot the region. A few miles to the northwest of the falls is a man-made lake — one of many — called Lake Gibson. Created one hundred years ago to catch the water runoff

The happy couple, Karla Homolka and Paul Bernardo. Little did the guests at their wedding know that just a few months previous, the pair had raped and killed Karla's little sister, Tammy.
Sun Media Corporation

from a nearby power plant, it's relatively small and nondescript; however, it has the most square miles of wetlands in the watershed system, making it a favorite of canoeists, birdwatchers, and hunters.

On June 29, 1991, a couple canoeing on Lake Gibson were taking in the sunset, noting how peaceful and quiet it was at that time of day. They were in shallow water when they saw a small slab of concrete with what looked like flesh on the outer edge. The couple pulled their canoe to the shore and found a local fisherman. The three went back to the spot and lifted the concrete from the shallow water. On closer inspection, they saw that it was encasing part of a human leg. They called the police, who discovered five more concrete slabs in the lake, each containing different parts of the body, which was quickly identified as that of Leslie Mahaffy, a fifteen-year-old girl from Niagara Falls who had gone missing two weeks before. The first clue was her braces.[1]

Leslie Mahaffy's parents didn't report her missing because she had a habit of going out and not coming home. She often stayed out past her curfew — a bone of contention between her and her parents — so her behavior on June 15 seemed to them typical of Leslie. That night, she had attended the funeral of a close friend, who had been killed in a car accident. A friend of hers walked her home, late of course. The front door of her house was locked, and her friend asked if she wanted him to hang around, but Leslie said it was fine, the back door would be open. Satisfied with this, her friend left.

When Leslie went to the back door, it too was locked. At the end of their tether with

Leslie's constant flouting of the rules, her parents had decided to teach their daughter a lesson. Oh well, Mahaffy probably thought, there's no real reason to go home, anyway. She walked back out to the street and saw an older guy, about twenty-five years old. He had blond hair, well-styled, and he was dressed nicely and spoke intelligently. He seemed normal. Leslie approached him and asked if he had a cigarette. He sure did, he said. In his car. Leslie followed him. When they reached the car, the guy pulled out a knife and told the teenager to get in.

Mahaffy was driven to 57 Bayview Drive in Port Dalhousie, St. Catharines, about an hour away, and forced at knifepoint to enter the Cape Cod style house, where the man lived with his fiancée. The teenager was held captive, drugged, raped, and videotaped by the pair for almost an entire day. They then murdered Leslie, dismembered her, and encased her remains in cement. The couple drove to Lake Gibson and disposed of the fifteen-year-old.

The day Mahaffy's remains were found in Lake Gibson, a lavish ceremony was taking place fifteen miles to the north, in the well-to-do town of Niagara-on-the-Lake. It was the killers' wedding day.

Paul Bernardo and Karla Homolka weren't going to let anything get in the way of their fun. The wedding ceremony had all the bells and whistles. Karla wore an expensive, traditional dress and arrived in a horse and carriage. Rings were exchanged, rice was thrown, the bouquet was tossed. Paul, dressed sharply in a black tux and white tie, had landed a job in 1987 with the prestigious tax firm Price Waterhouse. And Karla, holding a huge bouquet of white flowers, was clearly head-over-heels for her handsome new husband. They were the picture-perfect couple, the kind that wedding photographers use in their portfolios and showrooms.

But not all the wedding guests were perfectly pleased with the young couple, especially Karla's parents. They had asked her to postpone the ceremony. Karla's younger sister, Tammy, had died just six months earlier in a freak accident, and they were still in mourning. Tammy had taken drugs and choked on her vomit in her sleep. But Karla wouldn't have it. She had waited all her life for this day, and she wasn't going to postpone it for anything — even out of respect for her parents and the memory of her kid sister.

There was more to the situation than met the eye, though. Peter and Karla weren't just strangely blasé about Tammy's death. They were responsible for it. But no one knew.

On December 23, it turned out, the couple decided to act upon a decision they had already made: to drug and rape Tammy. Paul was apparently attracted to, some say obsessed with, the sixteen-year-old Tammy. And Karla, either out of spite (she was angry with Tammy for flirting with Paul and suspected that they had been together at least once) or due to her extreme sexual deviancy, was excited about it. At the time, she was working at an animal hospital and had access to a number of drugs. In the downstairs of the Homolka's house, after everyone went to bed, Karla and Paul crushed some powerful sedatives and spiked Tammy's drink. When her sister fell asleep, Karla put a cloth soaked with Halothane, an anesthetic, over Tammy's mouth and nose to induce unconsciousness.

The couple turned on the video camera and filmed each other raping Tammy. Within a few minutes, though, they realized that Tammy wasn't breathing. Unable to revive her, they scrambled to cover their crime and called an ambulance. She was pronounced dead on December 24, Christmas Eve. No major inquiries were made into Tammy's death. Karla and Paul went about their business as if the whole thing were just an accident.

This was the first in a string of sex crimes for Karla. Paul, though, was already a well-experienced sexual predator. Before he had even met his fiancée, Paul Bernardo had either raped or attempted to rape three teenagers in Scarborough, Ontario. His M.O. was mainly to hang around bus stops and wait for an attractive female to get off a bus. He would follow her and then attack when he felt it was safe. The victims would usually be dragged behind some bushes, tied, gagged, and beaten. Bernardo's attacks lasted anywhere from thirty minutes to an hour; he would sometimes leave for a short time and return to attack again. The first assault occurred on May 4, 1987, and the rapes continued well past the time he met Karla the following September. In all, Paul Bernardo stalked and sexually assaulted at least fifteen women as the "Scarborough Rapist."*

In August 1989, when Paul and Karla

*When he was arrested for murder, Paul Bernardo

425

were hot and heavy into their relationship (around the middle of the Scarborough Rapist's string of attacks), police followed up on a tip that Paul Bernardo, based on his physical description, was the perpetrator. They interviewed Paul at his home, where he happily agreed to submit DNA samples. The cops left with the samples . . . and Bernardo never heard from them again.[†]

Paul Bernardo and Karla Homolka had a chance meeting on October 17, 1987, in a hotel bar in Scarborough, a Toronto suburb about ninety miles from Karla's hometown of St. Catharines. Karla was working at a pet store at the time and was in town for a pet food convention. She was seventeen, he

---

admitted to fifteen rapes. He later admitted to ten more.

[†]The samples, which virtually proved that Bernardo was the Scarborough Rapist, sat on line in the lab for over two years according to various reports. Meanwhile, Paul continued his rape spree and is even suspected of an attack in Hawaii while he was there on his honeymoon; he continued raping women well after he was married. Karla Homolka claims not to have known her husband was the Scarborough Rapist until much later.

was twenty-three. The attraction was immediate and mutual; within hours they were having sex. The pair began seeing each other as often as possible. They were in love.

Karla would later claim that Paul began beating her a couple of years into their relationship. Yet, at the same time, she wrote letters to a friend saying that Paul was her dream come true, and she didn't hesitate to accept his marriage proposal. Their relationship seems to have been dependent on one thing and one thing only: their mutual taste for cruel, violent sex. They liked each other best when they were emotionally or physically hurting one another — or someone else. Tammy Homolka was their first victim.

Their second was Karla's own friend, known as "Jane Doe." By April 1991, Karla and Paul, two months away from marriage, were renting the house at 57 Bayview Drive. One night, Karla invited her friend over for some cocktails for a nice "girls' night in."

Paul wasn't home, of course, but he wasn't far away. And he was waiting anxiously for his fiancée's call. When the call came, it meant that Karla's friend was knocked out from a heavy dose of Halcion. Paul rushed home, and the couple raped their friend. Again, they took turns videotaping one another.

Jane Doe woke up the next morning at Karla's house with a killer headache. She couldn't remember a thing, other than coming over to the house and having a couple of drinks. She didn't think she drank enough to warrant passing out. She felt sick to her stomach, and threw up. She didn't have much experience drinking. She was only fifteen years old, after all. She was terribly embarrassed in front of her sophisticated older friends.

It wasn't until much later, when the couple's crimes were made public, that Jane Doe learned what happened that night.

When Paul and Karla were arrested for the strangulation murder of Leslie Mahaffy, each spouse blamed the other for actually killing the teenager. Bernardo has always claimed that he planned to let Mahaffy go. At one point, however, her blindfold had come off, allowing her to see and thus identify her captors. Karla had a needle and syringe that she had stolen from work. She wanted to kill Leslie by injecting an air bubble into her vein. Homolka, though, maintains that it was Paul's idea to murder Leslie. She took part in it only because she feared for her own life, since Paul was so abusive at this point.

They pretended to care about Mahaffy after their arrest, but they certainly weren't contrite about it before the police caught up to them. They were very much connected and on the prowl for more victims. They even invited Jane Doe over again. Paul and Karla again drugged her and began raping her. Then the teenager stopped breathing, and they got scared. They ended the assault and called 911. But then Jane Doe started breathing, and they called off the emergency services. Their victim again was fortunate to escape with her life.

Eight months later, Karla and Paul were driving around in search of another sex slave when they saw sixteen-year-old Kristen French, a Catholic-school student walking by a church. Karla and Paul pulled into the parking lot. Karla approached Kristen pretending to need directions, and the girl, totally unsuspicious of the pretty blonde woman, was happy to help. Paul then came up to her from behind with a knife and forced her into the car.

They did the same with Kristen French as they did with Leslie Mahaffy. Kristen, however, repeatedly resisted her captors.[*]

[*]As the Scarborough Rapist, Paul Bernardo didn't handle resistent victims well, usually running off

During her three-day ordeal, she insulted Bernardo and wondered out loud how his wife could stand being around him. Most of her insults are documented on videotape.[2] The tapes also show Bernardo forcing Kristen to tell him she loves him, as he rapes her.

The body of Kristen French was found in a ditch on April 30, 1992. Karla and Paul killed her on the nineteenth, just before leaving for a visit to Karla's parents' house for Easter dinner. French had been strangled. After their arrest, Karla again said Paul did it and Paul again said Karla did it.

At this point, Canadian police had no idea who did it, but in early 1993, they caught a big break when Karla Homolka turned up in the hospital with black eyes and bruises all over her face. Bernardo had beaten her so soundly with a flashlight that she could hardly walk. Little did he know at the time, but every blow with the flashlight took him closer and closer to life imprisonment for murder — and Karla closer to the notorious plea deal that would ensure her freedom after just twelve relatively enjoyable years in prison.

---

at the first sign that a woman was going to fight back.

Bernardo was arrested for assault with a weapon. And, shortly after, the old DNA results came in. The Scarborough Rapist was caught. Paul was released on bail and put on twenty-four-hour police surveillance. Then Karla told her aunt and uncle, with whom she was living after leaving the hospital, about the Mahaffy and French murders, including the fact that the rapes were videotaped.[*]

Karla Homolka was most definitely a victim of Paul Bernardo's chronic anger and hatred of women. But, like animals in the wild, victims can also be predators — and Karla Homolka clearly fit that role, too. However, she was crafty enough to play the victim until all bets were off, and she played it well. She immediately found a lawyer and instructed him to secure a plea deal for her. She spoke about how Paul had been abusing her for years and that she was fully under his control. Only now, with Paul at a safe distance, was she comfortable talking about it. She was sorry for the murders.

The DA had Karla Homolka evaluated by

[*]When her relatives had come to the house to take her to the hospital, Karla went back inside for something: she wanted to get the videotapes out of the house. She didn't succeed.

431

a number of psychologists, including those working for the FBI. They came to the conclusion that Karla was, indeed, a "compliant victim." That is, they bought her story about being a virtual slave of Paul Bernardo's sadism. The DA believed that Karla's identity had been suppressed, that she lived in mortal terror of Paul Bernardo, and that she remained in the marriage due to post-traumatic stress disorder. Sure, they were willing to deal with her in exchange for her testimony against Paul Bernardo. But they weren't willing to offer blanket immunity, as she wanted.

Eventually, Homolka and prosecutors arrived at a deal. She would cooperate completely with the investigation, testify against Bernardo, and plead guilty to manslaughter charges carrying a maximum sentence of twelve years. She told them all about her role in the abduction and rapes of Kristen French and Leslie Mahaffy, and how Paul had killed them both with a length of black cord. She never mentioned her role in the death of her sister Tammy or the sexual assault on Jane Doe.

After Bernardo's arrest for the rapes in Scarborough, meanwhile, police obtained a search warrant for the house on Bayview Drive to search for evidence against Paul for the rapes. They were hoping to find the many hours worth of video they believed to exist. However, after seventy-one days of searching, all they came up with was a tape a few minutes long of Karla performing oral sex on a woman they thought was Kristen French. (It was actually Jane Doe.)

Somehow, they missed the six videotapes hidden above a ceiling tile in the bathroom. But Paul Bernardo's lawyer Ken Murray didn't. Following the instructions of his client, Murray went to the house after the police search was over and took the tapes, which contained footage of the rapes of all four women. In them, Karla Homolka was far from the "compliant victim" she claimed to be. As the victims plead for mercy, Karla turns a deaf ear and eagerly participates in the rapes. In one segment, she even looks at the camera and pretends to pretty herself before an assault.

Bernardo wanted the tapes destroyed; Murray wanted to use them in court against Karla during her testimony. Unable to agree with his client, Murray dropped the case. Bernardo's new attorney went one step further than simply disagreeing with Bernardo. He handed the tapes over to the police.

Karla Homolka was exposed as the predator she was. Plea deals can always be reversed, and it's not unheard of for a judge to refuse to recognize an agreement between prosecutors and defendants. Karla had failed to confess to the assault on Jane Doe — a violation of her original agreement with prosecutors. And, when finally questioned about it, she pretended not to know anything about it. She did eventually confess to her parents about her involvement in her sister's death, and the DA felt that she had contributed so much to the case against Paul Bernardo that they didn't reverse the plea.

This, of course, raised a furor in Canada. A petition with 300,000 signatures urging prosecutors to change their minds was quickly sent to the DA's office. It's interesting to note, however, that Kristen French's mother supported the DA's decision.[3]

Bernardo stuck to his contention that Karla murdered Leslie Mahaffy and Kristen French, and that the deaths were accidental. Karla took the stand and said the opposite. The jury was shown the videos and in the end still believed her version of events. Paul Bernardo was sentenced to life imprisonment and eventually declared a "Dangerous Offender," a label in Canada's criminal justice system that almost ensures that the convict will not get paroled. The courts later turned down his application for appeal.

Karla and Paul were divorced before the trial. Today, Karla is a free woman, having served her twelve years in prison — if it can be called that. Karla Homolka has a talent for turning up roses whenever she finds herself knee-deep in trouble — and rubbing her fellow citizens' faces in the dirt left behind. Karla was initially assigned to a maximum-security women's prison but was soon transferred to Joliette Institution, a minimum-security facility that one former prisoner calls "adult day care."[4] Joliette is a place where some of Canada's most notorious convicts enjoy semiluxurious living — dorm-style bedrooms, civilian clothing, peaceful walks on the relatively scenic campus.

In 2000, the *Montreal Gazette* published photos that raised the ire of all law-abiding Canadians. Karla and her pals — two of Canada's most notorious female sex offenders — are shown having a birthday party, enjoying time with a pet cat, and posing on a couch with an unnamed, ridiculously coiffed male. And they all look *great*. They're dressed well, tastefully made up, and happy to mug for the camera.

In fact, to a certain extent Karla Homolka

has enjoyed less freedom outside the walls of Joliette. Released in 2005, she is one of the most despised people in the country, and journalists would just love an exclusive interview with her. She has been tracked down and approached by reporters attempting to goad her into a publishable remark, alas, to no avail. And the death threats she receives outside of prison must be a bit scarier to her than those she received in the safety of Joliette. As a condition of her release, she is subject to a number of restrictions, including updating police if she relocates, takes any trips, or changes her name.

For the most part, though, Karla has kept herself fairly well incognito. It was reported in 2006 that she had moved to Quebec and tried to change her name to Emily Chiara Tremblay. The rapist-murderer speaks French fluently and probably assumed that her story was less-known in French-speaking Quebec than English-speaking Ontario. Tremblay is among the most common names in Quebec.

In September 2005, the Canadian weekly *Maclean's* reported a story concerning Karla Homolka and the questionable company she was keeping after her stay in prison. A hardware store owner named Richer Lapointe convinced the ex-convict to take a job at his store. He said that he wanted to help the gal adjust to her new life of freedom. He employed a strange tactic, though: Lapointe taped certain conversations with Karla and then reportedly tried to sell them to the media. Lapointe claimed that Homolka was associating with at least two convicted criminals. He conveniently left one little detail out of his story, but *Maclean's* didn't: she was also friendly with at least one accused sexual predator — LaPointe himself.[5]

Eventually, Karla Homolka might fade into the background. Or maybe not. It's largely up to her.

The Time of Death

The most important factors in determining time of death are body temperature, rigor mortis, and the victim's food contents. While a forensic pathologist has to consider a number of variables, there are some general rules they go by.

First, a person's core temperature drops between one to two degrees Fahrenheit every hour after death, depending of course on such factors as ambient temperature, clothing, and the size of the victim.

Rigor mortis, which begins about three hours after death in the eyelids and jaws, spreads through the whole body within twelve hours. After full rigor mortis sets in, the body then begins to relax itself and becomes limber again within thirty-six hours after death. It's important to determine what stage a body is in right away since rigor mortis can cause the limbs to move after death. Thus, the position of the body when found might not be the same as when the suspect fled.

Generally speaking, within three

hours food has traveled from the stomach to the small intestine. It takes another five hours for it to move completely through the small intestine. Once food reaches the large intestine, a pathologist can guess the meal was eaten at least eight hours previous.

Twenty-Four

L&O SVU: ("Debt," Season 6) An illegal Chinese immigrant is held captive as a sex slave in New York.

TRUE STORY: In 1997, the FBI and U.S. Border Patrol raided six brothels in Florida run by a family of Mexican nationals. The young women working in the brothels had been smuggled out of Mexico, enslaved, and forced into prostitution.

The American woman was speaking to her in Spanish. Her voice was soft, soothing. *Everything will be all right. You're safe now. You can trust me.* Celia had heard those words before. A year earlier, she had put her trust in another woman. That woman, a fellow Mexican, had also spoken to her in a soft, soothing voice. She had smiled at Celia and patted her hand reassuringly. *Trust me. I will take care you.* But

440

she had betrayed Celia.

The Mexican woman was dressed in the finest clothes; her hair was perfect and she was adorned with expensive jewelry. Out of respect, Celia called her Senora. Although Senora had a beautiful house in Mexico, she spent much of the time in America, where her family owned several restaurants. She said the restaurants were doing so well that her family needed to hire additional staff. Of course, they could give the jobs to Americans but they preferred to hire their own kind, Mexicans who spoke their language and shared their culture.

Senora had grown up in Celia's hometown of Vera Cruz in southeastern Mexico. Her family, the Cadena-Sosas,[*] had found wealth and success in America. Senora smiled broadly as she described their wonderful lives across the border. Celia listened raptly, imagining what it would be like to have money, to live in a nice house with enough room for her siblings and her parents. Her own family was desperately poor;

[*]For editorial purposes the perpetrators will be referred to as "the Cadena-Sosa family"; there are, however, other members of the extended Cadena-Sosa family who were never involved in any criminal activity.

441

nearly everyone in the town struggled to make ends meet. Celia worked as a lemon picker; her salary was meager, just a few dollars a day. Senora promised her she would pay her $400 a week! That was ten times more than what Celia made in Mexico. It was an excellent opportunity; Celia could see that. Still, she was hesitant to leave her family. But Senora was persuasive, smiling and fingering her thick gold necklace. *Come work for us. You will be part of our family. We will be one big family, each of us looking out for the other.*

Senora assured Celia's parents that the Cadena-Sosa family would protect and care for her as if she were one of their own daughters. Celia would live with them in Florida. She would be free to return to Mexico at any time. It would cost $2,000 to smuggle Celia over the border, a reasonable fee considering the risks involved. The Cadena-Sosas would front Celia the money; she would pay them back from the wages she made working as a waitress. Senora said that a good waitress could make an extra hundred dollars a week in tips — Celia would be able to pay off her debt in no time. The offer was too good to pass up.

Celia, and several other girls from her town who had also been recruited to work as waitresses, traveled by bus to the border town of Matamoros. There they were met by *coyotes* — Mexicans who specialized in trafficking their countrymen into America. The girls crossed the Rio Grande River and were smuggled into Texas and then into Florida. Their handlers, men who worked for the Cadena-Sosas, picked them up and took them to the biggest store Celia had ever seen. It was filled with rows and rows of goods — food, clothing, toys, magazines, even cosmetics. They told the girls they were there to buy them clothing. Celia and the other girls were giddy looking at all the pretty dresses and blouses for sale. But the men chose the clothing the girls were to wear. Celia was alarmed; the clothes were skimpy and see-through, a number of the items were things that a woman might wear on her wedding night.

Celia saw Florida from the windows of a van. She was dropped off at a small white house. The other girls were taken away, presumably to other small white houses in Florida. Several tough-looking men relaxed on furniture inside the house. Celia was the only woman there. She was frightened by the way the men stared, and the way they talked to her, like a man might talk to a prositute. A man with a crooked eye reminded her that she owed the Cadena-Sosas a lot of money for bringing her into America. He told her that she would sell her body to pay the family back. Celia shook and felt her face flush. There must be a mistake, she told him. She had been hired to work as a waitress in the family's restaurant. The man with the crooked eye laughed. No mistake, he said. Celia told him she would do no such thing. He slapped her hard across her face. She started to cry. The other men watched, anxious, as if they were awaiting something. Suddenly, one of them grabbed her arms from behind. Another one ripped at her clothes. Celia screamed and tried to get free but they overpowered her. For the next three days, the men took turns raping and savagely beating her. Then, the man with the crooked eye held a gun to her head and asked her if she had changed her mind yet. "Yes," she said.

Celia was bruised and broken and sore in the most intimate parts of her body. She wasn't sure which was worse: the beatings or the rapes. She had barely recovered when she was sent to the brothel to begin working. The brothel was housed in a trailer; dirty mattresses covered the floor, bed sheets served as crude room dividers. Armed men stood guard outside. Celia worked alongside several other young Mexican girls; at sixteen, she was the oldest one. They worked twelve hours a day, six days a week. Each girl had sex with twenty to thirty men a day. The men, mostly Spanish-speaking undocumented migrant workers, paid the *ticketero* at the door twenty dollars for the honor of defiling the girls, three dollars of which the girls got to keep. The sessions lasted fifteen minutes. Celia despised the men and slowly began to despise herself for allowing them to touch her. Sometimes when she was alone in the bathroom she scrubbed her skin until it was red and raw.

At the end of their shifts, Celia and the other girls had to service their captors. If they refused, they were raped. Afterward, the girls slept on the same filthy mattresses on which they had had sex all day. Celia often cried herself to sleep. One night she and another girl huddled together, holding each other and crying until the sun came up. That girl was only fourteen.

Every two weeks, the girls were uprooted and relocated to another trailer in a different location. On the drive to a new trailer, Celia caught the scent of oranges from a nearby grove. It was a wonderful smell. The captors kept her inside all day; the air in the trailer was stale and stifling. She longed to inhale the scent of those oranges, to feel the Florida sun on her skin. She begged her captors to let her go outside but they refused.

Escape was not an option: the captors threatened to kill Celia's family if she ran away. They told her and the others that the American police had been paid off. What's more, they said that if the girls were caught in the country illegally they would be imprisoned for life. Police corruption was rife in Mexico and the girls were easily convinced not to trust local law enforcement officers. One young woman took a chance and called 911; she had learned about the number from watching a Spanish soap opera on the small TV the captors kept in the trailer. She dialed the numbers and hung up. An ambulance and a fire truck responded several minutes later. None of the emergency workers spoke Spanish and the girls were unable to communicate with them. The girls watched helplessly as one of their English-speaking captors assured the Americans that the call had been a false alarm.

Celia had been in Florida for almost a year. Her American Dream had turned into a nightmare from which she would not awake. The captors would never let her leave. She began to drink heavily to dull the pain. Sometimes she thought about killing herself. She had all but given up hope of being set free. And then the Americans came.

They arrived in a caravan of cars and trucks. Celia was certain the Americans were there to arrest them all and send them to prison for sneaking into the country. She thought about her family back in Vera Cruz and wondered if she would ever see them again. The Americans handcuffed the captors and loaded them into one of the trucks. The girls were escorted into a van and whisked away. Celia was ashamed to be seen in such a revealing outfit. She was grateful when one of the Americans gave her a T-shirt and a blanket. She pulled the T-shirt over her clothes and draped the blanket over her bare legs. They drove for a long time before arriving at a big official-looking building.

An American woman took her arm gently and led her into an office. In Spanish, the woman asked Celia if she was hurt. Celia had been tricked before and was reluctant to confide in this foreign woman. But the woman had such a kind face and such a soft voice. There were photos of children on the woman's desk, young children with chubby cheeks and big brown eyes. The photo made Celia smile. She hadn't smiled in so very long. She decided to trust the woman; she had nothing left to lose. *My name is Celia and I am from Vera Cruz . . .*

Celia was one of at least two dozen known young girls and women who were enslaved and forced into prostitution by the Cadena-Sosa family. Like the others, Celia was poor and had very little education, making her especially vulnerable to opportunistic human sex traffickers. The Cadena-Sosa enterprise was a family affair managed by Antonia Sosa; her sons Abel Cadena Sosa, Rafael Alberto Cadena Sosa, Hugo Cadena Sosa, and Juan Luis Cadena Sosa; Antonia's brother Rogerio Cadena; and several other extended family members. Over a two-year period, the Cadena-Sosas netted $2.5 million from brothels located across Florida and South Carolina.

In 1997, the FBI and U.S. Border Patrol launched a series of raids on the family's brothels. Family ringleaders, associates, and *ticketeros* were arrested; their victims were taken into protective custody. Initially, the agents were surprised by the cool reception they received from the young women they were there to emancipate. What they didn't know was that the women had been convinced not to trust them. "They hadn't determined who were the good guys and who were the bad guys," said FBI agent Alex Rivas. "So here we come knocking on their door saying, 'we're here to help you.' They didn't know who to believe."[1]

The young women that eventually confided in the agents recounted a terrible story of brutality and sexual exploitation. They were held captive, threatened with guns, raped, and degraded. Customers knew but didn't care that they were being held against their will. Some customers were as brutal as the captors. Many refused to use condoms; as a result, a few of the women got pregnant and were forced to have abortions. The cost for the procedures was tacked onto their smuggling debts. One teenager said her captors had kicked her repeatedly in the stomach until she had a miscarriage.

The captors had promised the women they could leave the brothel once their smuggling debts were paid in full. "I would take careful note of everything so that I would know when I paid off my debt," a young woman named Sarah said. "After four months, by my count, the debt was paid off."[2] Yet, Sarah was not allowed to leave. None of the women were.

In 1998, ringleader Hugo Cadena-Sosa and fourteen associates were indicted for conspiring to lure and hold Mexican women in involuntary servitude. Hugo Cadena-Sosa pleaded guilty and was sentenced to sixty months in jail and ordered to pay the victims one million dollars in restitution (to date, none of the victims has received a penny). Cadena-Sosa's associates, most of whom were low-level members of the crime ring pleaded guilty to human rights violations and were sentenced to two to six years in prison. U.S. District Judge Kenneth Ryskamp called the Cadena-Sosa case "one of the most base" and "most reprehensible" crimes he had ever handled.[3]

The case drew attention to the existence of human trafficking in the United States. Human trafficking is a global epidemic but until recently, Americans were unaware illegal immigrants were being trafficked in their own backyards. The U.S. Department of State estimates that fifty thousand illegal immigrants are trafficked into the country each year by criminal organizations and forced into indentured servitude or prostitution. Law enforcement agencies are determined to combat this growing problem. "The Justice Department is committed to protecting victims of human trafficking," said Ralph F. Boyd, Jr., Assistant Attorney General for Human Rights. "Those who seek to profit from modern-day slavery will be punished."[4]

In 2000, the Trafficking Victims Protection Act officially classified human trafficking as a specific offense punishable by twenty years to life in prison. Rogerio Cadena had the misfortune of being captured and indicted after the act went into effect. To avoid a life sentence, he pleaded guilty to slavery and prostitution charges. He was sentenced to fifteen years in prison.

Family matriarch and top recruiter Antonia Sosa died before she could be brought to justice. The remaining members of the Cadena-Sosa family — Carmen Cadena, Juan Luis Cadena, Rafael Alberto Cadena, Antonio Sosa, and Patricia Sosa — have gone into hiding. The FBI continues to pursue them.

Life remains a constant struggle for the young women victimized by the Cadena-Sosas. They are unable to forget the horrific ordeal they experienced; the emotional scars run deep. "When I see a tan van, I get scared because that's what they transported us in," said Sarah. "I wonder who's inside. When I see a van like that, I can't forget these things."[5]

Nor can Rosa. "I can't put it behind me. I find it nearly impossible to trust people," she said. "I still feel shame. I was a decent girl in Mexico. I used to go to the church with my family. I only wish none of this had happened."[6]

TWENTY-FIVE

L&O SVU: ("Bound," Season 5) Patients in a family-owned nursing home begin dying one after another. The investigation leads to the owner.

TRUE STORY: "Angel of Death" nurse Charles Cullen is suspected of killing as many as forty patients during his career.

They were waiting for him when he entered the courtroom. There were sixty of them, at least, and they were very angry. Charles Cullen walked in and took his seat at the defense table; it was as if he didn't even notice them. As a safety precaution, deputies had made him wear a bulletproof vest. Emotions ran high. Cullen didn't look like a monster but he had committed monstrous acts. As a nurse, Cullen had murdered at least forty people, injecting them with lethal dosages of medications or contaminating

Charles Cullen, a nurse who confessed to murdering more than forty hospital patients in New Jersey and Pennsylvania between 1988 and 2002, for which he received multiple life sentences. At the sentencing, the judge had Cullen's mouth duct-taped shut because the killer would not stop repeating the phrase, "Your Honor, you need to step down."
Courtesy of CNN

their IV bags with insulin. He had been hired to care for the sick and infirm; he killed them instead. In court, Cullen appeared docile, cowed. It was hard to believe that he was capable of such cruelty. But looks were deceiving.

The sixty people staring at him were there to give victim impact statements. One by one, they recounted the pain and anguish of losing their loved ones. Some sobbed, others shouted at him in anger. *Monster! Vermin! Trash!* Cullen sat silently through it all, head bowed, eyes closed. At times, he appeared to be sleeping. It enraged them that he wouldn't even look at them. *Look at me! Do you recognize me? I look like my mother — the woman you killed!* When it was all over, Superior Court Judge Paul Armstrong sentenced Cullen to eleven life terms in prison. "[W]hen you injected the bodies of your helpless victims, you unlawfully took their lives and are guilty of grievous murders," Armstrong told Cullen. "When you ignored the dignity and personhood of the human beings entrusted to your care, you betrayed the ancient foundations of the healing professions." Cullen stared blankly at the judge. "I have nothing to say, your honor," he responded before being led away in handcuffs. Cullen never addressed the sixty people who had come to confront him. Never told them why he did what he did. Never said he was sorry.

Charles Cullen was born in 1960 and raised in West Orange, New Jersey. The youngest of nine children, he suffered from frequent bouts of depression throughout his life. He was an infant when his father died; his mother died seventeen years later. Her death sent Cullen into a mental funk. He dropped out of high school and joined the navy. While assigned to submarine duty, Cullen made several suicide attempts. Alarmed by his mental instability, the navy discharged him after two years of service. Cullen got married, became a registered nurse, and fathered two children.

Over the next sixteen years, Cullen worked at nearly a dozen health care facilities, all within a forty-mile radius. His performance was substandard at best, life-threatening at worst. Cullen was fired numerous times; in other instances, he quit before he could be accused of harming patients. He claimed his first victim, John Wengo, in 1988, by injecting the seventy-two-year-old's IV bag with a deadly dose of insulin. Cullen killed ten more patients at that hospital. He resigned when hospital administrators began investigating the high number of insulin-related deaths on Cullen's watch.

Cullen had no problem getting another job. At the time, there was a nationwide shortage of nurses, and health care facilities, desperate for employees, weren't too picky about who they hired. On paper, Cullen seemed like a decent applicant; there was nothing negative in his employment record. Prospective employers calling for references were not told that Cullen had been linked to suspicious deaths. Fearful of being sued, his previous employers kept their suspicions about him to themselves. His employers also did not report Cullen to the state licensing board. He was allowed to continue working — and continue his killing spree.

Some serial killers are adept at fitting in and masking their evil intentions. Charles Cullen was neither successful nor charming. He had a long history of mental illness, which he was unable to hide. His strange and threatening behavior led his wife to file for divorce in 1993. She alleged Cullen was mentally unstable — an alcoholic who abused the family pets, set the children's books on fire, and poured lighter fluid into their guests' drinks. Cullen grudgingly moved out of the house and into a basement apartment nearby. To make himself feel better, he poisoned a few more of his patients. He also began stalking a coworker. He trailed the woman everywhere and even broke into her house while she and her son were sleeping. Afterward, he left numerous messages on her answering machine admitting to the break-in. The woman pressed charges against Cullen. He was sentenced to a year's probation and ordered to stay away from her. After another failed suicide attempt, he checked himself into a psychiatric institution.

Cullen was out and working at another hospital a few months later. His new co-workers were unnerved by his strange behavior. He had a habit of skulking about and always seemed to be around whenever a patient died under mysterious circumstances. A day before she died, ninety-one-year-old patient Helen Dean complained about a "sneaky male nurse" who had crept into her room to give her an unscheduled injection while she was sleeping. The nursing staff assumed Dean was simply confused. Her son, Larry Dean, was convinced his mother had been murdered. Dean tried to persuade the police to look into his mother's death and investigate Cullen. Believing Helen Dean had died of natural causes, the police refused to open an investigation.

Larry Dean was not the only one who was voicing concerns about Charles Cullen. In 1999, Northampton County Coroner Zachary Lysek became convinced a staff member of Easton Hospital was killing patients. He contacted the hospital's administrator. An internal investigation was conducted but failed to prove conclusively that any patients had been murdered. Three years later, Lyzek received a call from a nurse from St. Luke's Hospital in Bethlehem, Pennsylvania. She told him that the nursing staff believed Charles Cullen was responsible for a string of suspicious deaths. There had been an increase in fatal Code Blues when he was on duty, and Cullen had also signed out unauthorized medications. Further, the nurses had found unopened vials of medication hidden in a garbage can. Pathologist Isadore Mihalakis was assigned to look into the matter. He reviewed more than sixty cases but did not turn up any activities he felt warranted criminal investigation. Frustrated, St. Luke's contacted the Pennsylvania Board of Nursing with their concerns. For unknown reasons, the board did not censure or take any action against Cullen.

Cullen's final nursing job was at Somerset Medical Center (SMC) in Somerville, New Jersey. It was here that Cullen's killing spree finally came to an end — but not before he claimed another thirteen lives. In July 2003, SMC administrators detected an alarming increase in unexplained patient deaths. They discovered that all of the patients had been given lethal doses of the heart medication digoxin. All of the patients had also come into contact with nurse Charles Cullen. Administrators sent the patients' records and medical supply data to the New Jersey Poison Control Center. An analysis of the data revealed that Cullen had checked out and then inexplicably canceled orders of digoxin on the days the patients died. Poison Control confirmed what the hospital feared: SMC had an "angel of death" on staff. SMC fired him in October for falsifying his work history on his job application. During the hospital's investigation, he had managed to kill five more patients. With Cullen gone, the strange deaths at SMC stopped.

Somerset County prosecutor Wayne Forrest launched an official investigation into the mysterious deaths at SMC. Charles Cullen quickly emerged as the prime suspect. Forrest was shocked to learn that Cullen had been suspected of poisoning patients in multiple hospitals. He was also appalled that Cullen had been allowed to continue working in the health care field. Cullen was arrested on December 12, 2003, for the murder of Somerset Hospital patient Florian Gall, and the attempted murder of patient Jin Kyung Han.

In police custody, Cullen promptly con-

Crime Mapping

What if a cop could simply push a button to find out where an offender lives? It may sound like a hypothetical question, but it isn't. Crime-mapping programs are revolutionizing investigators' ability to track criminals right to their front doors — without even leaving the precinct house. If a detective equipped with crime-mapping software is investigating serial murders in the area, he will enter certain information about the crimes into his computer. The program then compares the information entered to known travel patterns of other serial killers to estimate a likely location of the offender's residence. It can be used to track any type of serial crime, including murderers, rapists, and arsonists. The most updated version of the computer program can reportedly track not only serial offenders but perpetrators of single crimes.

fessed to poisoning both Gall and Han — and up to as many as forty more patients. "My intent was to decrease suffering in people I saw throughout my career. I didn't intend for these patients, these people, to suffer, to go through unusual things," Cullen told detectives. "I would just cause them to pass away and not suffer or linger." His logic was faulty, and self-serving. Most of the patients Cullen murdered were *not* terminal and would have recovered from their illnesses. As it turned out, the majority of the murders occurred when Cullen was having personal problems or suffering from depression. Cullen told detectives that he had been poisoning patients for the duration of his career. "I wish I didn't do it," he said. "But I can't even remember all these people. It's like a fog, maybe that's how I've gotten to this point, you know. But I know I did it and I just don't remember the details. I don't remember faces."

One of the faces Cullen forgot was Helen Dean. For years, her son Larry Dean had fought to have her death investigated. In 2004, Helen Dean's body was exhumed and her death reclassified as a homicide. Sadly, Larry Dean died before he could see his mother's killer brought to justice.

Charles Cullen was the most prolific angel of death this country has seen. To escape the death penalty, he agreed to help prosecutors ascertain which — and how many

— patients he killed. Cullen pleaded guilty to murdering twenty-two patients in New Jersey and Pennsylvania. Most of the deaths had not been recognized as homicides when they occurred. At his March 10, 2006, hearing, Cullen caused a scene by demanding Judge William Platt — whom he felt was not impartial enough — recuse himself. "Your honor, you need to step down!" Cullen chanted over and over until the judge had him gagged. All told, Cullen was given eighteen life sentences.

As a result of the Cullen case, New Jersey, Pennsylvania, and numerous other states passed laws granting immunity from lawsuits to employers who give negative, truthful, appraisals of former employees.

ENDNOTES

One

[1] Phil Hirschkorn, "Man Accused of Rape Says Sex Was Consensual," *CNN*, April 22, 2003, cnn.com.

[2] Kevin Rivoli, " 'Bizarre' Kidnappings Probe Widens in NY," *USA Today*, April 21, 2003.

[3] Mike McAndrew and Mike Fish, "John T. Jamelske: The Unfolding Story," the *Post-Standard*, May 18, 2003.

[4] Ibid.

[5] Mike Fish, "Chamber of Horrors," the *Post-Standard*, May 4, 2003.

[6] Ibid.

[7] Ibid.

[8] Ibid.

[9] McAndrew and Fish, "John T. Jamelske: The Unfolding Story."

[10] Jim O'Hara, "Face to Face for Six Hours," the *Post-Standard*, July 16, 2003.

[11] Mike Fish and Mike McAndrew, "Victim:

I Hope You Die in a Cold Cement Cell,"
the *Post-Standard,* July 16, 2003.

Two

[1] Keith Sinclair, "Boy, Six, Kills Girl in Classroom Shooting," the *Herald,* March 1, 2000.

[2] *60 Minutes II,* "Murder in the First Grade," CBS News, August 24, 2000.

[3] Victoria Newton, "Gun Boy Six, and Victim in Class Picture," the *Sun* (England), March 2, 2000.

[4] Roger Rosenblatt, "The Killing of Kayla," *Time,* March 13, 2000.

[5] Ibid.

[6] The *Times* (London), "That Happens on Television, Says Killer, 6," March 2, 2000.

[7] Associated Press, "Six-year old's Shooting Raises Tough Questions," March 1, 2000.

[8] *Birmingham Evening Mail* (England), "New US Gun Call as Girl Aged 6 Shot," March 1, 2000.

[9] 60 Minutes II, "Murder in the First Grade."

Three

[1] Peter Vronsky, *Serial Killers* (New York: Berkley, 2004), 76.

[2] Ibid.

[3] Ibid.

[4] Casey Sherman, *A Rose for Mary* (Boston: Northeastern University Press, 2003), 50–51.

[5] Ibid, 52–53.

[6] Ibid, 55.

[7] Ibid, 85.

[8] Ibid, 87.

[9] Ibid, 91.

[10] Ibid.

[11] Ibid, 56–75.

[12] Jack Thomas, "In the Grip of Fear Forty Years Ago This Week," *Boston Globe,* June 13, 2002, D1.

Four

[1] Aphrodite Jones, *Cruel Sacrifice* (New York: Pinnacle Books, 1994), 150.

[2] Ibid, 140.

[3] Ibid, 151.

[4] Ibid, 22.

[5] Ron Grossman, "Fatal Affection?", *Chicago Tribune,* July 29, 1992.

[6] Ibid.

[7] Jones, *Cruel Sacrifice,* 324.

[8] Ibid, 213.

[9] Ibid, 327.

[10] Grossman, "Fatal Affection?"

Additional sources include court transcripts and police records.

Five

[1] Lona Manning, "Rapist, M.D.," *Crime Magazine,* April 2, 2003, crimemagazine .com.

[2] Ibid.

[3] Ibid.

[4] Ibid.

[5] Ibid.

[6] Mike O'Brien, "Doctor Guilty in Sex Assault Case," the *Leader-Post,* November 26, 1999.

Six

[1] Sue Russell, *Lethal Intent* (New York: Pinnacle Books, 2002), 30.

[2] Ibid, 27.

[3] Marlee Macleod, "Aileen Wuornos: Killer Who Preyed on Truck Drivers," *Crime Library,* www.crimelibrary.com/notorious_ murders/women/wuornos/1.html.

[4] Russell, *Lethal Intent,* 338.

[5] Ibid, 539.

[6] Macleod, "Aileen Wuornos."

Additional sources include court transcripts and police records.

Seven

[1] Stuart A. Wright, ed., *Armageddon in Waco* (Chicago: University of Chicago Press,

1995), 48–52.

[2] Ibid, 56.

[3] Angela Brown, "Survivors Remember Waco Raid," the *Western Mail,* April 18, 2003.

[4] Barbara Kantrowitz, et al., "Secrets of the Cult: The Messiah of Waco," *Newsweek,* March 15, 1993.

[5] Mark England and Darlene McCormick, "The Sinful Messiah," *Waco Herald-Tribune,* 1993.

[6] Ibid.

[7] Ibid.

[8] Ibid.

[9] Ibid.

[10] Brown, "Survivors Remember Waco Raid."

[11] Peter J. Boyer, "The Children of Waco," *The New Yorker,* May 15, 1995.

[12] *Waco: The Rules of Engagement* (DVD), New Yorker Video, 1997.

[13] Sen. John C. Danforth, "Interim Report to the Deputy Attorney General Concerning the 1993 Confrontation at the Mt. Carmel Complex," July 21, 2000, 172.

[14] Ibid, 166.

[15] Ibid, 167.

[16] *Assault on Waco,* Discovery Channel documentary, September 17, 2006.

[17] *Waco: The Rules of Engagement* (DVD), 1997.

[18] Danforth, 178.

[19] Ibid, ii–iii.

[20] Terri Jo Ryan, "Waiting for Koresh," *Tribune-Herald,* March 2, 2003.

Eight

[1] Michael Winerip, "Oddity and Normality Vie in Subway Killer's Confession," the *New York Times,* October 18, 1999.

[2] Ibid.

[3] Harriet Ryan, "An Elusive State of Mind," *Court TV Online,* October 18, 1999, www .courttv.com/archive/national/1999/1018/ goldstein_ctv.html.

[4] Ibid.

[5] Michael Winerip, "The Way We Live Now: The Jurors' Dilemma," the *New York Times,* November 21, 1999.

[6] Harriet Ryan, "Is It Crazy to Take Insanity Defendants Off Their Drugs for Trial?" *Court TV Online,* March 22, 2000, www.court tv.com/trials/news/032200_meds_ctv.html.

Nine

[1] Karen Roebuck, et al., "Clashing Views of Guards Emerge," *Tribune-Review,* March 30, 2006.

[2] CBS (KDKA) interview, March 22, 2006,

kdka.com.

Ten

[1] Allen Turner, "Experts Give 2 Views of Killers," *Houston Chronicle,* February 26, 1997.

[2] Allen Turner, "Prosecutors Tell of Burial Site in Woods," *Houston Chronicle,* February 21, 1997.

[3] Turner, "Experts Give 2 Views of Killers."

[4] Allen Turner, "Son Told His Father of Killings," *Houston Chronicle,* February 19, 1997.

[5] Turner, "Experts Give 2 Views of Killers."

Additional sources include court transcripts and police records.

Eleven

[1] Dick Bowman and Joseph Daughen, "Mom of 9 Quizzed in Fox Chase Death," *Philadelphia Daily News,* October 3, 1960.

[2] Joseph Barrett, "Carnival Family Quizzed in Boy-in-Box Slaying," *Philadelphia Bulletin,* February 2, 1961.

[3] *America's Unknown Child: The Boy in the Box Mystery,* "Case Summary," americas unknownchild.net.

[4] Sabrina Rubin Erdley, "Who is the Boy in the Box?" *Philadelphia Magazine,* Novem-

ber 2003.

Twelve

[1] *The Oprah Winfrey Show,* WABC, May 3, 2006.

[2] Editorial, "More Than a Clerical Error," the *Washington Post,* October 20, 2005.

[3] Ibid.

[4] Associated Press, "Misconduct Charges Filed Against Judge," May 3, 2006.

[5] Ruben Castaneda, "Embattled MD. Judge to Retire," the *Washington Post,* July 29, 2006.

[6] Allison Klein, "On 'Oprah,' a Wife's Tale of Terror," the *Washington Post,* May 4, 2006.

[7] Judson Berger, "Yvette Cade's Profile Rising," *Gazette.Net,* October 12, 2006.

Thirteen

[1] Carlton Smith, *The BTK Murders* (New York: St. Martin's 2006), 71.

[2] Murder details and many quotes from Rader's communiqués come from the Wichita DA's 92-page *States' Summary of the Evidence,* presented to the Eighteenth Judicial Court of Sedgwick County.

[3] *The BTK Murders,* 93.

[4] Ibid, 176.

[5] Ibid, 249.

[6] Ibid, 255–256.
[7] Ibid, 335–336.

Fourteen

[1] *60 Minutes II,* "Can A Video Game Lead to Murder?" CBS News, June 19, 2005.

[2] Ibid.

[3] Ibid.

[4] Associated Press, "Experts Disagree on Mental State of Man Who Allegedly Gunned Down Officers," August 9, 2005.

[5] Robert DeWitt, "Fayette Killer Sentenced to Death," *Tuscaloosa News,* October 6, 2005.

[6] Tony Smith, "Lawyer Vows to Prove Link Between Video Games and Murder," the *Register,* August 12, 2005.

[7] *60 Minutes II,* "Can A Video Game Lead to Murder?"

[8] Robert DeWitt, "Didn't Get Fair Trial, Killer Says," *Tuscaloosa News,* October 14, 2005.

[9] Jay Reeves, "Alabama Appeal in Game-Blame Killings Nixed," Associated Press, March 29, 2006.

Fifteen

[1] Rebecca Trounson and Nancy Wride, "USC Student Charged in Infant's

Death," *Los Angeles Times,* October 14, 2005.

[2] CBS News, Los Angeles, "Holly Ashcraft's Baby's Death Ruled Homicide," February 8, 2006.

[3] NBC News, "Student Accused of Infanticide Was Previously Investigated," October 15, 2005, www.nbc4.tv/news/5103037/details/htmls.

[4] Trounson and Wride, *Los Angeles Times.*

[5] Ibid.

[6] Bonnie Schindler, "Sex Ed May Have Impacted Ashcraft," *Daily Trojan,* October 28, 2005.

[7] Ibid.

[8] Joshua Sharp, "Experts Say Ashcraft's Baby May Have Been Dead at Birth," *Daily Trojan,* February 12, 2007.

[9] Ibid.

Sixteen

[1] ABC News, "Cut from the Womb," June 7, 2006, abcnews.go.com.

[2] The FBI affidavit can be found at Findlaw.com.

[3] Bob Meadows, et al., "How Could She Do It?" *People,* January 10, 2005.

[4] Local6, "Kansas Town Stunned by Kidnap-Murder Case," December 19, 2004, Local6.com.

Seventeen

[1] Joe Cantalupe and Lisa Petrillo, *Badge of Betrayal* (New York: Avon Books, 1991), 169.

[2] Ibid, 12–14.

[3] Ibid, 17.

[4] Ibid, 90–91.

[5] Ibid, 273.

[6] Ibid, 72–78.

[7] Ibid, 76.

Eighteen

[1] Testimony of Justin Berry before the Investigations Subcommittee of the House Energy and Commerce Committee, April 4, 2006.

[2] Kurt Eichenwald, "Through His Webcam, a Boy Joins a Sordid Online World," The *New York Times,* December 19, 2005.

[3] Ibid.

[4] Ibid.

[5] Ibid.

[6] Jack Shafer, "The New York Times Legal Aid Society," Slate.com, December 19, 2005.

[7] Generation Q.net, "How Old Am I?" July 14, 2006.

[8] Richard Casey, "A Letter from Casey," Generation Q.net, July 15, 2006.

[9] Jack Shafer, "The New York Times Legal

Aid Society," Slate.com, December 19, 2005.

[10] Jack D'Entremont, "Cop, Prosecutor, Hangman," The Guide.com, February 2006.

Nineteen

[1] Marilyn Bardsley, "Leopold and Loeb," www.crimelibrary.com/notorious_murders/famous/loeb/index_1.html.

[2] Ibid.

[3] Ibid.

[4] Ibid.

[5] Ibid.

[6] Ibid.

[7] Ibid.

[8] Douglas O. Linder, "The Leopold and Loeb Trial: A Brief Account," http://www.law.umkc.edu/faculty/projects/ftrials/leoploeb/Accountoftrial.html.

Additional sources include court transcripts and police records.

Twenty

[1] Susan Drumheller, "Slaying Victims Were Bound," *Spokesman Review,* May 19, 2005.

[2] Susan Drumheller and Erica Curless, "Victims in CdA Homicide Were Blud-

476

geoned," *Spokesman Review,* May 20, 2005.

[3] Drumheller, "Slaying Victims Were Bound."

[4] Richard Roesler, "Duncan a Charmer, Exploiter," *Spokesman Review,* July 15, 2005.

[5] Ibid.

[6] Ibid.

[7] Ibid.

[8] Ibid.

[9] Fifthnail.blogspot.com.

[10] Ibid.

[11] Ibid.

[12] James Hagengruber and Susan Drumheller, "Tense Late-Night Drama Ends Quietly, Safely," *Spokesman Review,* July 3, 2005.

[13] Taryn Brodwater, "Douglas Fights Videos' Duplication," *Spokesman Review,* October 28, 2005.

[14] Ibid.

[15] Taryn Brodwater, "Attorneys Agree: No Video Copy," *Spokesman Review,* November 3, 2005.

Twenty-One

[1] "Findings and Conclusions Regarding Defendant's Competency to Proceed to Trial," Case No. 031901884, Third Judi-

cial District Court, Salt Lake City, Utah, July 2005, 6.

[2] Ibid, 21.

[3] Ibid, 32.

[4] Ibid, 38.

[5] Ibid, 42.

[6] Ibid, 56.

[7] Ibid, 57.

Twenty-Two

[1] Shirley E. Perlman and Phil Mintz, "The House of Hell," *Newsday,* September 15, 1987.

[2] Associated Press, "Abused Girl Jailed in Dad's Slaying," October 6, 1987.

[3] Dena Kleiman, "Mail is Heavy in Killing Tied to Sex Abuse," Special to the *New York Times,* September 9, 1987.

[4] Betty Rollin, "Crime Mystery; The Girl Who Stopped Feeling Nothing," NBC News.

[5] Dena Kleiman, "Guilty Plea in Killing of Father," Special to the *New York Times,* March 25, 1987.

Additional sources include court transcripts and police records and the following articles:

Paul Vitello, "A Question of Motive," *Newsday,* March 25, 1987, 5.

Dena Kleiman, "Murder on L.I.," *New York Times,* September 14, 1986, A52.

Shirley E. Perlman and Laura Durkin, "A Homeroom Murder Pact," *Newsday,* October 14, 1990.

Twenty-Three

[1] Marilyn Bardsley, "Moving Up to Murder," *CourtTV's Crime Library,* Crimelibrary.com.

[2] Bill Hewitt and Fannie Weinstein, "Record of Horror," *People,* September 18, 1995, 235.

[3] *Maclean's,* "Clearing the Homolka Deal," April 4, 1996, 27.

[4] Paul Cherry, "Karla Homolka Lives Life of Birthday Cakes and Baseball," *Montreal Gazette,* September 22, 2000.

[5] Charlie Gillis, "Karla Parts Ways With Her Supposed Helper," *Maclean's,* September 5, 2005.

Twenty-Four

[1] Amy Driscoll, "A Case of Modern Day Slavery," *Miami Herald,* July 11, 1999.

[2] Ibid.

[3] Ibid.

[4] Department of Justice press release, "Florida Man Part of Mexican Trafficking Ring Pleads Guilty," September 13, 2002.

[5] Sean Gardiner and Geoffrey Mohan, "Smuggled for Sex — Teenagers Tell of Forced Prostitution," *Newsday*, March 12, 2001.

Twenty-Five

Sources instrumental in writing this chapter include:

Katherine Ramsland, "Charles Cullen: Healthcare Serial Killer," Crimelibrary .com, http://www.crimelibrary.com/ serial_killers/notorious/charles_cullen/ 1.html.

Max Alexander, "Killer on Call," *Reader's Digest,* November 2004.

Associated Press, "Monster Killer Gets 11 Terms," March 2, 2006.

Articles from the *Star Ledger,* the *Express Times,* and the *Pittsburgh Tribune Review.*

Additional sources include court transcripts and police records.

ABOUT THE AUTHOR

Kevin Dwyer and **Juré Fiorillo** are the authors of *True Stories of Law & Order*. They both live in New York.

The employees of Thorndike Press hope you have enjoyed this Large Print book. All our Thorndike and Wheeler Large Print titles are designed for easy reading, and all our books are made to last. Other Thorndike Press Large Print books are available at your library, through selected bookstores, or directly from us.

For information about titles, please call:
(800) 223-1244

or visit our Web site at:
http://gale.cengage.com/thorndike

To share your comments, please write:
Publisher
Thorndike Press
295 Kennedy Memorial Drive
Waterville, ME 04901